BACKROADS
& BYWAYS
OF
NORTHERN
CALIFORNIA

BACKROADS & BYWAYS OF NORTHERN CALIFORNIA

Drives, Daytrips & Weekend Excursions

Michele Bigley

THE COUNTRYMAN PRESS

A division of W. W. Norton & Company

Independent Publishers Since 1923

Excerpts from chapters 11 and 12 first appeared in the *Los Angeles Times Travel section*.

Chapter 11 includes text from Steven Streufert's blog http://bigfootbooksblog.blogspot.com.

Backroads & Byways of Northern California

ISBN: 978-0-88150-976-2

Interior photographs by the author unless otherwise specified
Maps by Erin Greb Cartography, © The Countryman Press
Book design by S. E. Livingston
Composition by Eugenie S. Delaney

Published by The Countryman Press, P.O. Box 748, Woodstock, VT 05091
Distributed by W. W. Norton & Company, Inc., 500 Fifth Avenue, New York, NY 10110

TO NIKKO:
THANK YOU FOR HITCHING A RIDE WITH THIS CRAZY FAMILY.

ACKNOWLEDGMENTS

As with the abundant size of this region, the wealth of people who helped make this book possible may be difficult to acknowledge fully. A hearty thanks goes out to Kermit Hummel, Lisa Sacks, Kim Grant, Kate Mueller, Doug Yeager, Caitlin Martin, and the Countryman Press team for believing that a pregnant mom of a three-year-old could birth this book and a child in the same month.

Buckets of gratitude go out to John Poimiroo, Tina Luster, Eden Umble, Steven Streufert, Tyffani Peters, Rita King, Al Hodgson, Richard Stenger, Jenny Zink, Karen Whitaker, Darcy Tunt, Bobby Richards, Christina Glynn, Andrea De-Trinidad, Jeanette Chin, Heather Thompson, Lindsay Wright, Sandy Gordon, Koleen Hamblin, Stephanie Fermin, and Lucy Steffens for their generous assistance crafting itineraries.

This book would not have been possible without the glorious wordsmith Linda Mastrangelo. Rachel Edgar and Autumn Cobb pulled through when I needed it most, and for that I owe you both big thanks. This book would not have been born without my parents, who trekked north to explore the farthest reaches of the state with me, offering plenty of encouragement along the way.

Most of all, not one syllable could have been crafted without the love and support of Eddie, Kai, and Nikko, my lifelong travel companions.

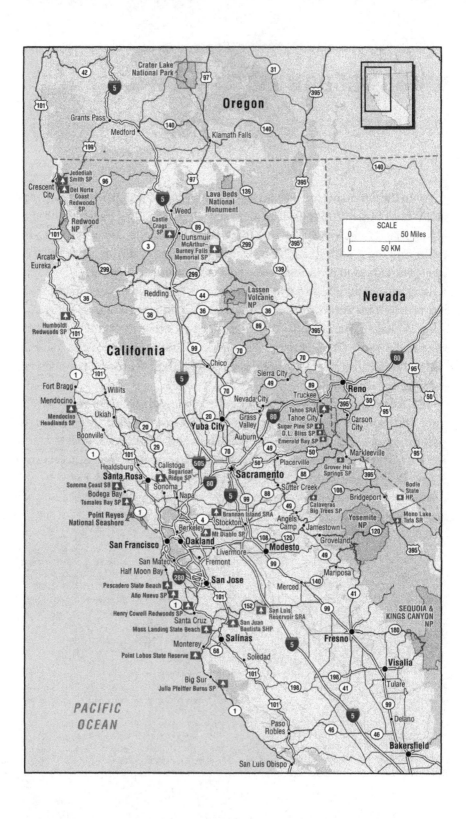

CONTENTS

The Shasta Cascade in spring

INTRODUCTION

E very summer, as a child, my parents packed us up in their van and drove for six weeks from Ohio to California and back. My father dutifully followed his AAA maps as my mom entertained my brother and me by counting license plates and schooling us on everything from Elvis to cornfields. Once we arrived at our destination—be it Yosemite or the beaches of Monterey—my dad would abandon the map and veer onto a back road, where we would always find our best adventures. Getting off the main road and into real communities where people (or animals, or Bigfoot, in the case of Northern California) live illuminates a place in a fresh way that cannot be accomplished by merely exploring Alcatraz and saying you know San Francisco. And on our warm weather jaunts across the continent, those friendly folks inhabiting the Gold Country towns around Yosemite, the sinuous drives along the Big Sur coastline, and the wooded marvels along the Avenue of the Giants all made this traveler fall in love with Northern California.

Yet, most people visit California's majestic northern half and rarely get off the main road. It is easy to see why with big-ticket destinations like San Francisco, Yosemite, Lake Tahoe, Monterey, and Napa. However, after visiting the best this swath of the state has to offer, visitors find it nearly impossible not to return—this time slowing down, turning off onto unchartered territory, and soaking up the wealth of nature located in this pristine environment.

Native Americans have a rich history stretching from the San Joaquin Valley, through Napa and Sonoma, and up into the Shasta Cascade. Many tribes consider this region sacred, with its abundance of healing hot springs, pristine lakes, and mystical mountains. When the forty-niners descended on the Sierra foothills, extracting hunks of gold from the earth during the largest human migration westward ever, the prospectors knew they had stumbled on a majestic area that offered more than mineral riches. They settled throughout the state, congregating in San Francisco, along the coasts, and in valleys and in mountain towns, creating new communities that still exist today.

This book is organized to introduce you to the range of natural and cultural experiences hidden in the depths of Northern California. Each chapter presents an itinerary for a road trip designed to last a weekend or a week. I've offered routes that showcase the tourist destinations of Northern California as well as some of the least traveled byways in the state. The first few chapters connect destinations by theme (for example in "The Tourist's Trek: The Best of Northern California" you'll explore San Francisco, Napa, Yosemite, and Carmel). Others focus on a speck of the region and can be stitched together with other itineraries to create a longer journey (see sidebar).

With this book, you'll be armed with tailored itineraries to suit varied travelers. You can hunt for Bigfoot; craft your own wine bottle label in Napa County; or shop for and then prepare your own gourmet meal created by world-renowned

A peek of San Francisco

BLENDING ITINERARIES

Many of these chapters can easily connect with alternative routes. Below are some recommendations of ways to extend your trip.

Wine and food lovers can blend the "Foodie Tour" with "Educational Escapades in Napa Valley," "Wacky Sonoma County," and "The Pacific Oyster Trail."

Outdoorsy travelers can stitch together "Great Outdoors Along the Mendocino Coast" with "Redwoods and Their Kitsch Counterparts," "Bigfoot Scenic Byway," and "Volcanic Legacy Scenic Highway."

Another option is to connect "Digging for Gold and Great Reds" with "Hunting for Ghosts in the High Sierra" or "Surf to Ski and Everything in Between."

Finally, you may use each itinerary to plump up a journey in a similar destination. For example, "Literary Northern California," "Highway 1 for Families and Adults Who Don't Want to Grow Up," "Foodie Tour," and "The Tourist's Trek" all cover similar destinations with varied themes. Feel free to mix and match for a more thorough exploration.

chef Josh Ash in Sonoma County. Travelers can shuck their own oysters in Marin County; drive along the historic Volcanic Scenic Legacy Byway to explore the subterranean caves carved by lava tunnels; surf and ski in the same day; or spot ghosts in the High Sierra. Sample the robust red wines of Gold Country or the best artichoke bread in the Central Coast; walk in the footsteps of America's greatest writers; or submerge yourself in the redwoods. These itineraries take you off the beaten track and into parts of California that natives don't even know exist, and hopefully, by getting on some of the United States' most beautiful back roads, you too will become smitten with Northern California, finding excuses to return and craft your own itineraries.

WEATHER, PACKING, AND ROAD CONDITIONS

What locals love so intensely about Northern California are the varied weather patterns experienced here. You can surf or ski in the same day (there's an itinerary for that!). That means travelers may need to pack for four seasons in one trip. As most of you know, the Northern California coast temperatures are moody, to say the least. Summers bring blasts of fog that force visitors into tchotchke shops for those emblematic San Francisco hoodies. Though it is common to have random beach days in February, generally it rains in winter. If you want warm beach

The symbol of San Francisco: the Transamerica Tower

A NOTE ABOUT FALL COLOR

by John Poimiroo

People who describe California as not having a change of seasons must not have ventured outside.

Each of California's seasons is spectacular and extreme, depending on where and when it's happening. Few locations in the U.S. get more snow than the Sierra Nevada in winter. Wildflowers grow in colorful profusion in springtime, providing a show that climbs in elevation for six months. Summer is seemingly endless throughout much of California, though it is hottest in the deserts and Central Valley. Yet, the most surprising seasonal discovery is that the Golden State has the longest and most dramatic displays of autumn color to be found in the country, rated for The Weather Channel by www.gorp.com, a national outdoor recreation website, as one of the best.

Whereas New England's impressive show appears by latitude, California's descends by elevation, revealing itself at a rate of about 1,000 feet in elevation per week. The display begins even before the first day of autumn above 9,000 feet in the Eastern Sierra, where stands of yellow, orange, red, and limey-hued aspen are reflected in blue alpine lakes. Then, the color marches downward, painting mountains, valleys, vineyards, and eventually California's urban forests with dazzling color. Networks of photographers and leaf peepers blog and tweet one another where it's happening and when, then venture outside to celebrate California's colorful autumn show.

For more on fall color and the best places to find Technicolor shows, visit John's blog at www.californiafallcolor.com.

days, book your trip in September or October for your best chance. The valleys offer more typical weather patterns with cool winters and blazing hot summers, which coastal Californians soak up when the fog rolls in. And while the mountains maintain a healthy dose of winter throughout the year (offering access to Lake Tahoe slopes in July), the lake gets more use than the slopes come summertime. For driving, I have noted when certain roads close in winter in the High Sierra, but it is always safer to check weather conditions before making the trek.

Yosemite Falls

1 The Tourist's Trek:
THE BEST OF NORTHERN CALIFORNIA

Estimated length: 543 miles
Estimated time: 7–10 days

Getting there: From San Francisco, follow US 101 north, crossing the Golden Gate Bridge. Exit CA 37 east to CA 121; follow the signs toward Napa. Turn left at CA 121/29 north and follow the signs to downtown Napa. Backtrack south on CA 29 to CA 12 east. Merge onto I-80 east; exit CA 12 east to I-5 south; drive for 40 miles to CA 4 east, which merges with CA 99 south. Travel for 11 miles to CA 120 east; follow the signs to weave up the windy road and into Yosemite National Park. From Yosemite Village, take CA 140 east for 70 miles to Merced; turn left on North Parsons, right on Merced Avenue, left on Carol Avenue, and right on East Childs Avenue. Travel left on CA 59 west toward Los Banos to CA 152 west, which merges with CA 156 west toward Monterey. Travel south on CA 1 to Monterey. To return to San Francisco, follow CA 1 north to merge onto US280 north.

Highlights: Experiencing San Francisco's radical spirit, artistic charm, and superfresh cuisine; sampling Cabernet in Napa's reinvigorated downtown; hiking past gushing waterfalls in Yosemite Valley; exploring the Pacific Ocean in Carmel.

San Francisco's 49 square miles house rolling hills begging to be hiked, beloved rainbow-hued Edwardians, parkland, and oodles of culture that will keep your camera snapping day and night. Surprisingly, San Francisco wasn't always the liberal lefty hub of radicalism. Gold rushers and railroad barons swelled the population and later helped the economy flourish until 1906 when a massive earthquake, and even more devastating fire, flattened much of the downtown. During this crisis, working-class folks banded together in parks, sharing food, water, and clothing, ultimately crafting the sensibility that would make

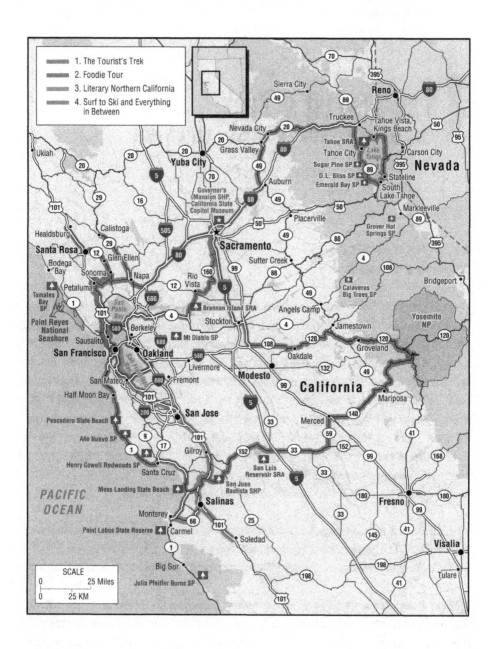

San Francisco into the tolerant city that leaves much of the nation's inhabitants scratching their heads.

Start your exploration of the city by the bay by checking the tourist destinations off your list. Hire a bike at Blazing Saddles and follow the GPS-assisted maps and pedal through the throngs in Chinatown, past North Beach (see chapter 3) and Lombard Street, until you arrive at Fisherman's Wharf. Though you will not locate fresh seafood straight from the fishing boats like folks used to, tourists congregate here to peep at the colony of sea lions on Pier 39, hitch a ride to Alcatraz (make reservations in advance to tour the former prison turned parkland), and purchase kitschy sweatshirts to protect them from the wind. On your tour of Fisherman's Wharf, snap photos of the white blanket of fog slicing the Golden Gate Bridge and embrace the tourist energy of San Francisco's most visited attraction before popping into Musee Mecanique, which showcases vintage arcade games and coin-operated—and occasionally naughty—picture shows.

As you pedal west up past Fort Mason (another spectacular photo op) and glide into the Marina District—a hub for the moneyed postcollegiate youth trying San Francisco on for size—head inland to Chestnut Street for a *poke* wasabi rice bowl at Pacific Catch or to Tacolicious to sample gourmet street tacos and sweet sangria. A couple of blocks east, walk off your meal window-shopping at the chic boutiques lining Union Street. The locally crafted creations at Gallery of Jewels or the designer wares at Sunhee Moon promise plenty of chances to inspire your credit card out of the wallet.

On the way back to the waterfront, take a detour to view the Palace of Fine Arts Theatre. Constructed for the 1915 Pan-Pacific Exhibition, this Parisian-style palace is a performance venue and home to the Exploratorium, one of the state's

Fisherman's Wharf from the bay

Fisherman's Wharf's resident sea lions

most innovative science museums. Numerous bird species nest in the trees surrounding the palace.

If the sun is bright and you care to dip your toes in the bay, Crissy Field offers a reasonably gentle experience (with relatively warm water, at least compared to the frigid temps of Ocean Beach). Nearby, the Wave Organ (part of the Exploratorium) showcases handcrafted pipes of gold rush–era tombstones for the bay waters to roar through. Note: the best time to hear the music is early in the morning, though at any time of day the views from the jetty are quite delightful.

Crissy Field's bike path is the gateway to the Golden Gate Bridge. You can pedal across its 1.7-mile length before descending the windy roads into Sausalito (for more detailed information, see chapter 4), which is the Bay Area's equivalent of a European seaside village. Stroll the shops and rest by the water with views of San Francisco before treating yourself to a glass of wine and a sweet treat at Poggio.

Instead of pedaling back to the city, book passage on the Sausalito–San Francisco ferry to marvel at the expanse of your journey. Conveniently, you'll arrive back at the Ferry Building. True to San Francisco's idealistic nature, after the 1989 earthquake toppled the Embarcadero Highway, the city rebounded, creating an oasis of locavore cuisine in the once run-down Ferry Building. Today, locals and tourists ooh and ahh past stands selling locally roasted coffee, vegan donuts, mushrooms, organic produce, sustainable hot dogs, lip-smacking gelato, and possibly the best truffles in the state, then head out to snap photos of the cargo ships passing under the Bay Bridge. Whether you want Chef Daniel Patterson's affordable lunch at Il Cane Rosso, a gourmet burger and fries at Gott's Roadside, or Chef Charles Phan's shaking beef at Slanted Door, it is nearly impossible to go hungry here.

After dark, hire a taxi and check out live music at the Fillmore Auditorium, a historic venue known for hosting the Grateful Dead, Prince, and its share of young notables (be sure to explore the upstairs gallery of rock posters). Or for something on the sophisticated side, Yoshi's Jazz Club hosts the biggest names in jazz alongside a sophisticated Japanese menu of bar snacks and full dinners.

Lay your head on the poster beds in North Beach's San Remo Hotel, whose historic budget rooms promise not to break the bank. Or cozy up under the anime-decorated walls of Japantown's funky Hotel Tomo—which happens to be within walking distance of the music venues listed above. If money is no worry, spring for the plush digs of Nob Hill's The Huntington Hotel (where you'll likely rub elbows with royalty as you chill out in their luxurious Nob Hill Spa), a recently renovated palace with stellar views of the city.

When the sun comes up, take the Muni (San Francisco Municipal Railway) to Church Street in the Castro District and breakfast on organic omelets in a casual diner setting at Chow. For decades, San Francisco's gay and lesbian community has congregated in the stretch between Castro Street and Church Street to stroll, protest, celebrate, and, of course, see and be seen. If people-watching appeals, you won't want to pass up the Castro.

With your belly full, take the Muni downtown to the Powell Street exit to explore the collection of modern art at the San Francisco Museum of Modern Art (SFMOMA). In addition to the array of photography, paintings, and sculpture on display, the building itself is a work of art. The rooftop garden promises a restful place for a coffee, and their in-house gift shop is my favorite place to shop for holiday presents. Across the street in Yerba Buena Gardens, you'll be rewarded with spectacular views of both this structure and the newly constructed Jewish Museum—a massive black cube, tilted on its side. Plus, in summer, there are free music events on the grass.

Take the N Judah Muni to Ninth Avenue/Golden Gate Park. Grab a bowl of

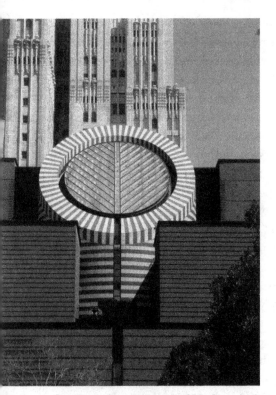 

San Francisco Museum of Modern Art's
exterior

California Academy of Sciences
Amazonian tunnel

ramen at Hotei, or enjoy some of the finest Thai food in the city at Marnee Thai before you enter San Francisco's largest swath of green—Golden Gate Park. As you travel north in the park, detour into Strybing Botanical Gardens to explore redwood groves, succulents, native plants, and abundant flowering magnolias. Follow the crowds to Music Concourse Drive to either geek out on fossils, massive fish tanks, and a re-creation of the Amazon at the California Academy of Sciences, or peruse the vast collection of South Pacific artifacts, as well as modernist sculptures and the bird's eye view of the park in the observation tower at the de Young Museum.

Returning toward downtown on the N-Muni, get off on Cole Street and walk north until you reach Haight Street. Though the collection of tie-dye, East Indian–inspired textiles, and used clothing shops have not waned—nor have the heaps of squatters with signs begging tourists for cash for beer—the neighborhood that was once home to Janis Joplin and Jerry Garcia now draws yuppies and hipsters into those lovingly restored Victorians. Take a seat at the bar of Magnolia

Brewpub for house-brewed beers, or sidle into the Alembic Bar to sample complicated cocktails that could be considered chemistry experiments.

With so many world-class eateries, deciding where to enjoy dinner might be the only challenge of your trip. For a classic San Francisco experience, order the chicken and bread salad at the venerable Zuni Café on Market Street. If you want something casual, but no less delicious, the Mission District's Flour + Water churns out delicately crafted pizza, pasta, and desserts that shine light on the seasonal bounty of the area. (Reservations are hard to come by, and though the staff leaves about half of the tables for walk-ins, you'll likely have to wait around for a while.) To really go big, Chef Corey Lee (the former chef at French Laundry) serves a complex 13-course tasting menu at his minimalist SOMA (south of market) restaurant, Benu. Items like a 1,000-year-old quail egg with handmade tofu, chrysanthemum, and black moss give you a sample of what's in store (make reservations well in advance).

In the morning, drive to SOMA's Fifth Street outpost of Blue Bottle Café—a laboratory of caffeine and sustainable morning treats. Then drive to Ninth Street and follow the signs to travel north on US 101 and cross the Golden Gate Bridge. Take CA 37 east to CA 121; travel toward Napa as you travel along the country

A Mission District mural

Blue Bottle Café coffee baristas operating the siphons

The Napa River

roads. Turn left at CA 121/29 north. Exit at First Street toward downtown Napa.

Though travelers have boasted about visiting Napa for years, rarely have they had any excuse to spend time in downtown Napa. All has changed. Today, restaurants, posh inns, tasting rooms, and jazz clubs hug the Napa River, finally creating a destination for people who are not keen on sampling wine and then getting behind the wheel. Check into the White House Inn's luxurious bed & breakfast rooms, housed in a 19th-century mansion and paired with a plentiful evening wine and cheese hour and a gourmet breakfast.

Enjoy lunch at Oxbow Public Market, specializing in gourmet local treats. Whether you choose freshly shucked oysters at Hog Island Oysters, spicy arepas at Pica Pica Maize, or a fanciful collection of gourmet hot dogs, croissant sandwiches, or triple-scoop organic ice cream at various vendors, this epicurean hub will set you up to sample plenty of vino.

Pop into the Napa Valley Visitor Center to find out about events going on in town during your stay; for assistance with winery visits, lodging, restaurant reservations; and to view the topographical map of the valley before purchasing your tasting card of downtown Napa—this deal gets you 10-cent tastings at participating wineries. Walk between tasting rooms and sample Cabernet, Chardonnay, and yummy chocolate.

Dinner at one of Napa's fantastic eateries is a must. Reserve early to sample some of Wine Country's best

Taking a break at Oxbow Public Market

wood-fired pizza and creative pastas at Oenotri, an Italian eatery that cures its own salumi and prides itself on serving cuisine often overlooked by Californians (for example, the last time I was here, lamb testicles graced the menu). Another option for more traditional Italian cuisine is Bistro Don Giovanni. Whether you enjoy fried olives and roasted chicken on the patio overlooking the vineyards or you dine inside at one of the sculptured tables, you will long remember this meal.

Cap off the evening at Napa River Inn's jazz club Silo's—a down-to-earth venue where you can hear innovative sounds. Or, if you still have energy, check to see if Ceja Winery is hosting salsa dancing at its downtown tasting room. This is *the* Napa event, lauded for the vibrant scene and welcoming attitudes toward nonhip shakers.

In the morning, hop on CA 29 east to I-80 west; merge onto US 780 east to US 680 south; then onto US 580 east, which passes through Livermore, a Bay Area suburb with a burgeoning wine scene, and L Street, a downtown drag populated with affordable women's clothing, brewpubs, and cafés. Continue onto CA 205 east, merging onto I-5 south for less than a mile and exit onto CA 120 east. This

Napa Valley from above

Groveland's Gold Country–era architecture

country road weaves through small towns like Manteca, Escalon, and Oakdale—all of which, unfortunately, won't inspire much exploration save a quick stop into Oakdale Cheese & Specialties, a decent spot for sampling gouda, preserves, and locally grown fruit. Follow CA 120 as it turns south, taking you past the Gold Country ghost town of Chinese Camp and zigzagging up the very windy mountain road. (If your brakes are not up to speed and the weather is fine, take the Old Priest Grade up the hill instead; this merges back with CA 120 at the top.)

When the alpine air begins to kick in, you've arrived in Groveland, a historic gold-mining town, once thriving with a strike-it-rich mentality and now the gateway to Yosemite. This is a decent option for stocking up on water, gasoline, and snacks before heading into the park. Besides serving coffee and morning goodies, Mountain Sage also hosts a weekly farmers' market (depending on the season) and sells a bountiful collection of outdoor gear, toys, and clothing. Worth a stop, if for nothing else than to look at the dollar-covered ceiling, the Iron Door Saloon easily brings to mind another era of gun-toting bandits and player pianos. Today, budding musicians and mountain climbers populate the wooden booths, sipping frothy beer, playing pool, and grubbing on burgers. For a dash of sophistication, enjoy early dinner at the Groveland Hotel's Cellar Door Restaurant. In summer, sip one of their hundreds of wines alfresco, while inhaling the scent of pine trees, then delight in specialties like braised angus ribs or wild mushroom ravioli.

Back on CA 120, the road carries you into Yosemite National Park—a treasure by all standards. First populated by the Miwok, gold seekers began to make their way west, only to be flabbergasted by the steep cliffs jutting up from the earth, with veils of waterfalls spraying the valley below. News reached naturalist John Muir, who, like most visitors, became smitten with the region; he then wrote a passionate letter to then president Roosevelt—a move that, coupled with a hiking trip with the head honcho himself, earned Yosemite its protected status. Today, the park surely experiences wear and tear from the thousands who visit each summer, turning this peaceful oasis into a sort of Disneyland; however, the shock of witnessing such beauty does not lessen regardless of how long you must wait for a park shuttle.

Follow the signs to Yosemite Village and check into Curry Village—a massive community of cabins and canvas tent cabins with beds (similar to those in the show *M.A.S.H.*). More summer camp than hotel, summer evenings include ranger shows, pizza-and-beer nights, and stargazing, as well as the occasional bear sighting. To feel like a dignitary, check into the stone Ahwahnee Hotel—a mountain palace favored by presidents. Though rooms are decorated in Native American motifs with comfy beds, you'll likely spend your downtime in the lofty lounge or in the bar sipping wine.

In the morning, hop onto the Yosemite Shuttle. Though it may

Curry Village cabins guarded by granite peaks

seem easier to drive to destinations, the park fills with cars and tour buses in the summer and trying to secure parking can take away precious hiking time. Also, the shuttle gains access to roads that cars cannot enter, making the hikes shorter (so you can fit more sightseeing in).

Take a short—though rewarding—walk to Lower Yosemite Falls (the fifth highest waterfall in the world). It is possible to trek up to the Upper Falls, though this is a very strenuous hike (if you plan to do this, check with the visitors center in advance for details and scratch the rest of the day's itinerary). After you explore the dramatic falls, the shuttle takes you to the Yosemite Valley Visitor Center in the village. Here you can gain information about wildlife and trails that fit your abilities. Meander around the Yosemite Village and poke into the Ansel Adams Gallery; the artist became enamored with the valley and captured some stunning images, which are on display. Grab deli sandwiches at Dengan's Deli before getting back on the shuttle for your big hike of the day.

Get off the shuttle at Happy Isles, which, in summer, is an interpretive nature center favored by families. Follow the crowds up to the Vernal Falls hike. The trail is a 1.6-mile very steep climb to the footbridge. The rewards of viewing the spewing waterfall, as well as the misty shower visitors receive on arrival, draw thousands. If you have more energy, continue for another 1.6 miles to the top where a cold alpine pool awaits.

Mirror Lake in spring

If you still have energy for walking, travel to the next shuttle stop: the 2-mile loop of Mirror Lake offers interesting views of Half Dome, as well as a bit of unchartered territory. In summer, the lake dries up, but last time I was here in peak season, we spotted a baby bear just off the path. This is one of my favorite destinations in the valley, especially in springtime.

By this point, you'll likely want to rest those dogs. Pop into the Yosemite Lodge's bar for a cocktail with unsurpassed views of the Yosemite Falls. Follow up with dinner (reservations are required in summer) at the Mountain

Room Restaurant, which honors local produce and serves imaginative mountain cuisine—think pistachio-crusted trout or mole-smothered steak.

After a restful sleep surrounded by granite peaks, wake to the joy of knowing you will eat a brunch served to presidents and kings at the Ahwahnee Hotel. The classic all-you-can-eat buffet—complete with ice sculptures, heaps of shellfish, and any type of griddle fare or omelet you can imagine—comes at a whopping cost, but sitting with a view of the valley as you sip mimosas is one of those memorable Yosemite moments.

Jump in the car and head over to Bridalveil Falls to take an easy 20-minute stroll up to this spectacular waterfall. Right near the falls, connect to CA 41 south toward Wawona until you reach the popular Mariposa sequoia grove. Parking can be tricky during high season, but an easy 1.6-mile walk through these giant trees makes up for the annoyance of waiting for a parking spot. This is where John Muir took Ralph Waldo Emerson hiking.

Backtrack north on CA 41, toward the historic Wawona Hotel. Sit on wicker chairs on the patio, and if you happen to be here on a summer Saturday afternoon, order a beer and enjoy the fun barbecue. If you are here for any other day, the dining room, decorated with a mural of sequoias, serves a popular turkey chili. When you can tear yourself from the beauty of this enchanting park, head back to CA 140 west, then turn left onto CA 140 east toward Mariposa. This historic gold-rush town was once the headquarters of California's largest county, cluttered with rowdy 49ers. Today, the shell of the original town still stands: see one of the oldest jails in California, tour the county courthouse, or take the historic walking tour of downtown (check into the visitors center for times). If shopping is your game, pop into the collection of antique shops lining the main drag. In town you'll find plenty of fine eateries, including the Butterfly Café, which serves a mean quiche; and for you burger lovers, don't miss a stop into Happy Burger Diner—a funky mainstay with walls papered in album covers and a menu that would take a lifetime to experience.

Travel for 30 miles to the town of Merced—an agribusiness community in the central valley of California. To honor the rich farming tradition of the region, stop in the Merced Fruit Barn, a decent place to picnic or grab some dried fruit before hopping back in the car. Turn left on North Parsons, right on Merced Avenue, left on Carol Avenue and right on East Childs Avenue. Turn left on CA 59 west toward Los Banos; merge onto CA 152 west. About 2 miles past I-5, pull into the San Luis Reservoir State Recreation Area to stretch your legs; this park is a favorite for wildflower seekers and fishermen, as well as a hunting ground for eagles and hawks. A popular trail is the 10-mile lakeshore trail around Salt

Pacific Grove's glimpse of the Pacific Ocean

Springs Cove, resulting in a fantastic immersion in a giant sycamore grove.

Back on CA 152, merge onto CA 156 west toward Monterey. Meander past fields of artichokes and sand dunes until you finally receive a long-awaited glimpse of the sea. Travel south on CA 1 to Pacific Grove. This drive should take about five hours, but arriving at California's most lovely stretch of oceanfront property is well worth the journey. The neighboring towns of Monterey, Pacific Grove, Carmel, and Big Sur cater to retirees, artists, winemakers, foodies, and salty outdoorsy folks.

After a long drive through California's Dust Bowl, unwind with a sunset stroll on Pacific Grove's Asilomar Beach. Known for its protected dunes, which are populated by deer and varied bird species, and the occasional glimpse of whales and dolphins, this surfer-favored beach spills out from the historic Asilomar Conference Grounds, known for their Julia Morgan–designed structures offered at a reasonable price. Wander the raised path to the plush Inn at Spanish Bay to sip fine Pinot noir with views of the Pacific. Dine at one of the fine eating establishments at the inn, such as Peppoli Northern Italian, then settle in for a night on Pebble Beach. Or you may want to stay the night at the Tickle Pink Inn, overlooking the sea in Carmel Highlands, or at the historic La Playa Hotel in Carmel, just a short walk to Carmel Beach. In the morning (if breakfast is not included with your stay) line up with the locals at Carmel Valley Coffee Roasting Company for a perfectly steamed café au lait and pastries (for more dining recommendations, see chapter 7).

Drive south on CA 1 to the beloved Point Lobos State Park. Originally home to Portuguese whalers, this park now draws naturalists who marvel at the breathtaking vistas. View whales spouting off the coast, otters resting on the cliffs below, the bluest sea in California, mating cormorants, and a dynamic coastal hike beneath the Cypress.

Travel north on CA 1 then turn onto Carmel Valley Road for a gourmet burger and *pomme frites* poolside at the luxe Bernardus Lodge. Splurge on a Chardonnay facial or a couple's massage at the award-winning Spa at Bernardus Lodge, and then relax in the eucalyptus steam room or take a dip in the pool. Before heading back to the beach, sample great white wines at Bernardus Winery Tasting Room up the street or at Heller Estate, which specializes in organic vino.

Stroll the galleries in Carmel, hoping to run into one of the town's famous

Point Lobos State Park

residents. Favorites include the Carmel Bay Company, a dizzying display of local artists who live within 35 miles of Carmel, and the Carmel Art Association, a co-op that has been showcasing sculptures, mixed media, and plenty of paintings depicting the region since 1926. Dinner in Carmel is serious business, and you'll be content whether you crave a Sonoma porterhouse hugged by root vegetable purée in a mint crust at the romantic Casanova, or a more casual (but no less delicious) margarita pizza or heaping plate of pasta paired with a fine Chianti at Cantinetta Luca.

Start your morning winding through the sinuous 17-mile drive, passing sea mammals and stunning views of the sea. Pop into the Lodge at Pebble Beach for breakfast at the

Downtown Carmel

low-key Gallery Café with views of the world-renowned Pebble Beach Golf Links and Stillwater Cove. If you dream of teeing off in California's most famous greens, book a spot up to two months in advance and prepare to be wowed at every turn. Since 1919, this course has drawn pros for five U.S. Open Championships as well as travelers eager to test out their skills on this gorgeous course.

Continue along the drive to Pacific Grove to peep the monarch butterflies (if you happen to be in the area in late fall early winter) that travel 2,500 miles to winter in the Monterey pines and eucalyptus trees of George Washington Park. The butterflies cluster together atop trees to avoid freezing (hint: they look like dead leaves). On warm days, catch them fluttering around in a magical display.

For a truly authentic Monterey experience—albeit not the most quaint location—Monterey's Fish House delivers local fare in gigantic portions (you can order half sizes even though they are not on the menu) to the tune of fresh oysters on the half shell, baby artichoke pasta, and grilled octopus. Make reservations if you plan to eat there for dinner; this old favorite gets packed. To return to San Francisco via the scenic route, reverse the itinerary in chapter 7.

IN THE AREA

ACCOMMODATIONS

Ahwahnee Hotel, 1 Ahwahnee Road, Yosemite National Park. Glorious accommodations in a historic stone building. Native American–inspired rooms, a stately lobby, and a brunch fit for presidents and kings. Call 801-559-5000. Website: www.yosemitepark.com.

Asilomar State Beach and Conference Grounds, 800 Asilomar Avenue, Pacific Grove. Affordable rooms in a Julia Morgan–designed building, formerly a YMCA, located on a state park. Group breakfasts, beach access, and a pool make this a family favorite. Call 888-635-5310. Website: www.visita silomar.com.

Bernardus Lodge, 415 Carmel Valley Road, Carmel Valley. Luxury rules the roost at this Carmel Valley resort. Two gourmet restaurants, Wine Country chic décor, a pool, and one of the finest spas around round out the offerings. Call 888-648-9463. Website: www .bernardus.com.

Curry Village, 9010 Curry Village Drive, Yosemite National Park. The largest accommodation in Yosemite. Sleep in tent cabins with beds or modest rustic cabins and enjoy the collection of restaurants (from pizza to tacos), nightly events in summer, and shared heated bathrooms. Call 209-372-8333. Website: www.yosemite park.com.

Hotel Tomo, 1800 Sutter Street, San Francisco. Anime-decorated rooms in San Francisco's Japantown might be small, but they are both affordable and located in a great shopping and dining region. Call 415-921-4000. Website: www.jdvhotels.com/hotels/sanfrancisco /tomo.

The Huntington Hotel, 1075 California Street, San Francisco. The largest independently owned hotel on Nob Hill. Royalty and celebrities fill the spacious (and newly renovated) rooms. The spa draws lunching ladies, and their indoor pool offers views of downtown. Call 800-227-4683. Website: www .huntingtonhotel.com.

The Inn at Spanish Bay, 2700 17-Mile Drive Pebble Beach. An exclusive Pebble Beach resort with a number of fine gourmet restaurants, a golf course, and nightly bagpipers that say adieu to the sun. Enjoy jazz and cocktails in the lobby area. Call 800-654-9300. Website: www.pebblebeach.com.

La Playa Hotel, Camino Real at Eighth Avenue, Carmel. Whether you want historic Latin-inspired rooms with ocean views or a private cottage complete with your own kitchen, La Playa is the only full-service hotel in Carmel. Their brunch is quite the affair. Call 831-624-6476. Website: www.laplayahotel.com.

The Lodge at Pebble Beach, 17-Mile Drive, Pebble Beach. An epic resort with fancy rooms, luxe restaurants, and a spa, as well as access to one of the country's most sought-after spots to tee off. Call 800-654-9300. Website: www .pebblebeach.com.

The San Remo Hotel, 2237 Mason Street, San Francisco. The 1906 Italianate Victorian, located in North Beach, provides small antique-decorated rooms with shared bathrooms. Spring for the rooftop cottage, which must be reserved three to six months in advance. Call 415-776-8688 or 800-352-7366. Website: www.sanremohotel.com.

Tickle Pink Inn, 155 Highland Drive Carmel. Located in the Carmel Highlands, across the street from the sea, but with some of the finest views around, this fancy hotel might sound like a girls' dreamy retreat, but there is nothing precious about the décor. Luxurious rooms lean on a modern aesthetic rather than pastels and doilies. Call 831-624-1244. Website: www.tickle pinkinn.com.

Wawona Hotel, 8308 Wawona Road, Yosemite National Park. Located in the southern end of Yosemite, this hotel draws families wanting to be close to the action but not stuck in summer traffic. Their restaurant serves BBQ on Saturday afternoons and traditional American favorites the rest of the time. Call 801-559-4884. Website: www .yosemitepark.com.

White House Inn, 443 Brown Street, Napa. A historic mansion in downtown Napa decorated with an eye on spare clean lines rather than B&B floral. High ceilings, gourmet cooked-to-order breakfasts, deep soaking tubs, and a garden pool make this property worth the splurge. Call 707-254-9301. Website: www.napawhitehouseinn.com.

Yosemite Lodge, 9006 Yosemite Lodge Drive, Yosemite National Park. This giant complex in the valley with basic to semiluxurious rooms, many with vistas of Yosemite Falls, sells out in summer; reserve early to dine in the dining room or join the masses in the bar for snacks and wine. Call 801-559-4884. Website: www.yosemitepark.com.

ATTRACTIONS AND RECREATION

Alcatraz Island. Tour the former prison, stroll the gardens, or explore the tide pools. Call 888-814-2305. Website: www.alcatraztickets.com.

Ansel Adams Gallery, Village Mall, Yosemite National Park. Call 209-372-4413. Website: www.anseladams.com.

Blazing Saddles, 2715 Hyde Street, San Francisco. Bike rentals in San Francisco by the hour or day. Call 415-929-8687. Website: www.blazing saddles.com.

California Academy of Sciences, 55 Music Concourse Drive, Golden Gate Park, San Francisco. Newly reimagined and transported into Golden Gate Park, complete with a rain-forest dome, giant aquariums, a living roof, a fantastic food court, and plenty of fossils for dinosaur lovers. Call 415-379-8000. Website: www.calacademy.org.

Carmel Art Association, Dolores Street between Fifth and Sixth, Carmel. Call 831-624-6176. Website: www .carmelart.org.

Carmel Bay Company, corner of Ocean Avenue and Lincoln, Carmel-by-the-Sea. Call 831-624-3868. Website: www.carmelbaycompany.com.

de Young Museum, 50 Hagiwara Tea Garden Drive, San Francisco. Exhibits range from masks from the Pacific to Andy Goldsworthy's nature creations. Special exhibits run the gamut— everything from fashion to light creations to Mayan ruins. Call 415-750-3600. Website: http://.deyoung.famsf.org.

Exploratorium, 3601 Lyon Street, San Francisco. A science museum for folks of all ages—grown-ups and kids delight in the trippy exhibits. Call 415-561-0360. Website: www.exploratorium.edu.

Ferry Building, 1 Ferry Building, San Francisco. A food mecca promising fresh produce, fancy chocolates, pricey burgers, Sunday suppers, and the best hot dog in California. Call 415-983-8030. Website: www.ferrybuilding marketplace.com.

Fillmore Auditorium, 1805 Geary Boulevard, San Francisco. Call 415-346-6000. Website: www.thefillmore.com.

Fisherman's Wharf. Call 415-673-3530. Website: www.visitfishermans wharf.com.

Gallery Café, 1200 Mason Street, San Francisco. Call 415-296-9932. Website: www.gallerycafe-sf.com.

Gallery of Jewels, 1506 Church Street, San Francisco. Call 415-550-0226. Website: www.galleryofjewels.com.

George Washington Park, 897 Pine Avenue, Pacific Grove. Call 831-648-5730. Website: www.ci.pg.ca.us /recreation/p-georgewash.htm.

Heller Estate, 69 West Carmel Valley Road, Carmel Valley. Call 831-659-6220. Website: www.hellerestate.com.

Jewish Museum, 736 Mission Street, San Francisco. Spare in design and exhibits, yet worth some time to view modern and classical Jewish artwork. Call 415-655-7800. Website: www.the cjm.org.

Musee Mecanique, Pier 45 Shed A at the end of Taylor Street, Fisherman's Wharf, San Francisco. A fun collection of penny arcade games at Fisherman's Wharf. Entrance is free. Call 415-346-2000. Website: www.museemechanique .org.

Palace of Fine Arts Theatre, 3301 Lyon Street, San Francisco. Built to honor the Pan Pacific Expo and newly refurbished, the structure looks like it jumped out of a European park. Notice the variety of nesting birds in the north end of the park. Call 415-563-6504. Website: www.palaceoffinearts.org.

Pebble Beach Golf Links, 17-Mile Drive, Pebble Beach. It's tough as nails to secure a spot at these links. If you do, you'll likely rub elbows with the finest names in the game. Call 800-654-9300. Website: www.pebblebeach.com.

Point Lobos State Park, Route 1, Carmel. One of my favorite state parks, here you can roam along the sea cliffs, spotting ocean coves, sea life, and cypress trees. Call 831-624-4909. Website: www.pointlobos.org.

San Luis Reservoir State Recreation Area, 31426 Gonzaga Road, Gustine. A popular Central Valley hiking spot. Call 209-826-1197. Website: www.parks.ca .gov/?page_id=558.

SFMOMA, 151 Third Street, San Francisco. The premiere modern art museum in Northern California, recent exhibits have included Diane Arbus, Gertrude Stein, and Olafur Eliasson. Call 415-357-4000. Website: www .sfmoma.org.

Strybing Botanical Gardens, Ninth Avenue and Lincoln Way, Golden Gate Park, San Francisco. Call 415-661-1316. Website: www.sfbotanicalgarden.org.

Wave Organ, 83 Marina Green Drive, San Francisco. Call 415-561-0360. Website: www.exploratorium.edu/visit /wave_organ.html.

Yerba Buena Gardens, 899 Howard Street, San Francisco. Call 415-543-1275. Website: www.yerbabuenagardens.com.

Yosemite National Park. Call 209-372-4386. Website: www.yosemitepark.com.

Yoshi's Jazz Club, 1330 Fillmore Street, San Francisco. Call 415-655-5600. Website: www.yoshis.com/san francisco.

DINING/DRINKS

Alembic Bar, 1725 Haight Street, San Francisco. Gourmet fixins like beef tongue sliders and nectarine and burrata salads are paired with artisan cocktails. Call 415-666-0822. Website: www.alembicbar.com.

Benu, 22 Hawthorne Street, San Francisco. A tough table to nab, so book well in advance for the tasting menu. Specialties like "shark fin" soup, without the actual shark parts, draws devotees. Call 415-685-4860. Website: www .benusf.com.

Butterfly Café, 5027 CA 140, Mariposa. Traditional American breakfast and lunch favorites served in a small café. Call 209-742-4114. Website: www.the butterflycafe.com.

Bernardus Winery Tasting Room, 5 West Carmel Valley Road, Carmel Valley. Call 831-298-8021 or 800-223-2533. Website: www.bernardus.com.

Bistro Don Giovanni, 4110 Howard Lane, Napa, Known by winemakers, local families and tourists as the best spot in town for a dependable meal for special occasions. Sample the house-made lemon ravioli or the pan roasted chicken. Call 707-224-3300. Website: www.bistrodongiovanni.com.

Blue Bottle Café, 66 Mint Street, San Francisco. Arguably San Francisco's best cup of coffee, this outpost of the Oakland coffee roasters looks like a science lab, complete with siphons, delicate brunch and lunch offerings, and high tables. Call 415-495-3394. Website: www.bluebottlecoffee.net.

Cantinetta Luca, Dolores Street between Ocean and Seventh, Carmel-by-the-Sea. Locals stream in and out of this Italian restaurant. Notice the house-made salumi hanging in the windows as well as the lovely wine collection. Call 831-625-6500. Website: www.cantinettaluca.com.

Casanova, Fifth and Mission Streets, Carmel. A legendary spot in Carmel, known for romance and class, serving European flavors in a sweet little house. House-made pastas are spruced up with local veggies and meats. Call

831-625-0501. Website: www.casanova restaurant.com.

Carmel Valley Coffee Roasting Company, Ocean Avenue, Carmel. Call 831-626-2913. Website: www.carmel-coffee .com.

Ceja Winery, 1248 First Street, Napa. Call 707-226-6445. Website: www .cejavineyards.com.

Cellar Door Restaurant, 18767 Main Street, Groveland. Dine outside in the garden or inside the Victorian dining room on California-style cuisine. The daily pasta special never fails, and their wine list is the best around. Call 209-962-4000 or 800-273-3314Website: www.groveland.com.

Chow, 215 Church Street, San Francisco. American favorites served in a diner setting using locally sourced produce. Breakfast scrambles never let me down, and the wood-oven-baked pastas make a great dinner. Call 415-552-2469. Website: www.chowfoodbar.com.

Dengan's Deli, Yosemite National Park. Sandwiches and snacks for hungry hikers. Call 209-372-8454. Website: www.yosemitepark.com/dining_yose mitevillagearea.aspx.

Flour + Water, 2401 Harrison Street, San Francisco. A challenging table to secure, but well worth the wait to dine at this popular Mission District eatery that takes Italian food seriously. Gourmet pizza and pasta, superfresh salads, and intriguing desserts make locals line up for hours. Call 415-826-7000. Website: www.flourandwater.com.

Happy Burger Diner, 5120 CA 140, Mariposa. Burgers and fries in a casual diner setting. Call 209-966-2719. Website: www.happyburgerdiner.com.

Iron Door Saloon, 18761 Main Street Groveland. Pub grub, beer, pool tables, and live music—this is the spot for meeting locals. Call 209-962-6244. Website: www.iron-door-saloon.com.

Magnolia Brewpub, 1398 Haight Street, San Francisco. Microbrews and healthy bar food make the locals drool. Their burger, quinoa breakfast, and egg creations make brunch a popular affair. Call 415-864-7468. Website: www.magnoliapub.com.

Merced Fruit Barn, 4526 East State Highway 140, Merced. You can pick up snacks and sandwiches as well as specialty and gourmet food items at this food emporium. Call 209-385-2222. Website: www.mercedfruitbarn.com.

Mountain Room Restaurant, Yosemite Lodge, Yosemite National Park. See Yosemite Lodge. Call 209-372-1281. Website: www.yosemitepark.com /dining_mountainroom.aspx.

Mountain Sage, 18653 Main Street, Groveland. Serving smoothies, coffee, and breakfast snacks, here you can shop, explore the gardens, and enjoy the small farmers' market in summer. Call 209-962-4686.

Oakdale Cheese & Specialties, 10040 CA 120, Oakdale. Picnic goods and snacks provide a good reason to break up the drive. Call 209-848-3139. Website: www.oakdalecheese.com.

Oenotri, 1425 First Street, Napa. Possibly the finest additional to Napa Valley since the wine grape, you'll be dreaming of their wood-fired pizzas, housemade salumi, mouth-watering desserts, and wine list for months. Call 707-252-1022. Website: www.oenotri.com.

Oxbow Public Market, 10 and 644 First Street, Napa. Food stalls serve arepas, ice cream, oysters, and hot dogs (all gourmet of course). There is also a burger joint, bakery, oyster bar, and more. Call 707-226-6529. Website: www.oxbowpublicmarket.com.

Pacific Catch, 2027 Chestnut Street, San Francisco. Sustainable seafood served every which way, including Hawaiian, Japanese, fried, raw, and Cajun spiced. Call 415-440-1950. Website: www.pacificcatch.com.

Peppoli Northern Italian, 2700 17-Mile Drive, Pebble Beach. Pricey Tuscan-inspired spaghetti and filet mignon served with views of the Pacific raging below. Diners must reserve in advance. Call 831-647-7433. Website: www .peppoli.com.

Poggio, 777 Bridgeway, Sausalito. A Sausalito institution for its Italian cuisine, wine list, and European flair. Score a table outside to rest those dogs before continuing your trek back to San Francisco. Call 415-332-7771. Website: www.poggiotrattoria.com.

Silo's, 530 Main Street, Napa. A fine wine bar and live music venue in downtown Napa; often showcases live jazz music. Call 707-251-5833. Website: www.silosnapa.com.

Tacolicious, 2031 Chestnut Street, San Francisco. Mexican street food served to moneyed recent college grads at this Marina District fave. Tacos are small but perfect. Call 415-346-1966. Website: www.tacolicioussf.com.

OTHER CONTACTS

Monterey Visitors Bureau, 765 Wave Street, Monterey. Call 831-657-6400. Website: www.seemonterey.com.

Napa Valley Visitor Center, 1310 Napa Town Center, Napa. Call 707 226-5813. Website: www.legendary napavalley.com.

San Francisco Visitor Information Center, 900 Market Street, San Francisco. Website: www.onlyinsanfrancisco .com.

Fiddlehead ferns 18.00 lb.

Farmers' market offerings

2 The Foodie Tour

Estimated length: 139 miles
Estimated time: 3.5 hours straight through, or 3 leisurely days

Getting there: From Berkeley, travel south on Telegraph Avenue to Oakland; follow the signs to the Waterfront; hop on I-880 south to CA 92 west. Continue to CA 280 north into San Francisco and merge onto US 101. Follow US 101 over the Golden Gate Bridge and through Marin County. Travel east on CA 116 and north on CA 12 through Santa Rosa to US 101 north. Exit in Healdsburg.

Highlights: Food, food, food, whether it's eating the best ramen in the state, sampling unique fixins served by a collection of food trucks, or gathering your own ingredients fresh from the farm and preparing a gourmet meal in your kitchen.

In the early '70s, food maven Alice Waters quietly opened Chez Panisse in a simple Berkeley neighborhood, coining a revolution of sorts in Californians,' and the rest of the planet's, relationship with what's on their plates. Phrases like *local, organic, slow food,* or *locavore* had yet to become notable entries in the dictionary. Yet people flocked to the shingled two-story restaurant, hidden behind a shady tree, to sample exquisitely crafted cuisine, fresh from the farm. Behind all its press and honors, Chez Panisse is a simple affair—wood-fired pizzas, salads that rely on a trio of ingredients, and a piece of fruit served in a fancy dish provide the mainstays for the café menu; while downstairs, diners enjoy a prix fixe menu of the finest produce and meats available to Bay Area chefs that day. Forty years later, and nearly every Bay Area restaurant worth its weight boasts a farm-fresh, sustainable menu; nearly every neighborhood promises a farmers' market; nearly every farm invites eaters to tour their ag-land, pick their own fruit, and maybe even subscribe to their CSA (community supported agriculture) to receive boxes of newly plucked produce each week.

To be frank, the options for food lovers in Northern California can be dizzying. California grows most of the organic food and half of the produce and nuts for the entire country and in addition lays claim to being the number 1 dairy producing state. To boot, San Francisco has more restaurants packed into its 49 square miles than any place this globetrotter has ever seen. This is why I have crafted the ideal itinerary for a food-lover wanting to eat his or her way through this bountiful agricultural region.

Assuming you are beginning your tour de cuisine in Berkeley, where the food revolution began, enjoy a café au lait and a bowl of perfectly sweetened granola at Alice Waters' French-inspired Café Fanny, and while you are at it, grab a loaf of freshly baked bread at Acme Bread Company, conveniently located next door. This outfit has been kneading the finest flours into edible creations since 1983, and devotees still line up out the door to sample the organic milled walnut levain and sourdough rounds. If the weather is cooperating, grab a seat outdoors and enjoy the rotating cast of characters streaming from these two Berkeley staples.

Sometimes it helps to let someone show you the ins and outs, and in Berkeley's foodie scene, this is especially beneficial. Epicurean concierge Lisa Rogovin leads tours of three of the Bay Area's most interesting food scenes—the Ferry Building, San Francisco's Mission District, and Berkeley's Gourmet Ghetto. If you have time (and the ability to not feel gluttonous by eating nonstop for three hours), I recommend all three tours. But if you have limited belly space (or time), to really understand how the slow food revolution began in this country, sign up for Edible Excursions' Gourmet Ghetto tour. In the short stretch along Shattuck Boulevard (where Alice Waters' shrine to cuisine sits center stage), you'll have the chance to sample artisan cheese at the local bakery/cheese co-op Cheeseboard, whatever soup is bubbling at Soop, mochas at the original Peet's Coffee, and much more.

Travel west on University Avenue until you reach Fourth Street. Enter the Bay Area's only sake distillery, Takara Sake. Tour the 2,500-square-foot warehouse; watch a short video on sake production; explore the only sake museum in the country; then sample the goods. If you need to walk off your buzz, the chic shopping district along Fourth Street houses plenty of stores hawking cooking goods (check out Sur la Table or the divine Pasta Shop), as well as bookstores and a few novelty shops ideal for picking up souvenirs.

Motor east on University, then south on Telegraph until you reach the Oakland foodie neighborhood of Temescal. In just 10 years, this once rough commu-

---

EAST BAY'S ANSWER TO WINE COUNTRY

Whether you find Napa and Sonoma too pricey, too far, or too overrun with drunken bachelorettes, wine lovers do not despair. There are plenty of under-the-radar wine destinations in the eastern part of the Bay Area.

East Bay Winery Bike Tours inspires folks to pedal from Oakland's Jack London Square to Alameda, and take the ferry back. One of the new trends in winemaking is urban cellars, and the East Bay (with its proximity to Napa, as well as the UC Davis wine program) has become a hub for garage winemakers who actually craft fine wines. The bike trip lasts five hours and includes a picnic lunch.

The swath of grape growers in **Livermore Wine Region** might not be fancy, but you can sample robust red wines in casual tasting rooms and rarely have to pay a tasting fee. In yet another attempt to get you out of the car, the **Livermore Valley Wine Tasting Tours** guides cyclists between tasting rooms and through the lovely vineyard-filled valley. If biking is not your deal, visit www.lvwine.org for more detailed tasting room information.

---

nity has morphed into a destination for eaters. During the day, people line up down the street at Bake Sale Betty's for the spicy fried chicken sandwich. And I have friends that travel from Los Angeles for the soft tofu soup at the Pyung Chang Tofu House, which serves up the spiciest Korean food I've ever had. On Sundays, this neighborhood hosts a hopping farmers' market, where you can grub on excellent pizza and purchase plenty of produce.

Continue traveling south on Telegraph and follow the signs to downtown Oakland's waterfront, which is quickly embracing its renaissance. Aided by cheap real estate, Oakland now provides a food lover with an abundance of sustenance, and between you and me, this city is well worth a bit of exploration—especially before the masses figure it out and descend upon the city. Check into the newly renovated Oakland Waterfront Hotel, which not only provides guests with bay views right in the heart of Jack London Square but also with modern nautical-themed guest rooms. Download an Oakland Waterfront Food Trail map to give you a glimpse of all the crafty cuisine in this small stretch of warehouses. Walkers can explore the waterfront by popping into Numi Tea for an authentic tea tasting, or maybe you prefer to sample cocoa at Barlovento Chocolates before heading back to the hotel for a sunset cocktail at Miss Pearl's Jam House.

Frankly, the most stressful decision you'll have to make is where to enjoy dinner. It seems like every day a new eatery opens in Oakland, and you may simply be pining for some of Alice Waters' goodness back in Berkeley (which you should enjoy at some point in your life). However, while you are in Oakland, it would be a shame not to embrace the innovative happenings on this side of the Bay Bridge. Local chef Daniel Patterson (known for his modernistic take on vegetables at San Francisco's Coi) brings his contemporary aesthetic to his new restaurant Plum. This is one of those places that you have to book a table ages in advance, but the reward is well worth the advance planning. Another less opulent option is former Chez Panisse chef Daniel Hallowell's Pizzaiolo, which is the Temescal neighborhood's answer to gourmet pizza in a casual atmosphere (and is another example of the East Bay's devotion to goodness; folks line up before the restaurant even opens). Prefer to walk to dinner near the waterfront? Bocanova serves Latin-inspired cuisine cooked with European stylishness—here you can sample fried shishito peppers, Brazilian-style fish stew, or duck posole.

In the morning, grab a cuppa joe at Blue Bottle Coffee, then walk up to Eighth Street to explore Oakland's bustling Chinatown. Many Bay Area locals consider this the real deal when compared to San Francisco's Chinatown. A venerable dim sum spot is Tao Yuen Pastry, a hole-in-the-wall serving fresh buns filled with everything from pork to taro for pennies; or brave the lines at Legendary Palace for scrumptious dumplings.

Travel south on I-880 and merge onto CA 84 west, exit on Ardenwood Boulevard and turn right. You'll arrive at Ardenwood, a historic 19th-century farm that is now luckily a part of the East Bay Regional Parks. In summer, kiddos ride the minitrain, view a blacksmith demonstration, or tour the historic mansion. Year-round, you can purchase organic veggies out front, tour the gardens, poke into the chicken coops, or peep the various farms animals scattered throughout the grounds.

Return to I-880 and cross the Dumbarton Bridge west to the Peninsula and travel north on US 101. Merge onto CA 92 west and then exit on El Camino Real south. In an unassuming San Mateo strip mall just a few structures down the road, you'll find the Bay Area's best ramen shop, Santa Ramen. Devotees line up (sometimes for up to an hour) to slurp freshly crafted noodles accompanied by a rich pork broth and a variety of additions—the local secret is to order fried garlic on the side, extra pork, roasted seaweed, and corn to add to your bowl. Seriously, folks, it doesn't get better than this.

While the Peninsula has its share of fine eateries, if ramen is not your thing, I recommend traveling back to San Francisco to continue your food tour—

OFF-THE-GRID SAN FRANCISCO

We can thank the fallen economy for one thing: food trucks. Gourmet chefs, often more creative than award-winning gourmands, prepare their creations in trucks, and hungry foodies line up for ages to sample everything from Korean tacos to burgers to tikka masala burritos to lumpia.

In the past, eaters had to follow vendors on their Twitter accounts, finding out when the crème brûlée guy would be haunting Dolores Park, or when those tasty Let's Be Frank dogs would appear downtown. Now, in addition to chasing trucks around town, diners can visit one of the food markets occurring daily. By far the largest collection of food trucks and tents (30 at last count) is on Friday nights at Fort Mason Center. Smaller gatherings occur during the day in the Mission, by Civic Center and downtown. For information, see www.offthegridsf.com.

especially if you have a soft spot for ice cream or pizza. Continue driving west on CA 92, then north on I-280 until you reach San Francisco. Exit on San Jose Avenue, which turns into Guerrero, and drive to 18th Street (turn left). Here you'll find a stretch of San Francisco that locals never tire of—aptly nicknamed the Gastro (for its gastronomic offerings as well as its proximity to the Castro district). Wait with the masses at Bi-Rite Creamery to delight in organic Strauss ice cream crafted by master tastemakers. Favorite flavors include the mint chip, honey lavender, and any of the seasonal fruit varieties. Also in this block, you'll find the Bi-Rite Grocery (same owners as the ice-cream shop)—one of San Francisco's finest gourmet grocers, specializing in local, organic everything. On a warm day, people grab picnic lunches from their extensive to-go counter and head to Dolores Park to pretend they are at the beach. The European-inspired Tartine Bakery crafts addictive sweet treats (he who gets that last bread pudding is one lucky eater), fresh-baked breads (served late in the day), and *tartine* sandwiches with spicy pickled veggies. Finally, Delfina Restaurant and its baby sister Pizzeria Delfina cater to another set of hipsters looking for farm-fresh Italian fare with a California aesthetic. Chances are you cannot leave this block without evoking your gluttonous evil twin, so afterward walk your bootie up Castro Street, one of San Francisco's infamous steep hills, toward Noe Valley to explore the stacks and get inspired at Omnivore Books, a food-centered book shop.

Ride the J Church Muni back to 18th Street to grab your car, then take Van

San Francisco's Lombard Street

Ness to Union Street (turn right) and check into the Union Street Inn, located in the Marina District, often considered the Los Angeles of San Francisco, with its share of boutiques, gourmet cafés, and ladies in big sunglasses pushing well-dressed babies (or tiny dogs) in top-of-the-line strollers. With such great real estate (the neighborhood is perched on the northern edge of San Francisco, hugging the bay and a short bike ride to the Golden Gate Bridge), prepare to pay a pretty penny to stay at this English-inspired inn, but your cash is well spent, especially considering this is the best breakfast you'll find in San Francisco. Though the owner David Coyle was the former chef for the Duke and Duchess of Bedford, his effusive wife, Jane Bertorelli, has learned his tricks, combined them with her own, and now prepares the decadent morning spread. Coyle does come out of retirement to prepare the afternoon sweets served daily.

Next, you'll motor down Lombard Street (which is not actually the curviest street in San Francisco—that honor goes to Potrero Hill's Vermont Street—but the drive is quite lovely all the same) to North Beach: a neighborhood that takes its food very seriously. Reserve in advance for a class at the Cheese School of San Francisco. A favorite is the whiskey and cheese class, but other highlights include Cheeses of Italy, Making Cheese at Home, and How to Taste Cheese. Classes last two hours and will spruce up your appetite enough to get you ready for dinner.

Truth be told, you can live in San Francisco for a decade (like me) and never make it to half of the restaurants in the city (though this gal can boast having made it to most of the good ones!). So ambition may be overrated in this regard. My recommendations are based on consistently good cuisine that won't make you take out a second mortgage and that also happen to support sustainable agriculture.

RESOURCES FOR SAN FRANCISCO'S RESTAURANT SCENE

If none of my recommendations satisfy your cravings, start with the *San Francisco Chronicle's* well-regarded Top 100 Restaurants list, a Who's Who in the restaurant scene compiled by local food critic Michael Bauer.

If you have a Mac device, my friends and venerable travel writers Jules and Effin Older have created an exhaustive list of their favorite dining establishments in their app *San Francisco Restaurants*.

Other places to explore include Marcia Galiardi's www.Tablehopper.com or www.sf.eater.com, both of which blog up-to-the-minute dining news and happenings.

For foodies who have been turned off by eating sushi because of the state of the ocean, chic Pacific Heights' Tataki sushi and sake bar allows diners to feel good about their food choices by only serving sustainable fish. Their sashimi platter exceeds expectation, highlighting seafood rarely seen in traditional sushi bars. Also in San Francisco's hub of high couture and gourmet eats is the breezy Dosa on Fillmore, a casual take on southern Indian cuisine, showcasing those thin pancakes (*dosas*) packed with a variety of spiced veggies and meats.

In the up-and-coming Nopa (north of the Panhandle) neighborhood along Divisadero Street, you can nosh on sustainable Mexican cuisine at The Little Chihuahua. While this isn't the place for margaritas or unlimited chips, you'll want to pop in here for spiced tofu burritos, hefty tostada salads, *grand carne asada*, and probably one of the best watermelon *agua frescas* I've ever had. Finally, for something a touch more high end, though still casual in terms of attire, Nopa restaurant lures local foodies with late-night service of organic comfort food like warm olives, grass-fed burgers, and flatbread pizzas dressed to the nines in farm-fresh produce. Their mixologists rock a mean cocktail, so take a taxi to this hot spot.

If you can hold off on dessert, table-hop yourself over to Citizen Cake's new Pacific Heights digs for a rich spread of sweets. Besides their hot chocolate and ginger cookies (which I go out of my way to attain), their house-made cakes and pies are all the rage with the sweet tooth set.

You cannot plan a food-themed itinerary without highlighting the Ferry Building, San Francisco's temple of cuisine. You'll want to peruse the above

SONOMA COUNTY SUMMER FLAVORS

Menu by John Ash

In addition to being a renowned chef, author, and food and wine educator, many refer to Chef John Ash as the Father of Wine Country Cuisine. In 1980, he opened his namesake restaurant, John Ash & Company, in Santa Rosa, California. It was the first restaurant in Northern California Wine Country to use local, seasonal ingredients to create dishes that complemented the wines being made in the region. Currently, Ash travels the world teaching cooking classes to both home cooks and professionals. Below is a menu crafted especially for you by Ash. (Website: www.chefjohnash.com)

CHILLED HEIRLOOM TOMATO SOUP
WITH SUMMER RELISH

SERVES 6–8

Unfortunately, regular hothouse tomatoes don't work in this recipe. Wait until summer heirloom tomatoes are in-season and select the most flavorful, vine-ripened ones you can find. For variety, I sometimes will separately add up to a cup or so of freshly juiced cucumber, sweet red bell pepper, or carrot to the soup mixture. Also a drizzle of fresh herb oil in place of the olive oil would be a nice little garnish.

4 pounds coarsely chopped ripe tomatoes
¼ cup or so balsamic vinegar, preferably white (or to taste)
Kosher or sea salt and freshly ground white pepper
Summer Relish (recipe follows)
1 large avocado peeled and cut into 6 fans

GARNISH:
Bellwether Farms Crème Fraîche
Fruity extra-virgin olive oil from one of Sonoma County's great producers such as DaVero, The Olive Press, McEvoy Ranch, or even a smoky drizzle from The Smoked Olive's Sonoma oil

Purée the tomatoes in a food processor and force through a medium mesh strainer with a rubber spatula to catch all the seeds and skins. Season to your taste with the vinegar, salt, and pepper. Cover and refrigerate until very cold.

To serve, ladle soup into chilled soup bowls. Place 1 to 2 tablespoons of the Summer Relish in the center and garnish with sliced avocado fans, a dollop of crème fraîche, and a drizzle of olive oil around.

SUMMER RELISH

1 tablespoon chopped fresh basil
2 teaspoons chopped fresh mint
¼ cup diced red onion
3 tablespoons diced red bell pepper

¼ cup seeded and diced cucumber
(lemon cucumber preferred)
2 teaspoons extra-virgin olive oil
Salt and freshly ground pepper to
taste

In a bowl, gently combine the relish ingredients. Correct the seasoning with salt and pepper.

WATERMELON, FIG, ONION, AND FETA SALAD

SERVES 6

This brings together four of the basic flavors: sweet, sour, salty, and peppery. As with all recipes, adjust these elements to your own taste.

1 medium sweet red or white onion,
peeled, cut in ¼-inch-thick
slices, and soaked in ice water
for 30 minutes
Raspberry Vinaigrette (recipe
follows)
1 bunch young watercress or other
peppery greens such as arugula,
woody stems discarded

8 cups chilled, seeded watermelon,
cut into 1-inch cubes (use
both red and yellow watermelon, if available)
6 large ripe fresh figs, fanned
3 ounces or so drained goat milk
feta from Redwood Hill Farm
or Achadinha Goat Cheese
Company

GARNISH:
Mint sprigs

Drain onions, pat dry, and separate into individual rings and pour vinaigrette over. Marinate onions for at least 30 minutes refrigerated.

On chilled plates, arrange a bed of watercress and top with cubed watermelon. Arrange onions and figs attractively around the bed and drizzle with vinaigrette. Crumble feta on top and garnish with mint sprigs. Serve immediately.

RASPBERRY VINAIGRETTE

1 tablespoon finely minced shallots
or green onions
¼ cup Kozlowski Farms raspberry
or other fruit vinegar
¼ cup raspberry purée made from
either fresh or frozen berries,
strained to remove seeds

¼ cup fresh orange juice
2 teaspoons honey (or to taste)
3 tablespoons olive oil
Salt and freshly ground pepper
to taste

Quickly whisk the shallots, vinegar, raspberry purée, orange juice, honey, and oil together to make a smooth mixture. Season to taste with salt and pepper.

GRILLED RIB-EYE STEAKS
WITH BLUE BUTTER AND ONION RINGS
SERVES 6

6 ten- to twelve-ounce well-
trimmed rib-eye steaks cut
thickly
Extra-virgin olive oil

Salt and freshly ground black
pepper
Blue Butter (recipe follows)
Onion Rings (recipe follows)

Brush the steaks well with olive oil and season liberally with salt and pepper. Heat two heavy skillets over medium-high heat and sear and cook steaks until desired doneness, about four minutes per side. Top with Blue Butter and Onions Rings and serve immediately.

BLUE BUTTER

2 heads roasted garlic
1 cup (2 sticks) unsalted butter,
softened
½ cup crumbled Point Reyes blue
cheese

2 tablespoons chopped chives
Salt and freshly ground black
pepper

Squeeze garlic from the cloves and mash in a small bowl. Mix in butter, cheese, and chives until relatively smooth. Season to taste with salt and pepper. Can be wrapped in a log shape with plastic and foil and stored refrigerated up to five days or frozen for one month.

ONION RINGS

3 cups buttermilk
2 large sweet variety onions such as
Maui or Walla Walla,
thinly sliced into rounds and
separated into rings
3 cups flour
2 tablespoons garlic powder

2 tablespoons pure chili powder
such as ancho (Tierra Vegetables
Farm Stand in Santa Rosa is a
great source for this)
2 teaspoons salt
Oil for deep frying

Add buttermilk and onions to a bowl large enough to hold them comfortably. Let stand for one hour. Mix flour, garlic powder, chili powder, and salt together in another bowl.

Preheat over to 350 degrees. Add two inches or so of oil to a deep skillet or saucepan and heat it to 350 degrees. Working with a few onions rings at a time, shake off excess buttermilk, then turn and coat in the seasoned flour mixture. Fry rings in the hot oil until golden brown, adjusting heat to maintain the 350-degree temperature, about two minutes or so. Drain onion rings on paper towels, and then place on baking sheet in oven while frying remaining rings. Serve immediately.

LEMON POLENTA CAKE WITH ROSEMARY SYRUP AND FRESH RASPBERRIES AND PEACHES

SERVES 8

This is a delicious rustic cake similar to those made in many parts of northern Italy. It's best eaten the day it is made. Key here is to not overbake the cake. The syrup can be made days ahead and is delicious drizzled on ice cream, pancakes, or a lusty blue cheese or as an unusual sweetener for iced teas. Other woody herbs such as lemon thyme or oregano make equally interesting syrups.

1 cup stone-ground cornmeal from Tierra Vegetables Farm Stand in Santa Rosa
½ cup all-purpose flour
1½ teaspoons baking powder
¼ teaspoon salt
1 cup sugar
2 large eggs plus 2 egg whites
¼ cup vegetable oil (plus 1 table-spoon for pan)
2 tablespoons softened butter

½ cup Clover plain yogurt
1½ tablespoons grated lemon zest
2 tablespoons fresh lemon juice
3 cups fresh raspberries
2 cups ripe fresh peaches, peeled if desired and sliced
Rosemary Syrup (recipe follows)

GARNISH:
Lightly sweetened and whipped cream or crème fraîche and rosemary sprigs

Line bottom of an 8-inch cake pan with parchment or wax paper and lightly oil. Sift cornmeal, flour, baking powder, and salt together in a bowl and set aside.

In a separate bowl, beat sugar, eggs, and egg whites together until creamy. Beat in oil, butter, yogurt, lemon zest, and juice until smooth. Fold in dry ingredients until just combined. Do not overmix.

Pour batter into prepared pan and smooth top with a spatula. Bake in a preheated 350-degree oven for 35 to 40 minutes or until toothpick inserted in center comes out clean. Cool for 15 minutes on a rack. Invert, peel off paper, and cool completely. Store wrapped in plastic in refrigerator for up to three days or frozen for one month.

TO SERVE: Cut cake into wedges and place on plates, scatter raspberries and peaches around, and drizzle a tablespoon or two of rosemary syrup over berries. Garnish with rosemary sprigs.

ROSEMARY SYRUP

¾ cup sugar
¾ cup dry white wine from any Sonoma County producer
⅓ cup water
3 tablespoons rosemary leaves

1 large bay leaf
½ teaspoon whole peppercorns
3 tablespoons fine balsamic vinegar, the Dry Creek Olive Company makes a nice one

Place all ingredients in a saucepan, bring to a boil, reduce heat and simmer for 10 minutes. Cool, strain, and store refrigerated.

Heirloom tomatoes—the perfect addition to dinner

dinner menu before entering this shrine, as next on the itinerary, you will start collecting goods to prepare your own meal. Producers to consider at this epicurean's delight that may be challenging to find elsewhere include spices, good oil and vinegar, and rib-eye steaks at Golden Gate Meat Company (they'll even teach you how best to butcher your own, if you plan ahead).

Cross the Golden Gate Bridge on US 101 north. Take CA 116 east (turn left off the freeway), left at Frates Road, and enter Green String Farm. This working farm hawks the freshest produce, oils, nuts, herbs, and even beef. While the farm is not certified organic, their sustainable farming methods are good enough for Alice Waters to serve at her restaurant. Poke around the chicken coop, spot the sheep, or just take a deep breath and smell what farm-fresh produce really smells like. FYI: Keep an eye out as you approach Sonoma. The owners of the farm also have two "beyond organic" Sonoma wineries: Cline Cellars (their ancient vine Mourvedre makes a lovely addition to a chocolate dessert) and Jacuzzi Family Vineyards (Italian wines like Barbera and Sangiovese shine here) are both good choices for dinner pairings.

Cheeseaholics swear by the creamy variations at Petaluma's Cowgirl Creamery, and on Wednesdays, you can tour their new cheese-making facilities and receive a bag of fresh *queso* for tonight's dinner. You must reserve in advance. However, if you happen to be passing through the area on any other day, your cheese needs can still be met by Epicurean Connection. From Green String Farms, continue east on CA 116 to CA 12 toward Sonoma. You'll find this adorable space, created in 2010 by cheese maker extraordinaire Sheana Davis. Learn to make crème fraîche (reserve ahead for this popular event) or just purchase your blue cheese for dinner.

Continue on CA 12 to Sonoma to indulge in one of my favorite California restaurants, the girl & the fig. Sit outside in the flowery garden, sip crisp Pinot gris, and consider the aesthetic of a chef using French techniques on local flavors. Ooh la la. Highlights include the hamburger, pastis-scented mussels and fries, house-smoked trout salad, and lavender crème brûlée.

Continue on CA 12 north through the Valley of the Moon wine region. Here, you'll want to begin collecting wines for your dinner. In the hamlet of Glen Ellen, tour Benziger Family Winery's organic vineyards via tram, then pick up a bottle of their famed Pinot blanc or Chardonnay to pair with your watermelon salad. Continue north on CA 12 into Kenwood (a blink and you'll miss this community that's home to one of Sonoma County's famed Kenwood Inn). Pull into Kaz Vineyard and Winery, a destination that's so organic they recommend that you bring

San Francisco's ferry building

Healdsburg's Barndiva Restaurant

your own jugs to fill. Wines here are as quirky as the owners, but nevertheless, the grounds, vibe, and complex red wine blends not crafted anywhere else are worth your time. (For more detailed information about this region see chapter 6.)

Once you have collected your goods, it is time to settle into your vacation rental. While you can sleep in everything from multimillion-dollar Wine Country villas to comfy cottages decked in subtle country antiques, you'll be hard-pressed to not find something in both your style and price range. Book in advance through the comprehensive list on www.sonomavalley.com. Spend the evening enjoying your summer bounty.

For noncooks wanting a memorable meal, travel north on US 101 to Healdsburg where you have a stellar choice of sustainable menus. Cyrus, the brainchild of Chef Douglas Keane, has made a name of itself in food-loving circles by serving up a divine prix fixe menu, highlighted by a cheese and caviar cart fit for Roman gods. You'll need to reserve well in advance for your expensive dinner here, and while not exactly the Superbowl of food (for that you need to travel to Yountville to sample the nine-course dinner at French Laundry), it may qualify as a semifinal entry. Alternatively, the regal Madrona Manor never fails to enchant eaters hunting for food alchemy—and I am not merely talking about the hydrogen ice cream made at your table. The cheese course, gamey entrées, and rich salads lure honeymooners and celebratory feasts. For something a touch more down to earth, settle in at an outdoor table at Barndiva, surrounded by modern art, a gravel floor, and fountains trickling in the distance. More a scene than a place to write home about the food, your simple dollop of french fries, heirloom salad, or the whole roasted chicken will not disappoint.

IN THE AREA

ACCOMMODATIONS

Kenwood Inn, 10400 Sonoma Highway, Kenwood. The 29 luxurious rooms in this Mediterranean-inspired inn offer numerous amenities, ranging from fireplaces to private patios and jetted tubs. Call 800-353-6966. Website: www.kenwoodinn.com.

Oakland Waterfront Hotel, 10 Washington Street, Oakland. Massive renovations to the hotel in 2008 resulted in upgraded guest rooms, a new lobby, and nautical-inspired décor. Call 800-738-7477 or 510-836-3800. Website: www.jdvhotels.com.

Union Street Inn, 2229 Union Street, San Francisco. This Edwardian-style B&B offers rooms with fresh flowers and fruit baskets, as well as a lovely garden. Call 415-346-0424. Website: www.unionstreetinn.com.

ATTRACTIONS AND RECREATION

Ardenwood, 34600 Ardenwood Boulevard, Fremont. A 19th-century working farm and country estate, complete with Victorian mansion and gardens. Exhibits illustrate agricultural practices from the 1870s to present. Call 510-796-0199. Website: www.ebparks.org.

Cheese School of San Francisco, 2155 Powell Street, second floor, San Francisco. With classes on everything from cheese and beverage pairings to demystifying blue cheese, you'll be an expert in no time. The school also arranges special events such as farm tours and cheese-making demonstrations. Call 415-346-8570. Website: www.cheeseschoolsf.com.

East Bay Winery Bike Tours, 530 Water Street, Oakland. A typical tour includes three to four wineries and a picnic lunch, with an experienced guide who will point out sites along the 10- to 14-mile bike route. Call 510-285-7884. Website: www.eastbaywinerybiketours.com.

Edible Excursions, 752 Duncan Street, San Francisco. Offers gourmet food-themed tours of the Mission District, the famed Ferry Building, and North Berkeley's Gourmet Ghetto. Call 415-806-5970. Website: www.ediblecursions.net.

Jack London Square, Broadway and Embarcadero, Oakland. Visit the farmers' market each Sunday from 9 AM to 2 PM, shop at the boutiques, or stop at one of the restaurants for everything from Mexican classics to Korean BBQ. Call 510-645-9292. Website: www.jacklondonsquare.com.

Livermore Valley Wine Tasting Tours, 871 Kottinger Drive, Pleasanton. Seasonal tours run from mid-May through mid-November. Tours include a gourmet lunch and the chance to taste private reserve wines. Call 925-399-6751. Website: www.livermorewineandcycletours.com.

Oakland Waterfront Food Trail, Oakland. The map includes over 45 food-related companies, including breweries, wineries, ice-cream shops, bakeries, and butchers in Oakland. Call 510-654-4400. Website: www.oaklandfood.org.

Omnivore Books, 3885 Cesar Chavez Street, San Francisco. Features a selection of new, rare, antiquarian, and collectible books on everything about food and drink. Call 415-282-4712. Website: www.omnivorebooks.com.

Sur la Table, 1806 Fourth Street, Berkeley. This shop offers a wide variety of cooking tools, cookware, bakeware, and cutlery. Call 510-849-2252. Website: www.surlatable.com.

DINING/DRINKS

Acme Bread Company, 1601 San Pablo Avenue, Berkeley. Artisan breads such as baguettes, rolls, and croissants are the stars at this bakery. Call 510-524-1327.

Bake Sale Betty's, 5098 Telegraph Avenue, Oakland. Besides the hugely popular fried chicken, other hits at this restaurant include chicken potpie and strawberry shortcake. Call 510-985-1213. Website: www.bakesalebetty.com.

Barlovento Chocolates, 638 Second Street, Oakland. Try a box of truffles, including flavors such as cardamom honey and tarragon. Call 510-238-8787. Website: www.barloventochocolates.com.

Barndiva, 231 Center Street, Healdsburg. Try seared Pacific halibut or a bacon-wrapped pork loin at this French-inspired restaurant. Call 707-431-0100. Website: www.barndiva.com.

Benziger Family Winery, 1883 London Ranch Road, Glen Ellen. The highlight of this vineyard is the tram tour, a 45-minute tour that includes a special tasting of the vineyard's biodynamic wines. Call 888-490-2739. Website: www.benziger.com.

Bi-Rite Creamery, 3692 18th Street, San Francisco. Try ice-cream flavors like salted caramel, honey lavender, and Ricanelas (cinnamon ice cream with snickerdoodles). Call 415-626-5600. Website: www.biritecreamery.com.

Bi-Rite Grocery, 3639 18th Street, San Francisco. Sells locally produced organic meat, fish, produce, cheese, and wine. Call 415-241-9760. Website: www.biritemarket.com.

Blue Bottle Coffee, 300 Webster Street, Oakland. If you're looking for a cup of authentic, rich coffee, this coffeehouse serves fresh organic coffee roasted on vintage gear. Call 510-653-3394. Website: www.bluebottlecoffee.net.

Café Fanny, 1603 San Pablo Avenue at Cedar Street, Berkeley. A casual stand-up food bar serving breakfast pastries and coffee, as well as soups, salads, and sandwiches for lunch. Call 510-524-5447. Website: www.cafefanny.com.

Chez Panisse, 1517 Shattuck Avenue, Berkley. Expect farm-fresh cuisine at this foodie mecca, which offers an expansive wine list and delicious entrées, such as braised duck breast or grilled lamb. Reservations for dinner can be made up to one month in advance and are highly recommended. Call 510-548-5525. Website: www.chezpanisse.com.

Citizen Cake, 2125 Fillmore Street, San Francisco. The menus change frequently at this patisserie and restaurant owned by pastry expert Elizabeth Falkner. Stop in for lunch, dinner, or snacks on weekdays and brunch on weekends. Call 415-861-2228. Website: www.citizencake.com.

Cline Cellars, 24737 Arnold Drive, Sonoma. Visit the vineyards and the mission museum, which is an exhibit of mission-style housing models from the 1939 World's Fair. The vineyards also feature a guest villa if you're inclined to stay overnight. Call 707-940-4010. Website: www.clinecellars.com.

Community Market, 1899 Mendocino Avenue, Santa Rosa. A huge vegetarian natural food store: a full grocery with produce, refrigerated, and bulk food sections. Call 707-546-1806. Website: www.srcommunitymarket.com.

Cowgirl Creamery, 105 H Street, Petaluma. The award-winning cheeses at this shop offer a wide variety, including a cheese wrapped with organic stinging nettle leaves (frozen before they are wrapped around the cheese to remove the sting). Call 866-433-7834. Website: www.cowgirlcreamery.com.

Cyrus, 29 North Street, Healdsburg. Try small plates from the tasting menu, such as gulf shrimp with banana blossoms and sea scallops in a watermelon and coriander broth, or choose the traditional five-course menu (with vegetarian options). Call 707-433-3311. Website: www.cyrus restaurant.com.

Delfina Restaurant, 3621 18th Street, San Francisco. Draws people from around the Bay Area to sample bucatini and pasta fagioli. Call 415-552-4055. Website: www.delfinasf.com.

Dosa on Fillmore, 1700 Fillmore Street, San Francisco. If you're looking for traditional South Indian cuisine, this restaurant serves up delicious *dosas* packed with spicy veggies. The restaurant also has a unique take on cocktails, using Indian spices, tinctures, and nectars. Call 415-441-3672. Website: www.dosasf.com.

Epicurean Connection, 18812 Sonoma Highway, Sonoma. The selection of artisanal cheeses, olive oils, organic meats, and fresh preserves is enough to satisfy any foodie with a curiosity for local goods. The restaurant serves amazing maple bacon waffles for breakfast on Saturday mornings. Call 707-935-7960. Website: www.theepicureanconnection .com.

Ferry Building, located along the Embarcadero at the foot of Market Street. Enjoy fresh pastries, produce, meat, and an excellent selection of coffee beans, loose-leaf tea, and wine. Stop by on a Tuesday or Saturday for the farmers' market. Website: www.ferry buildingmarketplace.com.

the girl & the fig, 110 West Spain Street, Sonoma. The three-course prix fixe dinner features dishes such as grilled steak with roasted summer squash. Locals sit on the patio or at the French-inspired bar and delight in the burgers. Call 707-938-3634. Website: www.thegirlandthefig.com.

Green String Farm, 3571 Old Adobe Road, Petaluma. The farm store offers a wide selection of produce, nuts, dried herbs, eggs, and cheese. Call 707-778-7500. Website: www.greenstringfarm .com.

Jacuzzi Family Vineyards, 24724 Arnold Drive, Sonoma. The complimentary tasting includes five wines. Call 707-931-7575. Website: www.jacuzzi wines.com.

Kaz Vineyard and Winery, 233 Adobe Canyon Road, Kenwood. The vineyard specializes in complex reds and rare varietals, such as Lenoir and Tannat, and uses organic farming methods. Call 707-833-2536. Website: www.kaz winery.com.

Legendary Palace, 708 Franklin Street, Oakland. Traditional dim-sum fare with over two hundred menu selections. Call 510-663-9188.

The Little Chihuahua, 292 Divisadero Street, San Francisco. Try the specialty black bean and plantain burrito along with a house-made *horchata*. Call 415-255-8225. Website: www.thelittle chihuahua.com.

Madrona Manor, 1001 Westside Road, Healdsburg. Build your own coursed meal with soft, delicate, smooth, meaty, or sweet foods. Call 800-258-4003. Website: www.madronamanor.com.

Miss Pearl's Jam House, 1 Broadway, Oakland. A waterfront restaurant with live music on the weekends. The food has a southern flair, with seafood jambalaya, gumbo, and BBQ as menu staples. Call 510-444-7171. Website: www.misspearlsjamhouse.com.

Nopa, 560 Divisadero Street, San Francisco. Specializing in organic wood-fired cuisine, the menu includes dishes such as Moroccan vegetable tagine and wood-roasted king salmon. Call 415-864-8643. Website: http://nopasf.com.

Numi Tea, 1050 22nd Avenue, Oakland. Organic, fair-trade loose-leaf teas served in a cozy, coffeehouse setting. Call 510-567-8903. Website: www.numitea.com.

Pasta Shop, 1786 Fourth Street, Berkeley. Stop by the cheese counter to sample artisan cheeses, or check out the specialty groceries section, which has hard-to-find baking ingredients and rare cookbooks. Call 510-250-6005. Website: www.pastashop.net.

Pizzaiolo, 5008 Telegraph Avenue, Oakland. Wood-fired pizzas with flavor combinations such as Monterey Bay squid, cherry tomato and aioli, or roasted eggplant with ricotta and mint. Call 510-652-4888. Website: www.pizzaiolooakland.com.

Pizzeria Delfina, 3611 18th Street, San Francisco. Traditional pizza topping combinations such as fresh tomato, basil, and mozzarella or prosciutto with panna and arugula are famous at this pizzeria. Call 415-437-6800. Website: www.pizzeriadelfina.com.

Plum, 2214 Broadway, Oakland. A great late-night spot serving gluten-free, vegetarian friendly cuisine, though the popular pork loin is a must for carnivores. Call 510-444-7586. Website: www.plumoakland.com.

Pyung Chang Tofu House, 4701 Telegraph Avenue, Oakland. Even tofu skeptics will be surprised by the dishes served here, such as the spicy tofu stew served with endless bowls of rice. Call 510-658-9040.

Santa Ramen, 1944 South El Camino Real, San Mateo. Traditional pork based ramen in a strip mall packs the house. Vegetarians will go hungry here. Closed Tues. Call 650-344-5918.

Takara Sake, 708 Addison Street, Berkeley. Visit the tasting room to sample sake and plum wine and the sake museum to see exhibits of sake artifacts and learn about the sake-making process. Call 510-540-8250. Website: www.takarasake.com.

Tao Yen Pastry, 816 Franklin Street, Oakland. Call 510-834-9200. Grab dim sum or pastries from this casual restaurant that serves everything from egg custard tarts to taro puffs.

Tartine Bakery, 600 Guerrero Street, San Francisco. A wildly popular bakery with lines out the door for bread pudding, fresh-baked bread, and hot pressed sandwiches. Call 415-487-2600. Website: www.tartinebakery.com.

Tataki Sushi and Sake Bar, 2815 California Street, San Francisco. Sashimi Delight, the signature dish at this Japanese-style sushi bar, is made with fresh, sustainable ingredients and offers 20 pieces of seared fish with an assortment of dipping sauces. Call 415-931-1182. Website: www.tatakisushibar.com.

Tierra Vegetables, 651 Airport Boulevard, Santa Rosa. Not your typical farm stand, this brother and sister team offers only produce they have grown at their own farm. It's as fresh as you can get without picking your own. Call 707-837-8366. Website: www.tierravegetables.com.

OTHER CONTACTS

Healdsburg Chamber of Commerce & Visitors Bureau, 217 Healdsburg Avenue, Healdsburg. Call 707-433-6935. Website: www.healdsburg.com.

San Francisco Visitor Information Center, 900 Market Street, San Francisco. Website: www.onlyinsanfrancisco .com.

Sonoma Valley Visitors Bureau, 453 First Street East, Sonoma. Call 866-996-1090. Website: www.sonomavalley.com.

Visit Berkeley, 2030 Addison Street, #102, Berkeley. Call 510-549-7040 or 800-847-4823. Website: www.visit berkeley.com.

Visit Oakland, 463 11th Street, Oakland. Call 510-839-9000. Website: www .visitoakland.org.

Enjoying a book in a park

3 Literary Northern California

Estimated length: 183 miles

Estimated time: 4 hours straight through, or 3 days

Getting there: From San Francisco, take the ferry to and from Oakland's Jack London Square. Hop on US 101 south to Salinas and drive about two hours. Connect to CA 68 west to Monterey.

Highlights: Getting to know the Bay Area's literary scene; exploring San Francisco's Chinatown and North Beach; sipping brews in Jack London's favorite watering holes; getting to know John Steinbeck's Monterey.

The San Francisco Bay Area has a history of being untamed: Not just because of its haunting beauty in the form of soaring redwoods atop dazzling cliffs leaning precariously over crystal waters like some vision out of a storybook, but also the Bay Area's true heart, bones, and spirit, which makes this area so unique, its writers. From John Steinbeck to Gertrude Stein, from Jack London to Jack Kerouac and the Beats of North Beach, the Bay Area has produced a number of bookish folk who have profoundly changed American culture. We will take you on the road starting at San Francisco's Chinatown/North Beach District, then east to one of Oakland's oldest neighborhoods, and finally south to the dramatic coastlines of Monterey Bay to find out what it truly means to be, well, literally a San Franciscan.

Author Amy Tan, though originally from Oaktown, has many of her works set in San Francisco's Chinatown district, including the critically acclaimed novel *The Joy Luck Club* (which was later adapted into a film). It was the formation of the People's Republic of China in 1949, coupled with corruption and political unrest, that forced many Chinese from their homeland to this very spot. Over the

---

STAR MAPS:
The Literary Scene in San Francisco

Because of the richness, beauty, and diversity of the landscape, it's no wonder the San Francisco Bay Area is home to poet laureates, Pulitzer Prize–winning authors, and the most eclectic writers of our time.

Isabel Allende Llona, *The House of the Spirits* (*La casa de los espíritus*), lives in San Rafael.

Michael Chabon, *The Amazing Adventures of Kavalier & Clay*, lives in Berkeley.

Diane di Prima, *Memoirs of a Beatnik*, lives in San Francisco.

Lawrence Ferlinghetti, *A Coney Island of the Mind*, lives in San Francisco.

Jonathan Franzen, *The Corrections*, lives in the Santa Cruz Mountains.

Amy Tan, *The Joy Luck Club*, lives in Santa Clara.

Alice Malsenior Walker, *The Color Purple*, lives in Mendocino.

---

decades, Little Shanghai grew, families thrived, and traditions were preserved, complete with religious temples, specialized markets, fortune cookie factories, and, of course, Chinese restaurants.

To begin your journey, enter through the ornate Chinatown Gate on Grant Avenue at Bush Street. A gift from the Republic of China in 1970 as a symbol of good faith between the countries, the bright-colored pagoda-topped doorway is like a portal into a tiny universe of bustling tourists and locals shopping for everything from live chickens to jade statues. Peruse in the many shops and wares on Grant Street just as it was decades ago. Chinese slippers, good luck charms, and

Morning tai chi in downtown San Francisco

Chinatown Gate in San Francisco

mechanical trinkets are just a few of the items you'll see by the basketful. So don't be surprised to find a ribbon-adorned phallus in one of the storefront windows.

To learn more about Tan's culture and Chinese heritage, head to the **Chinese Historical Society of America** located in San Francisco's original YWCA building. If you are interested in the Chinese American experience, this museum not only offers a historical perspective but also some interesting modern art.

For a yummy lunch and the best dim sum in town, try **Great Eastern Restaurant** on Jackson Street between Wentworth Place and Cooper Alley, an authentic experience complete with white tablecloths and aquariums of live delicacies. There's usually a decent wait time, but the food is well worth it. Highlights are shrimp dumplings (*har gow*), pork dumplings (*shumai*), and lava buns. If you miss out on the dim sum, Peking duck satisfies every time.

After lunch, mosey over to the Golden Gate Fortune Cookie Factory at Ross Alley at Jackson Street. The non-Chinese origin of these cookies is comically illustrated in *The Joy Luck Club* when Lindo Jong finds a job at a fortune cookie factory in Chinatown. After a few attempts at translating the fortunes in Chinese, she realizes the cookies contain "bad instruction" rather than good sense. Observe how cookies are made and purchase them fresh—they even have some racy fortunes. Or try the egg tarts and lotus pancakes.

For many, when they think of San Francisco, peace, love, and the summer of '69 wafts through the brain like a patchouli cloud. But the decade before that era was even more influential to the Bay Area's literary scene and, of course, the hippie counterculture. Meet the Beats of North Beach—a movement also known as the San Francisco Renaissance. The original Beat Generation gang included Allen Ginsberg, William S. Burroughs, and Jack Kerouac, who found each other in New York but later made their exodus west to San Francisco. This skeleton crew of bohemians grew into an iconic movement called the Beat Generation, the term first used by Jack Kerouac in 1948.

Take the Mason line of the cable car north to Columbus Avenue then travel south along Columbus Avenue, past the slew of alfresco cafes, and turn left on Kearny to the newly erected The Beat Museum. This tiny space packs a punch with a carefully selected collection, including Ferlinghetti paintings, Allen Ginsberg's typewriter, and first edition prints of Jack Kerouac's *On the Road*. The mu-

San Francisco's cable car

North Beach poets are serious about their cuppa joe.

seum also sells books and memorabilia and hosts special events like book signings, readings, and lectures.

Need to replace your college copy of Kerouac or Kesey? Turn right onto Columbus Avenue until you reach City Lights Bookstore. Founded in 1953 by Lawrence Ferlinghetti, it is the quintessential Beat headquarters, complete with a publishing house for fringe writers and dharma bums (Alan Ginsberg's *Howl* was published here). They also sell journals so you too can create your own literary masterpiece.

Newly inspired to write the great American novel? Then grab a table and an espresso at the original Caffe Trieste (from City Lights walk north to Vallejo and turn right). Opened in 1956 by Giovanni Giotta, this Beat haunt has housed many a writer including Ferlinghetti, Kerouac, Ginsberg, Hirschman (Poet Laureate of San Francisco), and a young Francis Ford Coppola, who wrote the screenplay to *The Godfather* here. Admire the archive of black-and-white photos on the wall or stay for the Caffe Trieste Saturday Concert series, the longest running show in San Francisco since 1971.

North Beach is not called the Little Italy of the West for nothing. There are a myriad of bakeries, delis, pastry shops, and restaurants to tempt your palette. And some spots are over a century old. Around the corner, on Grant Avenue, is Molinari's, the ultimate neighborhood deli and for good reason. This gem has been around since 1896 and is overflowing with hanging imported meats and cheeses (the *proscuitto di Parma* is to die for!). The sandwiches are especially generous, and if there's space, outdoor seating is available. If you are craving something sweet, the Italian French Baking Company of San Francisco just a block north on Grant Avenue offers breads crafted of their heirloom yeast (which is as old as the bakery), and the baking hearth has been in use since the spot opened. Come here for the coconut macaroon, which is the best in the city. For a high-end

---

DIANE DI PRIMA:
The Queen of the Beats

Though mostly a boys' club, one cannot mention the Beat Generation without speaking of Diane di Prima. Named the Poet Laureate of San Francisco in 2009, di Prima is also a prose writer, playwright, activist, and teacher. A bridge figure between the Beat movement and the hippie counterculture, she spent the late 1950s and early '60s in New York City with the original beatniks and was later at Millbrook with Timothy Leary's psychedelic crew. In the late 1960s, she made San Francisco her permanent home. A movement is currently underway to have a street in the city named in her honor. To learn more about her legacy, travel to **Bird and Beckett Books** in the Glen Park neighborhood, where she often hosts readings and signings.

California Italian fare, Rose Pistola is your place on Columbus Avenue. This spacious North Beach spot is a great choice for rustic cuisine of the highest quality. You can get everything from a pizza cooked in a wood-burning oven to family-style pasta. Pumpkin bread pudding with caramel gelato is heavenly! Another great eatery is Tomaso's, located on Kearny Street. This North Beach restaurant has been around for ages and still uses its original wood-burning oven for pizza.

After dark, North Beach is the place to be. Vesuvio's Bar, located at the corner of Columbus Avenue and Jack Kerouac Alley (check out the murals newly painted to honor Kerouac), is considered the epicenter of Beat locales. Like the volcano Mount Vesuvius, this little pub erupted into the Beat world on October 1955 when Neal Cassady (aka Dean Moriarity of *On the Road* fame) decided to grab a drink before heading to a poetry reading. This is also where the beatnik look became infamous thanks to Wally Hedrick, who sat in the window dressed in full Beat regalia—beard, turtleneck, and sandals—while creating improvisational drawings and paintings. Today, Vesuvio's has a great collection of Beat memorabilia as well as serving potent cocktails.

For that speakeasy vibe, head over to Specs' Twelve Adler Museum Cafe on Adler Place between Broadway and Columbus. This dive bar, which features a piano player, is literally frozen in time and has been serving the North Beach misfits for decades. Nautical paraphernalia, like a shark jaw, and memorabilia, including a photo homage to Jack London, make this a one-of-a-kind haunt for those that can appreciate the seedier side of life.

It wasn't just the Beat poets who made North Beach famous; its edgy comics and premier musicians have also contributed. At the **Purple Onion** playhouse, managed by Bud Steinhoff until his death in 1983, a foul-mouthed brood of performers has run the gamut from political satire to black humor. Lenny Bruce, Woody Allen, Richard Pryor, and Robin Williams, as well as the legendary music group the Kingston Trio, have all performed here. For campy fun, check out **Beach Blanket Babylon**. For 20 years, this cabaret has been entertaining the San Franciscans with outrageous musical numbers and costumes, or **Bimbo's 365 Club** on Columbus Avenue at the corner of Chestnut Street. This quirky venue is a throwback from the '30s, complete with a red velvet and topless mermaid décor, grand ballroom, and bathroom attendants. Enjoy first-class performances while kicking it old school.

Rest your bohemian bones at **Hotel Boheme** located right on Columbus. Hotel Boheme not only offers the bohemian experience similar to a Parisian hotel but also celebrates the literary roots of the North Beach neighborhood. The **Hotel des Arts** on Bush Street is located across from the Chinatown Gate and is a great spot for people who want to be in the center of downtown but don't want the run-of-the-mill type of room.

Start your day with a pastry and coffee at **Caffé Roma** on Columbus Avenue. Owner Tony Azzolini takes each cup as seriously as the bar. Sip your cappuccino and catch a glimpse of some local celebrities before heading north on Columbus to **Fisherman's Wharf's Pier 39** to catch a ferry to Oaktown's **Jack London Square**.

Interiors at Hotel des Arts

Although writer Gertrude Stein might have been disappointed, visitors to Oakland will more likely be delighted. Don't be surprised to see plenty of "I Hella Heart Oakland" adorning many a bumper and storefront window. This progressive city with a renewed downtown has come into its own especially with the recently renovated and vibrant Jack London Square, named for John Griffith "Jack" London, an American author, journalist, and

---

THE MISSION DISTRICT'S LITQUAKE:
Valencia's Literary Answer to the Bar Crawl

Litquake was the brainchild of writers, Jane Ganahl and Jack Boulware over beers at the Tenderloin's **Edinburgh Castle Pub** in San Francisco. What started as Litstock, a free one-day reading series in Golden Gate Park in 1999, erupted into Litquake, the largest independent literary festival on the West Coast—boasting national and international authors, youth programs, a spring season of literary events, and a fun litcrawl in October.

---

social activist best remembered as the author of *White Fang* and *Call of the Wild.* London was born in 1876 in San Francisco and later moved to Oakland with his family. In high school, London's moniker was the Boy Socialist of Oakland, and he even ran for mayor, but writing was his first true love. Jack London District, which surrounds the square, has undergone dramatic rehabilitation and was home to California governor (and former Oakland mayor) Jerry Brown.

Arrive at Jack London Square where you will dock at the Clay Street Terminal on Water Street. This waterfront property has become a popular tourist destination. Jack London spent much of his childhood here dreaming of adventures with pirate and sailors, which was surely the impetus for novels like *The Sea Wolf.*

Start your tour of the square by visiting the life-sized Jack London Statue located at the foot of Broadway near the flag; this tribute in bronze was lovingly created by artist Cedric Wentworth. For lunch, the Mexican fare at Cocina Poblana is *muy delicioso.* Try the *tacos al vapor* while you sip on one of over one hundred tequilas to choose from. On Tuesdays, the tacos are free! For you meat lovers, there's Everett and Jones: a true barbecue joint located on Broadway in a stunningly restored brick building. Though spacious, the brick and décor still makes for a cozy environment. The sauces tend to be on the spicier side, so go for mild if you can't take the heat.

Grab a cool one at Heinold's First and Last Chance Saloon (unofficially named Jack London's Rendezvous) at 48 Webster Street like London used to do as a lad. What once stood on stilts over the coastal mudflats has landed in the square like Dorothy's house. This crooked 125-year-old bar is just a shy of being 18 by 22 feet with just six barstools and cool memorabilia. You can just picture a 17-year-old Jack confessing to bar owner John Heinold of his desire to attend university and his dreams of becoming a writer.

After you imbibe, search the ground right in front of Heinold's and you'll see distinctive wolf tracks, which are placed throughout the square. This path is called Jack London History Walk. Follow the trail and discover diamond-shaped historic markers that explain the history of the area. The trail ends at the **Presidential Yacht Potomac,** aka FDR's Floating White House. This was Roosevelt's respite away from home (and was formerly owned by Elvis!). The yacht has been renovated and transformed into a museum with tours in honor of the former president.

Travel back to the Clay Street Terminal on Water Street and take the ferry back to the Fisherman's Wharf. Detour to Union Square's Hotel Rex's Library Bar for some American-inspired cuisine in a '20s-themed salon that's a tribute to Kenneth Rexroth. Then head back to North Beach for another night stay before packing up and heading south to Steinbeck country. A road trip through Central California reads like a classic novel, each turn of the road unfolding a dramatic, new chapter. Scores of writers have tried to capture Central California's unique essence, but few are as iconic as John Steinbeck, the author who achieved power in simplicity and beauty in gritty reality.

Explore Central California through Steinbeck's eyes with three special stops: Soledad Mission and River Road Wine Country, the setting of *Of Mice and Men;* Salinas, Steinbeck's birthplace and home of the National Steinbeck Center; and Cannery Row, the once industrial, canning district that is now home to luxury oceanfront hotels, boutique shopping, fine and casual dining, and exciting nightlife.

From San Francisco travel south on US 101 to the city of Salinas, the birthplace of Steinbeck. Steinbeck once wrote, "Not everyone has the good fortune to

---

CITY ARTS & LECTURES:
A San Francisco Institution

For over 30 years, the City Arts & Lectures series at the Herbst Theatre has been showcasing leading figures in the world of art and ideas, including outstanding icons in literature, as well as in science, the performing arts, and more. Located on 401 Van Ness Avenue between Cottage Row and Fillmore Streets, past performances include Beat generation poets Gary Snyder and Allen Ginsberg. Produced with KQED 88.5 FM in San Francisco, City Arts & Lectures programs can be heard on more than 170 public radio stations across the country.

> **GERTRUDE STEIN:**
> Oakland and Being "There"
>
> Gertrude Stein, though born in Allegheny, Pennsylvania, grew up in Oakland and San Francisco during the late 1800s. Her famous quote "There is no there, there" is a direct response to her visit back to O-Town only to find her childhood neighborhood had vanished. As a snarky retort, the city of Oakland has commemorated a statue by artist Roslyn Mazzilli in the **Oakland City Center,** where thousands of visitors regularly pass by the 1988 polychrome aluminum sculpture simply titled *There.*

be born in Salinas." There you will find the National Steinbeck Center, a cultural center with permanent and temporary exhibits that capture the essence of the Central Coast and Salinas Valley past and present. Enjoy lunch at The Steinbeck House. This Queen Ann Victorian, built in 1897 and lovingly restored in 1973, was Steinbeck's boyhood home and is now a museum and restaurant. Or check out the Grower's Pub for lunch; they have a prime-rib French-dip sandwich to die for. Afterward, take a leisurely stroll along Main Street, taking special notice of Buildings Nos. 201 and 247; both were featured in the novel *East of Eden.*

Travel south on US 101 through the Salinas Valley to the small town of Soledad, head west on Arroyo Seco Road to the scenic G17, which turns into River Road. Lining this two-lane road are rolling hills terraced with farmland and vineyards. Take your time to stop at Paraiso, Pessagno, and Marilyn Remark Vineyards to taste some of the very best in Monterey County wine. Don't miss Soledad Mission, built in 1791, located near the Salinas River. This lonely Spanish-style church has not changed much since the days Steinbeck wrote *Of Mice and Men,* the story of two migrant farm workers tending the "golden foothill slopes" around Soledad.

Travel north on US 101 and take CA 68 west for 3 miles to experience the town of Spreckels, where Steinbeck worked as a young man in the 1920s. Turn off to visit what used to be the largest sugar plant in the world (where Steinbeck worked) and is now just a few streets of what remains of a remarkably preserved company town called Spreckels: a place that inspired several of Steinbeck's novels including *Tortilla Flat* and was the location for the film adaptation of *East of Eden.*

If you continue west on CA 68 to the breathtakingly beautiful valley between Monterey and Salinas, you'll find the picture-perfect community of Corral de

Tierra ("fence of earth"). In his youth, John Steinbeck and his sister, Mary, played at the base of Castle Rock in Corral de Tierra, the striking sandstone cliffs that reach toward the heavens from the valley below, which Steinbeck described in his *The Pastures of Heaven.*

To truly get the Steinbeck experience, why not visit and work on an actual farm? Located off CA 68 (you can't miss the four giant statues of farmers working in the fields), The Farm is an agricultural education center and local farming business that offers fresh produce for sale, farm tours, and activities for the whole family.

When you arrive in Monterey, check into the Monterey Bay Inn, located on the quieter end of Cannery Row steps from San Carlos Beach. This boutique hotel is reminiscent of a 1930s cruise liner. Its oceanfront rooms with balconies overlooking the Bay contribute to the feeling of luxury at sea.

Make reservations ahead of time for dinner at the world-famous Sardine Factory, Monterey's most elegant and most romantic restaurant specializing in fresh seafood and USDA prime beef. With its lavish décor, impeccable service, and 35,000-bottle wine cellar, it is hard to imagine that the restaurant was once a cafeteria for sardine cannery workers. Among the plethora of wines on the menu, you will find your favorites from the River Road wineries you visited earlier.

Monterey's Cannery Row

In the morning, follow in Steinbeck's footsteps along the Cannery Row History Walk, detailed in a walking map for visitors, which includes a map of the murals and various historical markers and sites, a history, a time line, directions, and even a Canning Label Scavenger Hunt. Included on the walk is Steinbeck's home Lara-Soto Adobe, which he called "a house I have wanted since I was a little kid." It's now the admissions center at the Monterey International Institute. Along the way, stop at famous local chef John Pisto's Paradiso Trattoria for lunch, where you will find fresh, local seafood prepared with an Italian flair.

Before dinner, visit the Scheid Vineyard tasting room, where you can

OTHER CENTRAL COAST LITERARY STOPS

Robinson Jeffers Tor House

The story begins in 1914, when American poet John Robinson Jeffers and his wife, Una, glimpsed the unspoiled beauty of the Carmel-Big Sur coastline. They knew they had found their "inevitable place." Using granite boulders gathered from the rocky shore of Carmel Bay, Jeffers built Tor House and Hawk Tower as a home, where he wrote all of his major works, including the critically acclaimed adaptation of Euripides' *Medea* for the Broadway stage. There are docent-led tours of Tor House, Hawk Tower, and the old-world gardens.

Henry Miller Library

When hunting for a place to call home in 1944, Henry Miller drove into Big Sur and sighed the great audible sound of relief. He called Big Sur "his first real home in America," opting to stay until 1962. At various cabins around the area, he wrote some of his masterpieces, including *A Time of the Assassins, Sexus, Nexus,* and *Plexus.* Today, you can visit the library and view the lovely garden and structure honoring this legend. The library acts as a cultural hub for the area, drawing films, readings, performances, and more.

enjoy samples of award-winning, Monterey County wine in a relaxed lounge atmosphere. Then cross the street to the C restaurant + bar at the InterContinental The Clement Monterey for a fantastic dinner with expansive ocean views. Having spent years as executive chef for Wente Vineyards, Jerry Regester focuses on using local organic ingredients to create seasonal fare with rustic elegance and refined flavors. The C restaurant + bar complies with Monterey Bay Aquarium's Seafood Watch program and supports local, organic farming. The C bar offers a large selection of cocktails, an extensive selection of local wines, and a champagne menu featuring sparkling wines from around the world. After dinner, you might enjoy grabbing a drink and hitting the dance floor at Sly McFly's Refueling Station.

Before you hit the road the next day, rent some gear and try kayaking or stand-up paddling in the calm waters off McAbee Beach. The refreshing sea breeze and gentle exercise will energize you for a day on the road and will remind you why Steinbeck and so many others loved the Monterey Peninsula.

IN THE AREA

ACCOMMODATIONS

Hotel Boheme, 444 Columbus, San Francisco. This Parisian-style hotel has 15 small rooms each with an rod iron bed, mosquito net, striped carpet, and city views. If you ask for a room off Columbus Street (rooms 107, 207, and 208), you'll get views of Coit Tower. Call 415-433-9111. Website: www.hotel boheme.com.

Hotel des Arts, 447 Bush Street, San Francisco. Aside from the colorful murals, expect simple rooms with wainscoting, flat-screen TVs, low Japanese-style beds, and continental breakfast. Call 415-956-3232 or 800-956-4322. Website: www.sfhotel desarts.com.

Monterey Bay Inn, 242 Cannery Row, Monterey. Steps to San Carlos Beach and Breakwater Cove, this nautical-themed inn offers stellar bay views. Call 831-373-6242 or 800-424-6242. Website: www.montereybayinn.com.

ATTRACTIONS AND RECREATION

The Beat Museum, 540 Broadway, San Francisco. A great place to learn about the San Francisco Renaissance and see cool beatnik memorabilia. Call 800-537-6822. Website: www.thebeatmuseum .org.

Beach Blanket Babylon, 678 Green Street, San Francisco. For a wild night of singing, dancing, comedy, and drinks, you can keep coming back because the show changes as pop culture does. Call 415-421-4222. Website: www.beach blanketbabylon.com.

Bimbos 365, 1025 Columbus Avenue, San Francisco. A city favorite venue for live shows, the staff is superhelpful, and the décor makes you feel like you're in a giant aquarium full of mermaids. Call 4 15-474-0365. Website: www.bimbos365club.com.

Bird and Beckett Books and Records, 653 Chenery Street, San Francisco. This Glen Park institution has a carefully edited selection of books and occasional live poetry readings. Call 415-586-3733. Website: www.bird-beckett .com.

Cannery Row, between Prescott and David Avenues, Monterey. Live music, an IMAX theater, shopping, plenty of wine-tasting rooms, and bars give tourists lots to do, including the Cannery Row History Walk. Call 831-372-8512. Website: www.canneryrow.com.

Chinese Historical Society of America, 965 Clay Street, San Francisco. If you are interested in the Chinese American experience, this museum not only offers a historical perspective, but also some great modern art. Call 415-391-1188. We bsite www.chsa.org.

City Lights Bookstore, 261 Columbus Avenue, San Francisco. A San Francisco icon, Lawrence Ferlinghetti's bookshop and publishing house still attract bohemians. Call 415-362-8193. Website: www.citylights.com.

The Farm, 7 Foster Road, Salinas. Experience Steinbeck country by grabbing a hoe and tilling the soil to truly appreciate how we get our fruits and veggies. Call 831-455-2575 Website: www.thefarm-salinasvalley.com.

Fisherman's Wharf/Pier 39, San Francisco. Home to Ripley's Believe it or Not, the Wax Museum, a submarine tour, Historic Ships at Hyde Street Pier, Boudin Sourdough Bakery Museum, or the Aquarium By the Bay, so the best deal is to get a wharf pass. Call 415-440-4474. Website: www.wharfpass .com.

Heinold's First and Last Chance Saloon, 48 Webster Street, Oakland. For 125 years, this crooked little bar has stood on Jack London Square and is still the spot for a cool drink. Call 510-839-6761. Website: www.heinoldsfirst andlastchance.com.

Henry Miller Library, CA 1, Big Sur. It's not surprising that Henry Miller fell in love with Big Sur with its sea cliffs, majestic redwoods, and pine gardens, a visit (it's free!) to the library offers a tranquil destination, plus a glimpse at rare books about the region. Call 831-667-2574. Website: www.henrymiller .org.

Herbst Theatre, 401 Van Ness Avenue, San Francisco. Home to City Arts & Lectures, this gorgeous theater has some of the best acoustics in town for their popular reading series. Call 415-392-4400. Website: www.sfwmpac.org /herbst/ht_index.html

Jack London Square, 2 Broadway, Oakland. This homage to the author has revitalized Oakland with five-star restaurants, shopping, tourist attractions, and entertainment. Call 510-645-9292. Website: www.jacklondon square.com.

Litquake, 3512 24th Street, San Francisco. Writers from around the world participate in this free tribute to the pen, where you can bar hop and bookshop hop to hear hundreds of writers read their work. Call 415-750-1497. Website: www.litquake.org.

Marilyn Remark Winery, 645 River Road, Salinas. This out of the way winery has the finest Rhone varietals California has to offer (that's all Marilyn produces) and is well worth the trip. Call 831-455-9310. Website: www .remarkwines.com.

McAbee Beach, 1 Hoffman Avenue, Monterey. This well-protected cove provides a perfect respite after a long day of sightseeing or a great place to launch your kayak.

National Steinbeck Center Museum, 1 Main Street, Salinas. Located in historic downtown Salinas (grab a self-guided walking tour map while you are here), you can learn about John Steinbeck's life and then visit Oldtown Farmers Market outside. Call 831-775-4721. Website: www.steinbeck.org.

Oakland City Center, 1111 Broadway, Oakland. The hub of Oakland covering 12 city blocks with shops, restaurants, a hotel, and office spaces. Call 510-628-9170. Website: www.oaklandcity center.com.

Paraiso Vineyards, 38060 Paraiso Springs Road, Soledad. Owned and managed by three generations of the Smith family, this gorgeous vineyard is one of the original grape growers in Santa Lucia Highlands and specializes in Pinots. Call 831-678-0300. Website: www.paraisovineyards.com.

Pessagno Winery, 1645 River Road, Salinas. Free tastings, natural landscape and delicious Pinot noir makes Pessagno a must-visit. Call 831-675-WINE. Website: www.pessagno wines.com.

Presidential Yacht Potomac, 530 Water Street, Oakland. This meticulously restored majestic ship offers bay cruises on the weekends. Call 510-627-1215. Website: www.usspotomac.org.

The Purple Onion, 140 Columbus Avenue, San Francisco. Be a part of the San Francisco comedy scene where rising stars like Zack Galifianakis have been discovered. Call 415-956-1653. Website: www.purpleonionlive.com.

Robinson Jeffers Tor House, 26304 Ocean View Avenue, Carmel. You truly get a sense of Robinson Jeffers when you visit his home with breathtaking views from the tower, elegant gardens, and surprisingly cheap tours. Call 831-624-1813. Website: www.torhouse.org

San Carlos Beach, Cannery Row, Monterey. A grassy area with a little sand at the edge of Cannery Row marks the spots where divers head out on trips next to Breakwater Cove, a harbor with toilets and a decent, but pricey, snack bar. Website: www.mtycounty.com/pgs-parks/parks-reg/sancarlos.html

Scheid Vineyard, 751 Cannery Row, Monterey. Delicious wines, knowledgeable staff and location, location, location makes for a marvelous wine-tasting experience. Call 831-656-9463. Website: www.scheidvineyards.com.

Sly McFly's Refueling Station, 700 Cannery Row, Monterey. For a mellow evening, this is a great place to hear live jazz and blues while sipping on a beer or cocktail. Call 831-649-8050. Website: www.slymcflys.net.

Soledad Mission, 36641 Fort Romie Road, Soledad. Visitors often remark that Soledad is one of the loneliest of missions because it was ruined in a flood (plus the Our Lady of Sorrows altarpiece), though it seems to be getting a recent makeover. Call 831-678-2586

Specs' Twelve Adler Museum Cafe, 12 William Saroyan Place (formerly Adler), San Francisco. Frozen in time, this hidden dive bar is the closest thing you'll get to the real North Beach of the '50s. Call 415-421-4112.

Vesuvio, 255 Columbus Avenue, San Francisco. For a truly Bohemian experience, this bar has it all, complete with a laid-back vibe and delicious cocktails. Call 415-362-3370. Website: www .vesuvio.com.

DINING/DRINKS

Caffé Roma, 526 Columbus Avenue, San Francisco. After getting his law degree, owner Tony Azzolini bailed and opened this café with fantastic coffee, pastries, and soccer games on the TV. Open daily 6 AM–7 PM. Call 415-296-7942. Website: www.cafferoma.com.

Caffe Trieste, 609 Vallejo Street, San Francisco. Over 20 years old, this old Beat hangout is now a chain, but they still roast their own coffee and host the Caffe Trieste Saturday Concert series. Call 415-550-1107. Website: www.caffe trieste.com.

Cocina Poblana: The Art of Mexican Cooking, 499 Embarcadero, West Oakland. This festive eatery has fresh Mexican fare, live music, and outdoor seating. Call 510-451-4700. Website: www.cocinapoblana.com.

the C restaurant + bar, InterContinental The Clement Monterey, 750 Cannery Row, Monterey. A perfect location with spacious seating, attentive wait staff, and sustainable seafood, like arctic char, makes for a perfect evening. Call 831-375-4800. Website: www.thec restaurant-monterey.com.

Everett and Jones Barbeque, 126 Broadway, Oakland. Great atmosphere, huge portions, and the best collards and melt-in-your mouth brisket in town. Call 510-663-2350. Website: www .eandjbbq.com.

Golden Gate Fortune Cookie Factory, 56 Ross Alley, San Francisco. Pretty self-explanatory, this working cookie factory will show you how these sugar cookies are made, and it's free. Call 415-781-3956.

Great Eastern Restaurant, 649 Jackson Street, San Francisco. A Chinatown institution, GER's authentic Chinese cuisine and dim sum make it a must. Call 415-986-2500.

Growers Pub, 227 Monterey Street, Salinas. Great service and comfort food in an old-school atmosphere in the heart of Salinas. Call 831-754-1488. Website: www.growerspub.com.

Hotel Rex's Library Bar, 562 Sutter Street, San Francisco. Yes, it looks like a library but has a cool laid-back atmosphere and serves up potent drinks. With a menu split into short stories, novels, and textbooks, you'll get classic bar food spruced up—imagine truffle-infused and deep-fried mac and cheese. Expect live jazz on weekends. Call 415-433-4434. Website: www.jdvhotels.com/rex.

Italian French Baking Company, 1501 Grant Avenue, San Francisco. Bring your cash for some baked goodies and time to tour this 130-year-old bakery that is a San Francisco institution. Call 415-421-3796.

Molinari's, 373 Columbus Avenue, San Francisco. If you are craving an authentic Italian deli and grocery, you will do no better than Molinari's, who have been serving up sandwiches for over one hundred years. Call 415-421-2337. Website: www.molinarisalame.com.

Paradiso Trattoria, 654 Cannery Row, Monterey. Overlooking stunning Monterey Bay and Steinbeck's Cannery Row, Paradiso's is truly a Paradise known for their excellent seafood dishes. Call 831-375-4155. Website: www.paradisomonterey.com.

Rose Pistola, 532 Columbus Avenue. This popular eatery has everything from cozy ambience to live jazz to excellent Italian fare so make reservations. Call 415-399-0499. Website: www.rosepistolasf.com.

Sardine Factory, 701 Wave Street, Monterey. Reservations are recommended for this popular establishment with world-class cuisine, like abalone, prime rib, and crab ravioli, served in the windowed conservatory or head to the lounge where there is live entertainment. Call 831-373-3775. Website: www.sardinefactory.com.

Steinbeck House, 132 Central Avenue, Salinas. Come visit Steinbeck's childhood home more for the historic significance then the food. Call 831-424-2735. Website: www.steinbeckhouse.com.

Tommaso's, 1042 Kearny Street, San Francisco. This pizzeria provides an authentic North Beach experience, but if you can't take the long wait, you can always get their delicious pizzas to go and eat at Vesuvio. Call 415-398-9696. Website: www.tommasosnorthbeach.com.

OTHER CONTACTS

East Bay Ferry, Alameda/Oakland (Jack London Square). Shuttles people to Angel Island, San Francisco's Ferry Building, and AT&T Park. Call 510-522-3300. Website: www.eastbayferry.com.

Monterey County Convention & Visitors Center, 765 Wave Street, Monterey. Call 831-657-6400. Website: www.seemonterey.com.

San Francisco Visitor Information Center, 900 Market Street, San Francisco. Website: www.onlyinsanfrancisco.com.

Visit Oakland, 463 11th Street, Oakland. Call 510-839-9000. Website: www.visitoakland.org.

Like Henry Miller, you may be inspired to craft your own literary work on the Big Sur coastline.

Flying high over the Pacific Ocean

4 Surf to Ski and Everything in Between

Estimated length: 313 miles
Estimated time: 7 hours straight through, or 4 days

Getting there: Begin in Sausalito, just across the Golden Gate Bridge from San Francisco; drive north on US 101 to I-580 east; follow the signs to I-80 east toward Sacramento. Continue onto CA 4 east for 36 miles to CA 160 north; merge onto I-5 north to Sacramento and drive for 21 miles. Follow I-80 east for about 30 miles to connect to CA 49 north (this road often closes in winter). From Nevada City, take CA 20 east to I-80 east, and then you'll continue to CA 89 south (follow the signs through Truckee and onto Lake Tahoe).

Highlights: Kayaking in the San Francisco Bay; eating crawdads in the California Delta; getting to know California's state capital; book shopping in Nevada City; skiing the Olympic courses at Squaw Valley.

The Sierra Nevada Mountains began their lives during the age of dinosaurs. Glaciers exposed granite from deep underground and carved the cliffs that characterize these majestic mountains. These peaks house Lake Tahoe, the largest alpine lake in North America, as well as hot springs and a wealth of wildlife ranging from bears to affectionate squirrels. During spring, when the snow melts, the water plunges into scenic rivers, which continue westward, filling the bay and merging with the Pacific Ocean. This itinerary takes you backward on the water's route, examining in the San Francisco Bay, weaving along the California Delta, through Sacramento, and all the way up to the High Sierra, where you can ski most of the year.

Begin in the vacation town of Sausalito. Once a thriving Victorian village, today Sausalito attracts numerous tourists, most of whom arrive by ferry and bikes, and has an interesting blend of residents living on houseboats and in gazillion-dollar houses overlooking the San Francisco Bay. Along Bridgeway Street, visitors wander in and out of galleries and kitsch shops and stop for ice cream at Lappert's, a glass of wine and gourmet eats at Poggio, or a pint at the local watering hole Smitty's Bar. You, however, have other plans. North of downtown, follow the signs to the Bay Model Visitor Center, which showcases a 3-D model of the San Francisco Bay and delta areas. Over 1.5 acres in size, the model will give you a visual of your journey.

Rent a kayak and view a close-up of the Bay at Sea Trek Kayaking. This outfit rents gear for a short paddle or guided tours of the coast and Angel Island (an uninhabited island in the bay—where Japanese internment camps were located during World War II—popular with hikers and campers). Be on the lookout for the critters living in the waters, including sharks, jellyfish, manta rays, and over 70 species of native fish. If you aim to spend a night in Sausalito, splurge at the Inn Above Tides, which is literally perched above the water and decorated with fine Asian-inspired antiques.

Hop on US 101 north and take a quick detour to my absolute favorite pizzeria in Northern California, Pizzeria Picco. Exit on Tamalpais Drive toward Paradise Drive; turn left onto Tamalpais Drive. Veer left onto Redwood Avenue and right onto Corte Madera Avenue; this turns into Magnolia Avenue and the restaurant is on the right. Owned by restaurateur Bruce Hill, this pizzeria, which is attached to the also fantastic dinner joint Picco, specializes in baking their pies in ridiculously hot wood-burning stoves until they bubble to perfection. Talk about character: The pizzas are named for Italian bikes. The tiny alcove also doubles as a wine shop and soft-serve ice-cream stop.

Retrace your route back to US 101 north and then onto I-580 east to cross the Richmond Bridge to the East Bay. Follow the signs to US 80 east toward Sacramento. Merge onto CA 4 east, passing golden rolling hills blanketed in wildflowers in spring. Drive for 36 miles until you reach the 1,000-mile California Delta. Frankly, the delta has seen better days. During the gold rush, people, tired of digging for riches, moved to the waterway, built levees, and started steamboat service between Sacramento and San Francisco. Unfortunately, when the Transcontinental Railroad got going, they ended up poaching the steamboat travelers. Today, the delta draws the boating, hiking, fishing, and camping crowds. It's the kind of place where you crack open a can of beer, dine on crawdads, toss your floating lounge chair in the water, and let the sun fry you.

Travel north on CA 160 to the Brannon Island State Recreation Area, just a few miles south of Rio Vista. Here you can camp, hike, boat, bird-watch, and

DETOUR: LODI, NOR CAL'S BURGEONING WINE DESTINATION

It's a little known fact that Napa Valley growers source much of their big red wine grapes from a tiny town in the San Joaquin Valley called Lodi. Lodi might not look like much today, but mark my words, by the end of the decade, this community will be known for its wineries, a reputation already reaching savvy travelers hankering for free tasting rooms serving Rhone varietals without all the fuss of Northern California's more esteemed winemakers.

To get there from the delta, continue east on CA 160 and follow the signs to downtown. Pop into the **Lodi Wine and Visitor Center** to get a winery map. Favorites include **Cellardoor, Harmony Wynelands,** and **Michael David.** If you'd like a fancy (yes, you read right, fancy) place to dine and stay the night, the ambitious **Wine and Roses Hotel and Restaurant** caters to Wine Country tourists by serving up high-end delights, including seasonal produce, spa rooms, and a lovely array of massages.

learn about the islands, marshes, and wildlife populating the region. Continue north to the town of Isleton and grab some seafood or fried food at Pirate's Lair or Spindrift Restaurant, where you can also rent watercraft to get out and explore the waterways. If you'd like a place to rest for the night, keep driving north on CA 160 to the hamlet of Ryde to stay the night in the historic Ryde Hotel.

Continue until you reach I-5 north and motor for 21 miles to Sacramento—California's state capital, where, before the gold rush, an epidemic wiped out nearly 20,000 Native Americans. Entrepreneurs then staked claims on the land and forced the native people to work. The gold rush swelled the population, and with the help of the steamer routes between Sacramento and San Francisco (as well as the collection of rivers headed straight to the area), this city became an important business center for packing, transportation, and livestock. And while San Franciscans and Angelenos didn't quite get how ag-land could become a thriving state capital, Sacramento slowly grew into its role—first by erecting some of the state's most educational historical sites and, more recently, by becoming an emerging destination du jour for foodies, artists, and aspiring politicos.

Check into the Delta King Hotel, located in Old Town Sacramento. This former steamboat once carted passengers along the California Delta and into San Francisco. Today, it evokes the feeling of the 1800s with small rooms and the

Sleep aboard the Delta King Hotel.

Old Town Sacramento entertains the whole family.

gentle rocking of the water to help you fall into a slumber. If you are a history buff, Old Town Sacramento is constructed of various saloons and candy shops nestled in 19th-century architecture. Favored by families, but not a sophomoric endeavor, most will appreciate the California State Railroad Museum. Besides providing a decent lesson on everything train related—from dining cars to mail carriers—visitors can view a hefty collection of model trains, antsy kids can play with Thomas tracks, and on select days, everyone can ride the rails along the river.

Get up close with the ambling river by exploring the American River Parkway. With 23 miles of trails, picnic areas, fishing bars, and swimming holes, not to mention places to drop a boat in the water, you can begin to see why locals spend their summers congregating near the water—well, that and the scorching temps. The closest place to access the river from downtown is Discovery Park, though it gets a bit dodgy after dark and is considered the dirtiest swimming area in town. Or hop on US 50 east and take the Howe Avenue off-ramp north. Make a left on Fair Oaks Boulevard, then a right on Carlson Drive. You will find Paradise Beach. This is where college students congregate in the water and picnic.

To really get to know Sacramento, you'll have to get out of Old Town and head to the Grid. Within the last decade, the tree-lined streets of midtown have morphed into an it-destination, cluttered with galleries, alfresco eateries, shops, and renovated Victorian architecture. Stroll along I, J, and K streets (between 17th and 26th streets) and get to know the latest fashion creations, antique shops, and art offerings of the valley folks.

Since the majority of California's produce is grown and nourished in this valley, you'd think Sacramento would have a thriving culinary community, and in the recent years, the state capital has finally delivered. Probably the most famous Sactown restaurant is Biba Caggiano's Bologna-inspired Biba, where you'll get heaping plates of traditional handmade pastas and likely spot a senator or two. Another good choice, Hot Italian, serves fantastic flatbreads in a mod setting, decorated with Italian motorbikes. A fun stop for margaritas and Mexican cuisine served outdoors is Zocalo. Healthy eaters may prefer the seasonal offerings at Café Bernardo, which has one of the best breakfasts around. Another great spot for pancakes and eggs is the ever-popular Tower Café, decorated with a globetrotter's collection of souvenirs; sit on the patio if the weather cooperates.

When night falls, your best bet to find live music and stage shows is the free weekly *Sacramento News and Review*. If you'd like to sip and sample California's wine history, you'll enjoy the Discover California Wine Bar. Beer drinkers will

Sacramento's Hot Italian restaurant

be content in Sacramento, with heaps of breweries to choose from. Favorites include Pyramid Alehouse Brewery and BFD. Or if you dig the coffeehouse vibe, don't miss a visit to Temple Fine Coffee and Tea, serving one of Northern California's best cups of coffee.

Follow I-80 east for about 30 miles. Here you'll find the historic town of Auburn, which is the gateway to Gold Country and Lake Tahoe. While the historic downtown is quite a looker, most merely pass through, grab a slice of pie and road trip snacks at Ikeda's, and then continue on to their destinations. In downtown, there is an informative Gold Country Museum and a few creative restaurants, but I recommend connecting to CA 49 and heading north. (This road often closes

> ## EVENTS WORTH HEADING TO TOWN FOR
>
> Like any good state capital, Sacramento hosts some of California's most interesting seasonal events. In March, if you are a fan of fast planes and air stunts, the **California Capitol Air Show** delights (though it is quite loud). In August, Sactown hosts the over 150-year-old **California State Fair.** For Labor Day, the city carts in plenty of dirt to cover Old Town, and horses strut through the streets as the city gears up to celebrate its raucous **Gold Rush Days.**

in winter, so check traffic listings. If it is closed, you can continue on I-80 all the way to Truckee.) Once you begin your trek on CA 49, you have officially arrived in Gold Country. The road winds into the foothills toward Grass Valley, which dates back to the 1850s and was once the epicenter for gold (over $900 million in gold have been found here). For a history lesson, begin your trip at the Empire Mine State Historic Park to educate yourself on hard rock gold mining. This mine operated for over a hundred years and produced almost 6 million ounces of gold.

Or, if you'd prefer to get out into nature, detour to the South Yuba River State Park (to access the park from CA 49, take Edwards Crossing or Purdon Crossing). This 20-mile stretch of the river offers some of the best rafting, kayaking, and fishing around. You'll also find the longest single-span covered bridge in the world and the first wheelchair-accessible trail in the country, the Independence Trail. There are loads of swimming holes around the park as well; check with the local ranger station for water levels and tips. Gold panning is a popular activity; make sure to bring your gear.

Grass Valley's Main Street collects antique shops, green eateries, and historic hotels. Check into The Holbrooke Hotel for Victorian-era antiques, fireplaces, fluffy brass beds, and claw-foot tubs. Their lively bar The Golden Gate Saloon was brought to Grass Valley in the 1850s from Italy and is a fine place for a shot of whiskey. Alternatively, sleep in a former hospital, the Swan Levine House, which has morphed into an art gallery, for the owners as well as the guests.

Food options are plentiful, ranging from the organic coffee, sandwiches, and picnic goods at Briar Patch Co-op and Deli to the colorful décor and Latin-inspired seafood served at Diego's Restaurant. For breakfast, Tofanelli's serves 101 different types of omelets to devoted locals and tourists.

Grass Valley's sister city, Nevada City, just a few miles north on CA 49 is a Gold Country gem. She manages to be both historic and modern, without feeling dusty, tired, or too ambitious. Many local writers and artists make their homes up here, resulting in a surprisingly sophisticated community. Broad Street is considered Booktown, USA, as there are more books per block than people in the county. My favorites include Mountain House Books, Harmony Books, Brigadoon Books, Toad Hall Book Shop, Main Street Antiques and Books, Inner Travel Books, and Inner Sanctum Books.

However, downtown doesn't just please bibliophiles. Check into the lovely National Hotel, a resting spot for weary travelers for over 130 years. Then gear up for some of the finest food in Gold Country; start at the New Moon Café for organic seasonal menus in a candlelit dining room. You cannot go wrong with the ravioli or fish specials. For something more low key, Ike's Quarter Café serves organic New Orleans–style goods like biscuits and gravy, po'boys, and sweet potato pie. After your meal, drop into the Old Nevada Brewery: a historic building that used to churn out libations before the prohibition. This is a lively spot for a beer and pub food.

After exploring the riches of Gold Country, you'll be ready to hit the slopes.

ATTENTION MOUNTAIN BIKERS

If racing down a mountain on a two-wheeler energizes your blood, go to Downieville, Northern California's mountain-biker haven. Favorite trails include **North Yuba Trail, Halls Ranch, Fiddle Creek Ridge, Downie River Trail,** and the **1st, 2nd, and 3rd Divides** west of Downieville off CA 49. For committed mountain bikers, the steep **Badenaugh Trail** offers views of eastern California and western Nevada in the Sierra Valley just east of Loyalton off CA 49. If you happen to be in the area in July, check out the three-day **Downieville Classic Bike Race.**

DETOUR: THE REAL LOST SIERRA

To really get off the beaten track, continue traveling north on CA 49 until you reach the community of Sierraville. Seemingly in the middle of nowhere, you'll find **Sierra Hot Springs,** a clothing-optional hot springs resort, where you can camp, rent a room, and spend your days relaxing beneath a canopy of oaks in hot springs. On the premises are a shared kitchen, an organic restaurant, and plenty of hiking trails.

From here, you may want to spend a day traveling east to the **Lakes Basin Recreation Area** where you'll find 15 lakes situated in mountains and trees. Hikers head to the **Gray Eagle Creek** and **Lily Lakes** trails off Gold Lake Highway, **Bear Lakes Loop** from the Lakes Basin campground, and the Pacific Crest Trail. Anglers favor **Gold Lake.**

Take CA 20 east for 26 miles until it reaches I-80 east. Drive for 23 miles to Truckee (for more information on the town of Truckee, see chapter 14). Six miles south of Truckee on CA 267 south is Northstar at Tahoe. For folks heading up to Northstar, you have plenty of options—from condos to modest guest rooms all the

way up to the newly constructed Ritz Carlton, Lake Tahoe. Throw in pools, bike rentals, tennis, kids' clubs, and six restaurants, and you begin to see why families favor this mountain above others.

Little tykes take on the Tahoe slopes.

Another option is to travel south from Truckee on CA 89 to Squaw Valley USA, the site of the 1960 Olympics, catapulting this lovely area into one of the biggest, most famous ski resorts in California. With 100 trails on 4,000 acres, all levels of skiers, boarders, and hot cocoa sippers will enjoy getting to know the six peaks, the wealth of restaurants and watering holes (including Plumpjack Café, Mamasake, and Graham's), an invigorating pool, Adventure Center, ice rink, cable car, the decadent spa, and the plush Resort at Squaw Creek.

Perched at the northern edge of the lake is Tahoe City—a hub for serious adventurers and families and one of the more developed stretches of the lake. Local skiers populate Alpine Meadows and Homewood Mountain Resort for dependable snowpack and reasonable rates. When the muscles tire from that downhill fun, the town of Tahoe City is worth a wander. In summer, grab groceries and light up a beachside BBQ at the Tahoe City Commons. Or sit yourself on a colorful chair and order up some margaritas and tacos at Caliente. Other than ski resort hotels, Tahoe City hosts some affordable destinations, including the popular River Ranch Lodge, which may not be the snazziest, but it sells out every season. Families flock to Rustic Cottages Resort, located

A typical sight in winter

across from the lake in Tahoe Vista. For breakfast, there are two wildly popular breakfast options: Fire Sign Café specializes in benedicts, while the Log Cabin Café slings massive portions of griddle fare and egg creations.

Hunting for something on the more modest side? Continue traveling south on CA 89 to Historic Camp Richardson Resort. Built in the 1920s, this 40-unit lodge, campsite, and recreation area provides an affordable place to bring the entire clan to snowshoe, cross-country ski, play in the lake, cook your meals, and ride horses. It isn't fancy, but the views of the lake (and the access to slopes and water fun) cannot be beat.

If you stay at Camp Rich, as locals call it, then you will be a stone's throw from South Lake Tahoe's bustling Heavenly Mountain, a playland almost too popular for its own good. Whether you choose to merely ride the gondola up the mountain for some of the best views of the area, ski, ice skate, drink at one of the bars, eat at the slew of restaurants, shop in the high-end stores, or throw snowballs, you'll find Heavenly a celestial spot for activities of all persuasions.

IN THE AREA

ACCOMMODATIONS

Delta King Hotel, 1000 Front Street, Sacramento. This floating hotel offers two acclaimed restaurants for casual and fine dining, two professional theaters, and a wine school. Call 800-825-5464. Website: www.deltaking.com.

Historic Camp Richardson Resort, 1900 Jameson Beach Road, South Lake Tahoe. Perfect for large groups, who can either get hotel-style lodging, private cabins with basic kitchens, or camp, with views of the lake for a steal compared to other parts of Tahoe. Call 800-544-1801. Website: www.camp richardson.com.

The Holbrooke Hotel, 212 W. Main Street, Grass Valley. Check out the guestbook of this historic hotel. Former guests include former president Ulysses S. Grant and writer Mark Twain. Call 530-273-1353 or 800-933-7077. Website: www.holbrooke.com.

Inn Above Tide, 30 El Portal, Sausalito. All 29 elegant rooms and suites face the San Francisco Bay. Call 415-332-9535 or 800-893-8433. Website: www.innabove tide.com.

National Hotel, 211 Broad Street, Nevada City. Forty-two antique decorated rooms and suites have access to the restaurant and pool. Call 530-265-4551. Website: www.thenationalhotel.com.

Northstar at Tahoe Resort, 5001 Northstar Drive, Truckee. This 270-unit megaplex of a resort offers everything from hotel rooms to condos. This super family-friendly environment has so many activities to offer (including free lift tickets, pool, bikes, tennis, fitness center, kids' club, golf course, six restaurants, hot tub, and teen center) that you won't need to leave the resort.

Call 530-562-1010 or 800-466-6784. Website: www.northstarattahoe.com.

Resort at Squaw Creek, 400 Squaw Creek Road, Squaw Valley. A 6,500-acre complex offering every amenity imaginable: a winter chairlift, a fly-fishing center, waterslide, and ski-in/ski-out lodging, 405 rooms with warm tones (some kitchens and fireplaces), pools, tennis, four restaurants, concierge, kids' programs, spa, gym, golf course, and bar. Call 530-583-6300 or 800-327-3353. Website: www.squawcreek.com.

Ritz Carlton, Lake Tahoe, 13031 Ritz-Carlton Highlands Court, Truckee. Rooms feature fireplaces, floor-to-ceiling windows, and private balconies with views of the mountain. Call 530-562-3000. Website: www.ritzcarlton .com.

River Ranch Lodge, CA 89 and Alpine Meadows Road, Tahoe City. This hotel sits on the banks of the Truckee River and features a riverside patio and two dining venues. Call 530-583-4262 or 866-991-9912. Website: www.riverranch lodge.com.

Rustic Cottages Resort, 7449 North Lake Boulevard, Tahoe Vista. Originally the sawmill and labor camp of the Brockway Lumber Company, the property was converted to vacation cottages in 1925. Each cottage includes Benicia Iron Beds, a microwave and refrigerator, and a porch. Call 888-778-7842. Website: www.rusticcottages.com.

Ryde Hotel, 14340 CA 160, Walnut Grove. Rooms feature an art deco aesthetic and many provide panoramic views of the Sacramento River. Call 916-776-1318 or 888-717-7933. Website: www.rydehotel.com.

Swan Levine House, 328 South Church Street, Grass Valley. Antiques, poster beds, plush comforters, breakfast, and friendly service make this a great choice for families and couples looking for something different. Call 530-272-1873. Website: www.swan levinehouse.com.

Wine and Roses Hotel and Restaurant, 2505 West Turner Road, Lodi. This 80-room hotel features a fitness center, pool, and jacuzzi, and a continental breakfast. Call 209-334-6988. Website: www.winerose.com.

ATTRACTIONS AND RECREATION

Alpine Meadows, 2600 Alpine Meadows Road, Tahoe City. Offers ski and snowboard lessons, a ski shop, and dining. Call 530-583-4232 or 800-441-4423. Website: www.skialpine.com.

American River Parkway, 5700 Arden Way, Carmichael. Fishing, boating, and rafting opportunities are available, along with picnic sites. Access to the parkway is available at various points off of I-50.

Bay Model, 2100 Bridgeway, Sausalito. Offers the unique opportunity to view the bay-delta system at a glance. Call 415-332-3871. Website: www.spn.usace.army.mil.

Brannan Island State Recreation Area, 17645 CA 160, Rio Vista. The area offers great fishing, including striped bass, sturgeon, catfish, bluegill, perch, and bullhead. Frank's Tract, a protected wetland marsh, is home to beaver, muskrat, river otter, mink, and 76 species of birds. Call 916-777-6671 Website: www.parks.ca.gov.

Brigadoon Books, 109 North Pine Street, Nevada City. Call 530-264-7183.

California Capital Air Show, Mather Airport. Enjoy jet demonstrations, aerobatic performers, and vintage aircraft displays. Call 916-876-7568. Website: www.californiacapitalairshow.com.

California State Fair, 1600 Exposition Boulevard, Sacramento. Call 916-263-3247. Website: www.bigfun.org.

California State Railroad Museum, 125 I Street, Sacramento. The museum features 21 lavishly restored locomotives and cars, some dating back to 1862. The museum also has a full-scale diorama of an 1860s construction site high in the Sierra Nevada and a bridge. Call 916-445-7387. Website: www.parks.ca.gov.

Camp Richardson Marina, 1900 Jameson Beach Road, South Lake Tahoe. They rent everything from boats to water skis, jet skis, WaveRunners, kayaks, and canoes. Call 530-542-6570. Website: www.camprichardson.com.

Discovery Park, Sacramento. From I-5, take the Richards Boulevard off-ramp, then go west to get to the south entrance of the park. Enjoy the 32-mile Jedediah Smith Memorial Trail or the picnic area by the river.

Downieville Classic Bike Race, Downieville. Bikers gather in these foothills to race in this three-day event. Call 530-289-3010. Website: www.downievilleclassic.com.

Empire Mine State Historic Park, 10791 East Empire Street, Grass Valley. Offers tours, living history events, a scale model of the underground workings of the mine, and 14 miles of hiking trails. Call 530-273-8522. Website: www.empiremine.org.

Gold Country Museum, 1273 High Street, Auburn. Includes exhibits of a miner's cabin and a mining camp saloon, a replicated hard rock mine, and a stamp mill. You can also pan for your own gold in an indoor stream. Call 530-889-6500. Website: www.placer.ca.gov.

Gold Lake, Plumas National Forest. A great place to catch rainbow trout, with campsites and hiking trails nearby. Gold Lake Road is closed during the winter months, but snowmobiles may gain access.

Gold Rush Days, at Old Town Sacramento. Activities include gold panning, pony rides, arts and crafts, and costumed performances. Call 916-808-7059. Website: www.sacramentogold rushdays.com.

Harmony Books, 231 Broad Street, Nevada City. Call 530-265-9564.

Heavenly Mountain, 4080 Lake Tahoe Boulevard, South Lake Tahoe. Ski, ice skate, or view the snowcapped mountain. Call 800-587-4430. Website: www .skiheavenly.com.

Homewood Mountain Resort, 5145 Westlake Boulevard, Homewood. Groomed boulevards and trademark hidden powder stashes. About 15 percent of the runs are at a beginner level and 50 percent are intermediate level.

The view from the Heavenly Mountain gondola

Call 530-525-2992. Website: www.ski homewood.com.

Independence Trail, located within the grounds of South Yuba River State Park, 175660 Pleasant Valley Road, Penn Valley. The trail features waterfalls, scenic vistas, and a gentle switchback descent to a mountain stream on a wooden flume accessible by wheelchair. Call 530-432-2546. Website: www.parks .ca.gov.

Inner Sanctum Books, 308 Broad Street, Nevada City. Call 530-478-9905.

Inner Travel Books, 14618 Tyler Foote Road, Suite 171, Nevada City. Call 530 478-7792. Website: www.innertravel-books.com.

Lakes Basin Recreation Area, off CA 49, east of Sierra City. Fifteen lakes situated in mountains and trees offer more than a weekend's share of exploration. Call 530-836-2575 or 877-444-6777. Website: www.reserveusa.com.

Main Street Antiques and Books, 214 Main Street, Nevada City. Call 530-272-7949.

Mountain House Books, 418 Broad Street, Nevada City. Call 530-265-0241.

North Yuba Mountain Bike Trail, Downieville. Take CA 49 toward Downieville. Make a right at Goodyear's Bar crossing, cross a single-lane bridge, make a left at the T intersection; as soon as the road turns to dirt, the trail head is on the right. This 16-mile trail out and back is best for advanced riders.

Paradise Beach, at the intersection of Carlson and Sandburg Drives. Offers river swimming as well as a supervised public pool. Call 916-277-6071. Website: www.riverparksacramento.net.

Resort at Squaw Creek Spa, 400 Squaw Creek Road, Olympic Valley.

Call 530-583-6300. Website: www.squaw
creek.com.

Sea Trek Kayaking, 85 Liberty Ship
Way, Sausalito. Single or double kayaks
and stand-up paddleboards available
for rent. Offers classes as well as group
or private guided tours. Call 415-332-
8494. Website: www.seatrek.com.

Sierra Hot Springs, 521 Campbell Hot
Springs Road, Sierraville. Hike to a private pool beneath a canopy of oaks, or
meditate in the private Phoenix pools.
Note that most people are nude. Call
530-994-3773. Website: www.sierrahot
springs.org.

South Yuba River State Park, 175660
Pleasant Valley Road, Penn Valley. Besides rafting, kayaking, and fishing, the
park offers docent-led history, nature,
and gold-panning tours at selected
times throughout the year. Call 530-
432-2546. Website: www.parks.ca.gov.

Squaw Valley Adventure Center, next
to the Olympic Village Lodge, Olympic
Valley. Take a ropes course, or play on
the giant swing, bungee-trampoline,
and other heart-dropping activities.
Open daily. Call 530-583-7673. Website:
www.squawadventure.com.

Toad Hall Book Shop, 108 N. Pine
Street, Nevada City. Call 530-265-2216.

DINING/DRINKS

BFD, 3527 Broadway, Sacramento.
Enjoy all-you-can-eat hot chicken
wings and crawfish with a cold beer.
Closed Tues. Call 916-476-5034. Website: www.brewfermentdistill.com.

Biba, 2801 Capitol Avenue, Sacramento.
Traditional Italian cuisine made with
fresh ingredients. Try the prix fixe
menu, which includes a seasonal choice
of soup or salad, entrée, and dessert for
$30 per person. Call 916-455-2422.
Website: www.biba-restaurant.com.

Briar Patch Co-op and Deli, 290
Sierra College Drive, Grass Valley. Food
offerings range from Rahlene's Beautiful (a sandwich of sunflower seeds,
cheese, and avocado) to burgers. Call
530-272-5333. Website: www.briarpatch
.coop.

Café Bernardo, 1431 R Street, Sacramento. A European-style café serving a
menu of fresh pastries, sandwiches, and
pizzettas made with local ingredients in
a certified green kitchen. Call 916-930-
9191. Website: www.paragarys.com.

Caliente, 8791 North Lake Boulevard,
King's Beach. Enjoy chicken mole enchiladas, crab chimichangas, and
paella. Try the restaurant's signature
drink, a Chupacabra, or order from the
extensive tequila menu. Call 530-546-
1000. Website: www.calientetahoe.com.

Cellardoor, 21 N. School Street, Lodi. A
tasting room collaboration by Bokisch
Vineyards, Jessie's Grove, Van Ruiten,
and Michael David Winery. Small bites
such as cheese platters and tapenades
accompany an extensive wine list. Call
209-339-4394. Website: www.lodicellar
door.com.

Diego's Restaurant, 217 Colfax Avenue, Grass Valley. Fish tacos, rellenos,
and tres leches accompany live music
on Friday evenings. Reservations recommended on weekends. Call 530-477-
1460. Website: www.diegosrestaurant
.com.

Discover California Wine Bar, 114 J
Street, Sacramento. Call 916-443-8275.
Website: www.discovercal.com.

Fire Sign Café, 1785 West Lake Boulevard, Tahoe City. Breakfast is the most
popular meal here. Try the Baker's
Benedict, eggs Benedict served with
fresh sausage. Open for breakfast and
lunch. Call 530-583-0871.

Golden Gate Saloon at the Holbrooke, 212 W. Main Street, Grass Valley. Call 530-273-1353 or 800-933-7077. Website: www.holbrooke.com.

Graham's at Squaw Valley, 1650 Squaw Valley Road, Olympic Valley. Serves classics like salmon and duck breast in a mountain lodge setting. Call 530-581-0454. Website: www.dinewine .com.

Harmony Wynelands Winery, 9291 East Harney Lane, Lodi. Call 209-369-4184. Website: www.harmonywynelands .com.

Hot Italian, 1627 16th Street, Sacramento. Pizzas, calzones, and panini are popular menu items. Call 916-444-3000. Website: www.hotitalian.net.

Ikeda's, 13500 Lincoln Way, Auburn. The Burger Bar satisfies, and the bakery features pies baked with fruit straight from the orchard. Call 530-885-4243. Website: www.restaurant-bakery -auburn-ca.com.

Ike's Quarter Café, 401 Commercial Street, Nevada City. Using organic ingredients, this New Orleans–style bistro serves diners either inside the little house or beneath the trees on the patio. Cash only. Call 530-265-6138. Website: www.ikesquartercafe.com.

Lappert's, 689 Bridgeway, Sausalito. Hawaiian-inspired ice-cream flavors such as Kauai Pie (Kona Coffee Ice Cream, Macadamia nuts, toasted coconut, and chocolate fudge). Call 415-331-3035. Website: www.lapperts.com.

Log Cabin Café, 8692 North Lake Boulevard, King's Beach. Traditional breakfasts, eggs Benedict with smoked trout, or Arizona French toast (dipped in crushed cornflakes and steel-cut oats) make this café a winner. Call 530-546-7109. Website: www.logcabin breakfast.com.

Mamasake, 1850 Village South Road, Suite 52, Olympic Valley. A Cal-Asian restaurant that offers dishes with Japanese, Italian, and Latin American influences. Specialties include Mamas Balls (inari pocket stuffed with a fresh seafood salad), tempura, and sashimi. Call 530-584-0110. Website: www .mamasake.com.

Michael David Winery, 4580 West Highway 12, Lodi. Call 209-368-7384. Website: www.michaeldavidwinery.com.

New Moon Café, 203 York Street, Nevada City. Elegant cuisine in a casual setting. Save room for desserts, which change nightly, but if there is something with lemon, order it. Reservations recommended for dinner. Call 530-265-6399. Website: www.thenewmooncafe .com.

Old Nevada Brewery, 107 Sacramento Street, Nevada City. The first floor serves casual classics such as onion rings, nachos, and pizza, with a fine-dining venue on the second floor. Call 530-265-3960.

Picco, 320 Magnolia Avenue, Larkspur. Favorites include local halibut, California lamb T-bone, and a daily special risotto. Call 415-924-0300. Website: www.restaurantpicco.com.

Pirate's Lair, 169 W. Brannan Island Road, Isleton. Serves American classics such as hamburgers, hot dogs, and tuna melts. Open daily for breakfast and lunch. Call 916-777-6565. Website: www .korthsmarina.com.

Pizzeria Picco, 316 Magnolia Avenue, Larkspur. Expect primo Neapolitan-style pizzas and organic salads. Call 415-945-8900. Website: www.pizzeria picco.com.

Plumpjack Café, 1920 Squaw Valley Road, Squaw Valley. Chefs use seasonal organic ingredients, which make this urbanesque restaurant hip: Here you'll get a stellar wine list and some of the best food around. Reservations recommended. Call 530-583-1578. Website: www.plumpjack.com.

Poggio, 777 Bridgeway, Sausalito. Dine on seasonal Italian cuisine from the wood-fired roasting oven or rotisserie. Expect classics with a twist such tagliatelle with local braised rabbit and spaghetti with Dungeness crab. Call 415-332-7771. Website: www.poggio trattoria.com.

Pyramid Alehouse Brewery, 1029 K Street, Sacramento. Enjoy one of the Brewer's Plates, dishes crafted to complement the beer selection. Call 916-498-9800. Website: www.pyramidbrew .com.

Smitty's Bar, 214 Caledonia Street, Sausalito. The star here is the shuffleboard table, which draws a crowd during league season. Originally a soda pop and beer bottling plant, Smitty's is a great place to grab a beer and relax. Call 415-332-2637.

Spindrift Restaurant, 841 West Brannan Street, Isleton. Serves classic American cuisine along with a special "South of the Border" menu, which features Mexican favorites such as burritos, enchiladas, and tostadas. Call 916-777-4944. Website: www.the spindrift.com.

Temple Fine Coffee and Tea, 1014 10th Street, Sacramento. This coffee shop and teahouse is situated in a former bookstore with Danish-inspired architecture. Call 916-443-4960. Website: www.templecoffee.com.

Tofanelli's, 302 W. Main Street, Grass Valley. A slew of omelets populate the breakfast menu, while dinner heads to Europe for Italian specialties. Call 530-272-1468. Website: www.tofanellis.com.

Tower Café, 1518 Broadway Street, Sacramento. Serves a varied menu of world fusion dishes. Specials include Brazilian chicken, East African veggie burgers, and Florentine ravioli. Call 916-441-0222. Website: www.tower cafe.com.

Zocalo, 1801 Capitol Avenue, Sacramento. Signature sides such as green rice and black beans are served family style, and the corn tortillas are homemade on-site with freshly ground nixtamal. Call 916-441-0303. Website: www.zocalosacramento.com.

OTHER CONTACTS

California Delta Chambers and Visitor's Bureau. Call 916-777-4041. Website: www.californiadelta.org.

Grass Valley/Nevada City Convention & Visitors Bureau. Call 530-273-7934. Website: www.grassvalleynevadacity cvb.com.

North Lake Tahoe Chamber of Commerce. Call 530-581-6900. Website: www.laketahoechamber.com.

Sacramento Convention and Tourist Bureau, 1608 I Street, Sacramento. Call 800-292-2334. Website: www.discover gold.org.

Sausalito Chamber of Commerce, 10 Liberty Ship Way, Bay 2, Suite 250, Sausalito. Call 415-331-7262, ext 10. Website: www.sausalito.org.

Truckee Donner Chamber of Commerce, 10065 Donner Pass Road, Truckee. Call 530-587-8808. Website: www .truckee.com.

Napa Valley grapes

5 Educational Escapades in Napa Valley

Estimated length: 100 miles

Estimated time: 1–4 days

Getting there: From San Francisco, take US 101 north, crossing the Golden Gate Bridge. Exit CA 37 east to CA 121; follow the signs toward Napa as you travel along the country roads. Turn left at CA 121/29 north and take this all the way to Calistoga.

Highlights: Learning about all the elements that make Napa Valley special— cooking, winemaking, art, food pairing, and even history.

Just the image of Napa Valley creates visions of the high life, where art, wine, food, wellness, and history all seep into daily life. However, this prolific agricultural valley wasn't always so peaceful. Native Americans and gold country settlers battled it out for the right to farm the land, and after the eastern migrants won, Mother Nature had her say, creating drought, plant diseases, and flooding to challenge the brave folks who laid down roots along the rolling hills. After a small agricultural honeymoon, this abundant valley experienced a metamorphosis that some might call a fluke: At a blind tasting in France, the guys from Calistoga's Chateau Montelena wowed judges with their delicately crafted vino, and suddenly this valley was all the rage.

Today, Napa Valley is the second most visited destination in California—a mouse and his cartoon friends still have the valley beat by a mile—which means that it can occasionally be challenging (especially during the crush from August through October) to secure accommodations and reservations for tastings and dinner.

Begin in the small community of Calistoga—at once both homey (yes, everyone does know each other in town) and sophisticated, not to mention accessible.

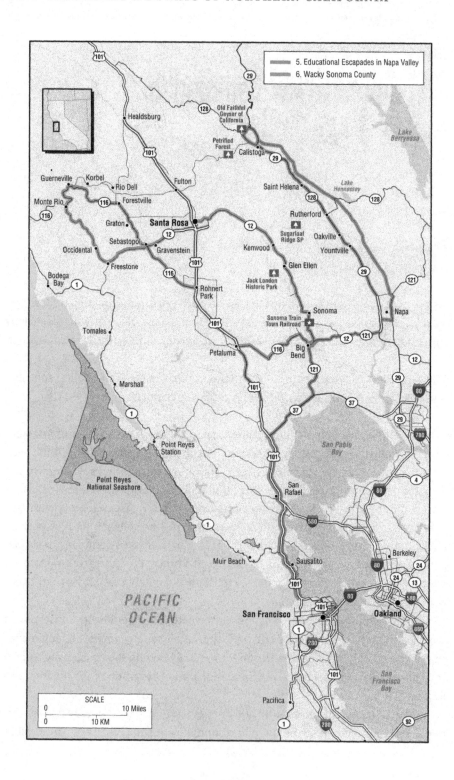

Pop into the Sharpsteen Museum to gather up some interesting tidbits about the history of the town that put Napa Valley on the map before beginning your experiential vacation. Reserve early to wake up your nose at W.H. Smith and the Wine Sensory Experience. This carefully crafted course gets you in touch with how to interact with wine and chocolate before they even enter your lips. Sniff, sample, and enjoy this crash course in waking up the senses.

For something completely new to the valley, book a seat at Kate Stanley's fanciful table to craft lavender wreaths, grapevine baskets, picture frames, cards, or whatever is on the menu at this world-class craft studio. Kate Stanley is one of Wine Country's hottest event designers, with an eye for creating accessible artsy experiences for all types. Top off your craft making with a catered lunch under the garden trellis, paired with plenty of yummy bevies.

Fall in Yountville

Check into your artist cottage at the Mount View Hotel and Spa. This lovely historic building blends a sophisticated aesthetic (think slick furniture and flat-screen TVs) with classic touches like landscaped gardens and a cabana-hugged pool, popular with lunching ladies. Each cottage offers guests an easel and paints to express themselves with, and then asks guests to submit their creations for a complimentary night stay. The hotel's nightly poolside wine tasting, spa, and two hopping eateries make guests feel as if they have arrived at the hippest spot in town. If you prefer something on the splashier side, Indian Springs Resort and Spa has long been a Calistoga favorite. With a hot spring pool once favored by local Native Americans, a sculpture garden, and a lovely spa, this property caters to those enamored by the good life without wanting anything too decadent (or overpriced).

If you can tear yourself from the pool for a few hours, hop in the car and head south on CA 29 to the dynamic castle of the Culinary Institute of America. For

Kate Stanley's lovely studio

Calistoga's art on display

those visitors with time, sign up for one of their cooking classes that range from bread-making workshops to grilling basics to full-on meal-prep techniques; otherwise explore their amazing cooking accessory store and stumble upon the **Flavor Bar**—a new addition to the property. Sample artisan olive oil, chocolate, wine and cheese pairings, and seasonal treats under the supervision of a video feed crafted by a chef/professor who guides you through your tasting experience. I'll say this: For 15 bucks, I scored enough chocolate to keep me going for my entire trip.

Afterward, stroll through the precious town of **St. Helena,** learning about the self-proclaimed Beverly Hills of Napa Valley. This collection of historic buildings houses luxe boutiques, shockingly expensive galleries, and a smattering of hole-in-the-wall eateries. That being said, St. Helena also manages to feel like a farming town, where the community gathers annually for the pet parade and the open house at the fire station—which draws so many adoring locals, you'd think Britney Spears was doing a surprise show.

When you need to replenish, this village has more than enough by way of sustenance. To educate your palate on the farm-to-table movement, there is no better stop than Long Meadow Ranch's Farmstead Restaurant. Headed by one of the pioneers in organic farming, the restaurant sources much of its produce and meat from their own long-standing farms located a short drive from town. Chef Sheamus Feeley dutifully crafts down-home recipes (oh those chicken and dumplings) for a clientele of celebrity chefs like French Laundry's Thomas Keller. Try to arrive early enough to sample their rich Cabernet or fresh olive oil, and then explore their lovely gardens.

In the morning, enjoy a hearty breakfast at **Café Sarafornia** before taking CA 29 south to Conn Creek Winery's AVA Room Barrel Blending Experience. Here, you can taste and blend wines from grapes grown throughout the entire valley. If you ever dreamed about becoming a winemaker, here's your chance to enhance your skills. Blend a bottle (with the guidance of seasoned wine educators) and take it home to enjoy on a special occasion.

Join the locals and celebs as you grab a bite to eat at Solage Resort's Solbar. Either dine inside by the toasty fireplace or out on the patio gazing at the pool as you educate yourself on the subtleties of seasonal favorites like a yellowfin tuna sandwich lathered in kimchi or maitake mushroom pizza. Less adventurous eaters may prefer Mexican favorites at the locally favored Miguel's. Long heralded for its wonderful *chilaquiles,* you cannot go wrong with nearly anything you sample. From quesadillas to burritos, they manage to pull off most south-of-the-border faves with style.

The chocolate tasting at the Culinary Institute of America's flavor bar

Travel up to Calistoga's CasaLana for your one-day culinary lesson. An esteemed chef, Lana Richardson, owner and operator of CasaLana, teaches you cooking techniques, rather than merely offering a handful of recipes. Chop, sauté, and ultimately delight in your own fantastic meal, served outside (and accompanied by wine) in her lovely garden. Or, if you prefer a more intensive class, Lana offers three- to five-day cooking classes tailored for newbie cooks to pros.

At the end of the day, gather up your newfound friends and settle in at the Calistoga Inn and Brewery's hopping bar to hear live music and sip house brews. Ask the bartender to school you on the variety of brews crafted for this restaurant/bar, and if you are lucky, you may even score a tour of the brewery. Then retreat to your domicile to soak your arm muscles in the hot tub.

Wake early and check out of your hotel. Drive south along the Silverado Trail to view vineyards and fantastically designed wineries. Then follow the signs westward to reach Yountvillle, a small Wine Country town that packs a big punch. Known for its world-renowned restaurants—Chef Thomas Keller rocks three sit-down eateries plus a bakery and, at press time, was hard at work creating a hotel to complement his award-winning French Laundry restaurant—as well we its dynamic collection of boutique wineries, travelers flock to this one-street town.

You will be experiencing a food and wine-pairing lesson from a wine guru at Girard Winery. Make an appointment to settle down at the communal table and learn about how to best combine flavors with a variety of wines. Sample everything from cheese to salumi to sweet treats; you'll be surprised at what flavors pair with wine and how these foods actually make the wine taste better.

Learn what pairs with most flavors at Girard Winery.

Follow up your experience by sampling a meal crafted by masters. Here in town you have two to choose from—Thomas Keller and Michael Chiarello. Lunch at Keller's French-inspired Bouchon promises inspired palate pleasers like a *tartine du jour* or mussels. If you prefer a more decadent meal, Chiarello's Bottega hits a home run with foodies for its rich takes on Italian cuisine highlighted by the finest California-grown ingredients. The pecorino cheese pudding, twice-cooked pork chop with honeyed applesauce, or Chiarello's famed braised short ribs paired with a bottle of Cabernet make this gal giggly at every visit.

Travel south on CA 29 to downtown Napa and check into the Napa River Inn. This historic property, located on the banks of the Napa River, has recently been renovated and now, coupled with the benefits of the reinvigorated Napa scene, draws plenty of foot traffic. More like a resort than hotel, this property offers a nightclub, a variety of restaurants, spacious river-view rooms decked out in fine sleek furnishings, and a few shops.

Put on your walking shoes and stroll through downtown, experiencing a self-guided audio tour of the Napa ARTwalk. View public art sculptures as well as a variety of galleries populated with an array of mixed media art. Don't miss a chance to marvel at the new Gordon Huether Gallery, which just might be the most dynamic new house of art to grace Napa Valley.

Dinner in Napa used to be a snore. Today, you can sample delicacies from around the globe, crafted with care, style, and plenty of locally sourced ingredients. For some spicy contemporary Indian cuisine, Neela's highlights the delicacies of all regions, including various breads, veggie dishes, and a wealthy selection of curries and tandoor specialties. Japanophiles appreciate the delicate cuisine at Morimoto's Napa, where you can get a selection of shared plates like fig tempura and bone marrow, or select entrées to the tune of whole roasted lobster *épicé* or *ishi yaki buri bop* (a fanciful selection of seafood prepared in a clay bowl at your table). For more dining options, see chapter 1.

For your last night, take a salsa dancing class hosted by Ceja Vineyards at Bistro Sabor. Partner up to swing, sway, and shake your thang at the most exciting weekend event in the entire valley.

In the morning, enjoy breakfast at the Oxbow Public Market. Sample everything from salmon croissants at the Model Bakery to sweet corn arepas at Pica Pica Maize. Then return to your hotel to take a historic tour of downtown Napa. The hotel itself is a historic building and former mill, but that's not all. This educational experience helps visitors understand how far the lively reinvention of downtown has brought this small city.

Cap off your trip by trying out your wine education. Grab a map from the new Napa Valley Visitor Center and visit the collection of downtown Napa wineries. Smell, swirl, and sample the finest red wines in California, all located within walking distance of each other.

And when you've had enough education, take CA 29 south to CA 37 west until you reach US 101.

IN THE AREA

ACCOMMODATIONS

Indian Springs Resort and Spa, 1712 Lincoln Avenue, Calistoga. Lovely rooms and cottages just a short walk to downtown Calistoga provide ample romance and family-friendly amenities, including a giant mineral spring pool. Call 707-942-4913. Website: www.indian springscalistoga.com.

Mount View Hotel and Spa, 1457 Lincoln Avenue. Though the building is historic, the modernist aesthetic of the small rooms, and the bohemian flair of the cottages, draw creative types. Two restaurants, a spa, and a pool round out the offerings. Call 800-816-6877. Website: www.mountviewhotel.com.

Napa River Inn, 500 Main Street, Napa. Nautical-themed rooms overlooking the Napa River. Throw in three restaurants, a bar, a café, and history walks, and this historic structure begins to lure people uninspired by the B&B crowd. Call 877-251-8500. Website: www.napariverinn.com.

ATTRACTIONS AND RECREATION

CasaLana, 1316 South Oak Street, Calistoga. Book one- to five-day cooking classes in Lana Richardson's glorious teaching kitchen. You can stay the night in her lovely B&B as well. Call 707-942-0615. Website: www.casalana.com.

Ceja Vineyards, 1248 First Street, Napa. Call 707-255-3954. Website: www.cejavineyards.com.

Chateau Montelena, 1429 Tubbs Lane, Calistoga. Call 707-942-5105. Website: www.montelena.com.

Conn Creek Winery's AVA Room Barrel Blending Experience, 8711 Silverado Trail, St. Helena. Call 800-793-7960. Website: www.conncreek.com.

Culinary Institute of America, 2555 Main Street, St. Helena. Book serious cooking classes on weekends to amp up your grilling or veggie preparation, or sit at the Flavor Bar to sample cocoa, olive oil, and other fun treats. Call 707-967-1010. Website: www.ciachef.edu.

Girard Winery, 6795 Washington Street, Yountville. In addition to wine tasting, reserve a seat at the food and wine-pairing lesson. Call 707-968-9297. Website: www.girardwinery.com.

Gordon Huether Gallery, 1821 Monticello Road, Napa. Call 707-255-5954. Website: www.gordonhuether.com.

Kate Stanley's, 1347 Lincoln Avenue, Calistoga. Craft classes accompanied by a catered gourmet lunch from the master artist Kate Stanley must be booked in advance. Call 707-942-4244. Website: www.katestanley.net.

Napa ARTwalk. Call 707-257-2117. Website: www.napaartwalk.org.

Sharpsteen Museum, 1311 Washington Street, Calistoga. A simple museum showcasing the history of Calistoga. Call 707-942-5911. Website: www.sharp steen-museum.org.

W.H. Smith and the Wine Sensory Experience, 1367 Lincoln Avenue, Calistoga. Learn to rely on your sense of smell as you sample wine and chocolate. Call 707-942-1194. Website: www .winesensoryexperience.com.

DINING/DRINKS

Bottega, 6525 Washington Street, Yountville. Michael Chiarello's stab at fine Italian dining has crafted a niche for itself in foodie Yountville. Creative dishes like ancient grain polenta or whole fish wood-roasted in Meyer lemon have wowed visitors and locals. Call 707-945-1050. Website: www .botteganapavalley.com.

Bouchon, 6534 Washington Street, Yountville. With a name meaning traffic, you can gather how popular Thomas Keller's tribute to all things French truly is, especially after you sample the mussels, frites, and wines. The attached patisserie has fabulous sweet treats and breads. Call 707-944-8037. Website: www.bouchonbistro.com.

Café Sarafornia, 1413 Lincoln Avenue, Calistoga. A hopping breakfast tradition in Calistoga, known for friendly servers, heaping omelets, and yummy griddle fare. Call 707-942-0555. Website: www .cafesarafornia.com.

Calistoga Inn and Brewery, 1250 Lincoln Avenue, Calistoga. Eat outside with the local winemakers under the landscape trellises. Traditional dishes like steak, chicken, and seafood pair well with the inn's homemade brews. Call 707-942-4101. Website: www.calistoga inn.com.

Long Meadow Ranch's Farmstead Restaurant, 738 Main Street, St. Helena. New on the dining scene, this lofty restaurant pays tribute to the farm in delightful ways, with a garden and wine-tasting room on-site. Diners can sit and enjoy bone marrow, chicken and dumplings, or hearty steaks. Call 707-963-4555. Website: www.longmeadow ranch.com/Farmstead-Restaurant.

Miguel's, 1437 Lincoln Avenue, Calistoga. I have one word for you—chilaquiles. Miguel's is a hole-in-the-wall, serving the best Mexican food in Napa Valley. Don't come here for fancy. Just plain old good eats. Call 707-942-6868.

Model Bakery, 644 First Street, Napa. Pastries and sandwiches are on the menu at this patisserie. Call 707-259-1128. Website: www.themodelbakery .com.

Morimoto's Napa, 610 Main Street, Napa. The Napa outpost of the Morimoto's chain never fails to inspire diners. Delicately presented Japanese staples—from sushi to skewered meats—fill the menu. Call 707-252-1600. Website: www.morimotonapa .com.

Neela's, 975 Clinton Street, Napa. Indian food has arrived in Napa with a splash. Neela's serves traditional dishes paired with Napa style. Call 707-226-9988. Website: www.neelasnapa .com.

Oxbow Public Market, 610 and 644 First Street, Napa. A collection of farm stands, restaurants, and take-out joints that all accompany wine. Get ice cream, arepas, oysters, hot dogs, coffee, and more. Call 707-226-6529. Website: www .oxbowpublicmarket.com.

Solage Resort's Solbar, 755 Silverado Trail, Calistoga. Join the LA crowd in a massive dining room, or outside near the pool, to dine on seasonal salads, sandwiches, and pizzas. Wines and cocktails delight the Sex in the City crowd. Call 707-226-0800. Website: www.solagecalistoga.com.

OTHER CONTACTS

Calistoga Chamber of Commerce, 1133 Washington Street, Calistoga. Call 707-942-6333. Website: www.calistoga chamber.com.

Napa Valley Welcome Center, 600 Main Street, Napa. Call 707-251-5895. Website: www.legendarynapavalley .com.

St. Helena Chamber of Commerce, 1010 Main Street, Suite A, St. Helena. Call 707-963-4456. Website: www.st helena.com.

In case you get lost, this sign illuminates the way to Sonoma's charms.

6 Wacky Sonoma County

Estimated length: 132 miles
Estimated time: 1–4 days

Getting there: From San Francisco, take US 101 north to CA 116 east; connect to CA 12 north (first toward Sonoma, then to Santa Rosa). Travel north on US 101 to Healdsburg, then backtrack south to Sebastopol. From there, head west on CA 12, north on the Bohemian Highway, and east on CA 116. Then return to US 101 south to San Francisco.

Highlights: Seeing agricultural feats from fermentation festivals to landscaped gardens; visiting fun wineries; hiking in cemeteries; staying at the only American luxury tent accommodation where you can view giraffes from your door; soaking in a cedar enzyme bath.

Wine Country evokes visions of Athena-dressed gals holding up flutes of bubbly to toast their tanned linen-clad hubbies. While Sonoma County does harbor folks who embody this image—one merely needs a night in the posh **Hotel Healdsburg** to get the perfect Wine Country couple photo—the true essence of Sonoma County is refreshingly otherwise. In truth, spending some time traveling around this wacky county (a fairly large collection of towns and hamlets) affords visitors a glimpse into all that makes Northern California unique—funky wineries, hippie festivals, unlikely tributes to art, and even one of the largest collections of wild animals outside a zoo. Sonoma County promises to shatter your perception of Wine Country chic, while not completely depriving you of a well-deserved dash of class.

As you travel north from San Francisco on US 101, exit on CA 116 east and connect to CA 12 toward Sonoma. If time permits, drop into the enchanting

Cornerstone Gardens, a collection of four wineries, a gourmet food shop, an art store, and an inspiring presentation of landscape architecture crafted by recent graduates from California's most prestigious universities. This is one of my favorite destinations to bring families as the gardens are ideal for children to explore—and folks of all ages get a kick out of the giant chair by the entrance.

Cornerstone Gardens

Continue traveling toward Sonoma, a town rich with an unlikely history (the evidence can still be spotted today in the city's Mission San Francisco Solano de Sonoma—the only California mission erected after Mexican independence from Spanish rule). The town of Sonoma was a Mexican city until 1846 when it became the short-lived capital of the "Bear Flag Republic." After 25 days, when California annexed itself into the United States, Sonoma's freedom fighters retreated to agriculture, constructing one of the richest grape-growing areas in California.

To view the evidence of history, Sonoma Segway Tours leads Sonoma journeys via motorized scooter. Zoom for 7 miles past vineyards, stopping at one of four historic wineries to sample vino, as well as testing out some cheese at the sustainable Vella Cheese Factory. Tours include a bottle of wine to take home. You can tack on the deluxe option to include a picnic lunch; or grab a massive sandwich at the Sonoma Cheese Factory and plop down under the shady oaks in the eight-acre Sonoma Square (California's largest, and eldest)—a favorite destination for picnicking locals whose kids play everything from soccer on the grass to tag on the play structures. Before departing Sonoma, poke your head into Tiddle E. Winks Vintage 5 & Dime, which houses a staggering collection of antique toys and candies, not to forget a classic soda fountain and an effusive staff ready to transport you back to 1953.

Back in the car, continue traveling north on CA 12 until you arrive in Glen

Ellen; in summer, follow the signs to Morton's Warm Springs. Cool off with a dip in the one of three geothermal heated pools, play a game of ping-pong in the arcade, or kick a ball around under the oaks. Since 1934, families have gathered here to barbecue along the creek and soak in the pools—though don't expect *hot* pools; these are naturally heated to about 80 degrees Fahrenheit. The pools can be a scene on weekends, and the cost of parking and swimming can seem obscene to people not used to California's overpriced fun, but the retro flavor and all around good-time character makes for a good resting point in the midday summer heat.

As you enter the town of Kenwood (just north of Glen Ellen), notice a winery with a giant John Deere tractor out front—you've arrived at Landmark Vineyards, home to the kin of *the* John Deere, with plenty of kitsch souvenirs for tractor-loving visitors. Beyond the farm equipment, this winery works to not only please imbibers with fine Chardonnay, but also invites folks to sit back, and enjoy the luscious flowery grounds. While musicians play on summer weekends, people tour the vineyards in horse-drawn carriages or play a round of bocce ball near the duck pond. For a real treat, book a stay in one of the vineyard's cottages to watch bunnies trying to score grapes from the vines and experience the particular enchantment of sleeping surrounded by a farm.

For dinner, it pays to be reminded that Wine Country quirkiness doesn't have to equate to oddity. Rather, we'll call it difference, and leave it at that. Kenwood's Vineyards Inn might look like a roadside diner from the outside, but inside you'll find unparalleled organic Spanish and Basque cuisine. Chef and owner Steve

Landmark Vineyard's gardens are ideal for tasting and relaxing.

WALK TO PLUTO? IN SONOMA?

In the hills high above the hamlet of Kenwood lies **Sugarloaf State Park,** home to the Valley of the Moon's favorite hiking, a waterfall, guided docent tours, and a bounty of wildlife—all standard operating procedure for a park, wouldn't you say? However, hidden in the park's **Robert Ferguson Observatory** lie a wealth of cosmic information and activities. Most people head up here at night to view the stars from their collection of telescopes—peeks of the stars are free! However, once a month, the good astronomers shrink the universe and allow eager minds to walk along the galaxy all the way to Pluto. Kids can see how grand the size of the sun truly is when compared to its orbiting planets. For more information view www.rfo.org.

Rose not only grows most of his produce on his farm, but he also instructs his staff to use diners' unfinished glasses of water to drench the restaurant's abundant herb garden. Continuing with the homegrown appeal, a visit to Santa Rosa's Zazu Farm and Restaurant will not disappoint either. To get here from Kenwood, travel on CA 12 to US 101 north, exit on Guerneville Road/Steele Lane, and drive west for 4.2 miles. It appears you are driving into nowhere, and then this roadside farm and restaurant magically appear. Claiming to combine Americana with northern Italian cooking, Zazu focuses on what's growing in its gardens—imagine a summertime star-anise-rubbed duck combined with apricot *sambal* and a spicy rice cake paired with a local Riesling grown a few miles down the road. The tiny interior gets crowded with devotees, so book ahead for a table.

After dinner, travel west on Guerneville Road, turn left on Fulton Road, then right on River Road; continue onto Mark West Springs Road and then merge onto Porter Creek Road, and you arrive at Sonoma County's most curious destination—Safari West. Hidden in the mountains between Santa Rosa and Calistoga, animal-lover Peter Lang scooped up this 400-acre stretch of rolling hills and began filling it with African wild animals of all things: so if you thought you saw a giraffe poking over a fence along your drive, your eyes were not deceiving you. Part zoo, part drive- through animal park, Safari West brings a dash of madcap to Santa Rosa. Book one of their luxury safari tent cabins and sleep on heated beds, surrounded by the sounds of African birds throughout the night. Spot giraffes grazing on the plains as you enter the mess hall to enjoy a family-style breakfast. Fill up, because you'll be embarking on a wild ride through the preserve for a couple of hours to spot everything from ostriches to cheetahs to rhinos (tours are open

A giraffe smooch at Safari West

NOT 100 PERCENT NONGHOSTLY CEMETERY HIKES, BUT CLOSE

When I heard that the **Santa Rosa Rural Cemetery** offers a variety of guided walks, I chalked it off to kitsch. However, I quickly learned that this group of volunteers so adore this historic place of rest that they really want people to congregate here. And locals do! Picnicking, hiking, and even walking their dogs. The area's oldest cemetery is foremost home to a variety of old rose bushes hard to spot in today's hybrid plant culture. Horticulturalists will delight in the flora tours. For people interested in the history of the area told through the dead, sign up for the cemetery's educational history tours. The most popular tours are, of course, the monthly Night Walks. You'll need to bring a flashlight and prepare to be slightly spooked. But you only live once . . . or do you?

to people staying elsewhere, but everyone must book in advance). Other perks of a visit here include guided hikes, morning Behind the Scenes tours to feed the animals, and a lively dinner/campfire complete with ghost stores, wine, and catfish feeding.

When you've exhausted the offerings of Safari West (or merely need a respite from the action), take Mark West Springs Road back to US 101 and travel north to Healdsburg. Within the last 20 years, the town of Healdsburg has morphed from a backward country town that locals aimed to escape from to one of the hottest tickets in Wine Country. Now, gourmet eats dot the area around the picturesque square and high-end hotels populate this zip code. That being said, Wine Country is never without its dash of fun—especially when it comes to eating, so grab a burger and a beer at the wildly popular Bear Republic Brewery.

If you are finding yourself enamored with Healdsburg's artsy aesthetic, two pricey hotels deliver a nontraditional experience. Hotel Healdsburg provides guests with a design-forward look at Wine Country, with mood lighting creating shadows along the walls, slick furnishings, and one of the best breakfast spreads around. This hotel makes for a fanciful getaway if you want stylish quirkiness. Alternatively, for people who can't get enough of modern art, the Duchamp Hotel, hidden by a grove of olive trees, is a gallery come to life. Large sculptures dot the pool area, and each cottage promotes luxury in the sparest sense— imagine concrete floors covered in animal-fur carpets and a sumo-wrestler-sized shower, plus wine tastings at the hotel's winery and plenty of personal attention sans the typical B&B bubbly hostess.

Travel north on US 101 to Geyserville and reach Francis Ford Coppola Winery's newly refurbished wine park. Families gather around the pool, sipping cab in a cabana; movie buffs explore the collection of cinematic artifacts, including the desk from *The Godfather*, Coppola's Oscars, and ship models from the film *Marie Antoinette*; others sample the hearty red wines (the tasting rooms stays open until 9 PM!), and then settle into Rustic Restaurant to enjoy Coppola's favorites—a dizzying collection of Italian foods notable for their ambition (much like the owner of this property).

In the morning, grab a cappuccino at Flying Goat Coffee and pastries at Downtown Bakery and then travel south on US 101 to CA 12 west. In Sebastopol, drive south on Gravenstein Highway to explore the wealth of antique shops housing wacky finds; or take a peek into California Carnivores, the largest carnivorous plant store in the country. Stop into Coffee Catz, a local coffeehouse with plenty of sass. Not only do they serve a variety of organic blends and sandwiches, but they also host local events like a Science Café and open-mike nights. If you want some true local flavor, this is the spot to explore.

Back on CA 12, make a quick right onto Sebastopol's Florence Avenue, a five-block residential street festooned with over 150 colorful sculptures made by local junk artists Patrick Amiot and Brigette Laurent. These whimsical statues run the gamut, showcasing everything from a rat driving a car to a mermaid resting on a lawn.

Continue on CA 12 to the Bohemian Highway and turn right. Pull into the gravel road of Wildflour Bread Bakery. These bakers sell out of over 900 loaves of wood-oven-baked breads each day. Prime buying time is around 10:30 AM for the most exhaustive selection, but anything you get when you arrive will make carb lovers giddy. I have to admit the 100 percent rye may be the best I've ever had. Next, stop into Osmosis Day Spa to dive into the only cedar enzyme baths in the country. Inspired by the Japanese, these wood-chip-filled tubs are meant to extract all the yucky stuff from your insides as well as clear up your skin. If nothing else, the view from the tubs of the Japanese gardens, followed by a luxurious shower and a deep massage, make this spa a must on your itinerary.

As you continue north on the Bohemian Highway, you enter the hamlet of Occidental—quite possibly the funkiest town in Sonoma County. Home to a cast of characters ranging from European transplants to families escaping the bustle of city life, here you can find off-the-wall shops, a comprehensive wine store, a

WILD AND WACKY FESTIVALS OF SONOMA COUNTY

For fans of unique festivals, Sonoma County offers a handful well worth a special trip. My absolute favorite is the **Harmony Festival**—a celebration of music and kookiness, currently coming into its own. Every June, hippies, music lovers, families, and more gather at the Santa Rosa Fairgrounds to enjoy big name musicians (Lauren Hill, Flaming Lips, and Primus have performed in recent years). But that's not all. Imagine a kids' section with its own cast of entertainers, bubbles, and free snacks; a Sustainability Living Roadshow (which is a dressed-up circus); a parade; ecofriendly booths; and a Silent Disco. Regardless of your musical taste, this festival should not be missed, if only for the people-watching. Bring your camera.

Another highlight is the wacky **Handcar Regatta** in Santa Rosa's railroad square each September. Call it punk, or pedal madness, but whichever way you spin it, this creative collection of handcrafted pedal-powered machines, in the guise of giant elephants and golden zeppelins, promises to wow your idea of machinery and its general usefulness. Throw in costumed participants of all varieties, music, and, of course food, and you begin to get a sense of how wacky Sonoma's inhabitants really are.

Finally, the **Freestone Fermentation Festival,** which occurs each May, honors all things fermented—from bread to wine to kombucha and more. Whether you dig kimchi or yogurt, or just want to see what the hype is all about, a visit to the town of Freestone is a trip.

Scratch Sonoma and instead have Santa Rosa's Harmony Festival.

Stay along the Russian River.

lovely inn, gourmet restaurants, and the popular Howard Station Café. Hippies love the vegan offerings, and farmers populate the tables for the café's steak and eggs. You will rave about nearly everything you receive here—save the fact that they only accept cash.

Now that you arrived in nature, you likely don't want to get back in the car so fast. Instead, book a trip with the Sonoma Canopy Tours, which takes you on a zipline through the tops of redwood trees. Zipline at speeds up to 25 miles per hour to 11 different platforms scattered through the forest, and you'll find your heart pumping to the exhilarating tune of glee.

As you travel north on the Bohemian Highway, passing groves of long-standing redwoods, travel east on CA 116 through the Russian River Valley and into the funky town of Guerneville. This beloved vacation village has long drawn both San Francisco families and the gay community, eager for summertime sun. To cater to the wide variety of inhabitants, Guerneville provides kookiness as the main event. From decidedly posh B&Bs to woodsy cabins lining the riverbed, plus hemp shops, taco trucks, and lively brewpubs, this quiet town swells in summer no matter what your persuasion. My favorite destination here is the Pee Wee Golf Course, a colorful collection of miniature golf holes showcasing cannibals cooking a man over a flame (fake, of course) to a tribute to Jerry Garcia—no matter your golf skills, you've never seen a course quite like this one.

On your way back toward Healdsburg, you'll pass a variety of wineries, and most any are worth a stop. If you are hungry, Hop Kiln Winery, a California landmark cum wine destination, provides guests with food and wine pairings. Sample their gourmet treats and soak up the luscious growing conditions for white wines.

Head east on River Road for a few miles until you reach Forestville. For travelers wanting to end their Sonoma County experience with a fanciful splash of decadence, check into the Farmhouse Inn, a renovated barn and community of cottages spruced up by the careful eyes of a brother/sister team of artists. Each room has its own enchanting theme, from the poems stenciled on the walls to the soaking tubs that fill from the ceiling. Most rooms have radiant-heated floors, luxe bedding, and carefully chosen amenities, plus a lovely collection of locally crafted bath salts and sweets and treats is available in the office. If the price is too steep (though I often find deals online), opt to reserve dinner at their award-winning dining room to enjoy their famed Rabbit, Rabbit, Rabbit—which is, as the name implied, rabbit served three ways— before retreating to your quarters in Healdsburg (just 9 miles north on US 101); or travel back to San Francisco by continuing south on US 101.

Poetry lines the walls of the Farmhouse Inn.

IN THE AREA

ACCOMMODATIONS

Duchamp Hotel, 421 Foss Street, Healdsburg. Spare and mod rooms fit for design-forward hipsters. Pricey. Call 707-431-1300. Website: www.duchamp hotel.com.

Farmhouse Inn, 7871 River Road, Forestville. Creatively crafted rooms and cottages might be pricey, but the charming aesthetic, the Michelin-starred restaurant, and the pool, fire pits, and spa call to people wanting decadence in a rustic environment. Call 707-887-3300. Website: www.farm houseinn.com.

Hotel Healdsburg, 25 Matheson Street, Healdsburg. Quite possibly the hippest hotel in Wine Country, imagine rooms that seem to have hopped off the pages of a glossy magazine with modern furniture that manages to be comfortable as well as hip. Call 800-889-7188. Website: www.hotelhealds burg.com.

Safari West, 3115 Porter Creek Road, Santa Rosa. Sleep in a luxury tent cabin complete with private bathroom, heated bed, and African art. Call 707-579-2551. Website: www.safariwest.com.

ATTRACTIONS AND RECREATION

California Carnivores, 2833 Old Gravenstein Highway, Sebastopol. Call 707-824-0433. Website: www.california carnivores.com.

Cornerstone Gardens, 23570 Arnold Drive, Sonoma. Four tasting rooms, a landscape architecture garden, kids' play area, gourmet grocery, and gallery make this destination a worthy stop as you enter Sonoma County. Call 707-933-3010. Website: www.cornerstone gardens.com

Francis Ford Coppola Winery, 300 Via Archimedes, Geyserville. A new wine park offers a public swimming pool, red wine tastings until after dark, a movie museum, and a restaurant. Call 707-857-1471. Website: www.franciscoppola winery.com.

Freestone Fermentation Festival, 1935 Bohemian Highway, Sebastopol. Call 707-874-1963. Website: www.free stonefermentationfestival.com.

Handcar Regatta, 738 Wilson Street, Santa Rosa. Call 707-490-5039. Website: www.handcar-regatta.com.

Harmony Festival, 1350 Bennett Valley Road, Santa Rosa. Website: www .harmonyfestival.com.

Hop Kiln Winery, 6050 Westside Road, Healdsburg. Call 707-433-6491. Website: www.hopkilnwinery.com.

Landmark Vineyards, 101 Adobe Canyon Road, Kenwood. Sample Chardonnay in the gardens or spend a night in the cottage. Call 707-833-0053. Website: www.landmarkwine.com.

Mission San Francisco Solano de Sonoma, 114 East Spain Street, Sonoma. Call 707-938-9560. Website: www.parks.ca.gov.

Morton's Warm Springs, 1651 Warm Springs Road, Glen Ellen. Grab your summer energy and dive in the mineral-spring-heated pools. They have BBQ pits, basketball courts, and access to a creek. Call 707-833-551. Website: www.mortonswarmsprings.com.

Osmosis Day Spa, 209 Bohemian Highway, Freestone. Book a spa treatment or soak in the cedar enzyme baths. Call 707-823-8231. Website: www.osmosis.com.

Pee Wee Golf Course, 16155 Drake Road, Guerneville. Possible the wackiest minigolf course in the country; you have to check it out for yourself. Call 707-869-9321.

Robert Ferguson Observatory, 2605 Adobe Canyon Road, Kenwood. Explore the galaxy for free up in the mountains. Call 707-833-6979. Website: www.rfo.org.

Santa Rosa Rural Cemetery, 415 Steele Lane, Santa Rosa. Hike in the most peaceful spot in Santa Rosa. Call 707-543-3282. Website: www.santarosa rec.com.

Sonoma Canopy Tours, 6250 Bohemian Highway, Occidental. Zip through the treetops, hopping from canopy to canopy like a monkey. Call 888-494-7868. Website: www.sonoma canopytours.com.

Sonoma Segway Tours, 375 First Street East, Sonoma. Balance your way through Sonoma, sampling wine and cheese as you go. Call 707-938-2080. Website: www.sonomasegway.com.

Sugarloaf State Park, 2605 Adobe Canyon Road, Kenwood. A beloved state park that draws hikers of all levels. Call 707-833-5712. Website: www.parks.ca.gov/?page_id=481.

DINING/DRINKS

Bear Republic Brewery, 345 Healdsburg Avenue, Healdsburg. This hopping brewery serves pub grub to families and folks who prefer beer to vino. Call 707-433-2337. Website: www.bear republic.com.

Coffee Catz, 6761 Sebastopol Avenue #300, Sebastopol. A great coffeehouse offering pastries, sandwiches, and delicious desserts alongside a good cup of coffee. Call 707-829-6600. Website: www.coffeecatz.com.

Downtown Bakery, 308 Center Street #A, Healdsburg. Pastries, breads, and coffee served atop silver tables. Call 707-431-2719. Website: www.downtown bakery.net.

Flying Goat Coffee, 324 Center Street, Healdsburg. The best latte in Wine Country draws locals and tourists. Call 707-433-3599. Website: www.flyinggoat coffee.com.

Howard Station Café, 3811 Bohemian Highway, Occidental. This cash-only eatery still has locals lining up for everything from vegan scrambles to meaty breakfasts. Call 707-874-2838. Website: www.howardstationcafe.com.

Rustic Restaurant, 300 Via Archimedes, Geyserville. Italian specialties served in Francis Ford Coppola's new wine park, including everything from traditional faves to creative concoctions. As you might expect, the wine selection satisfies. Call 707-857-1485. Website: franciscoppola winery.com/rustic.

Sonoma Cheese Factory, 2 Spain Street, Sonoma. Order heaping sandwiches at the counter, then take them across the street to the square to enjoy under the oaks. On summer weekends, they fire up the BBQ outside. Call 707-996-1931. Website: www.sonomacheese factory.com.

Vella Cheese Factory, 315 Second Street East, Sonoma. Call 707-938-3232. Website: www.vellacheese.com.

Vineyards Inn, 23000 Arnold Drive, Sonoma. Gourmet and seasonal cuisine, served in a roadside diner setting. Call 707-938-2350. Website: www.sonoma vineyardinn.com.

Wildflour Bread Bakery, 140 Bohemian Highway, Sebastopol. Specialties of this bakery include its sourdough breads made in a wood-fired brick oven, scones, and biscotti. Call 707-874-2938. Website: www.wild flourbread.com.

Zazu Farm and Restaurant, 3535 Guerneville Road, Santa Rosa. Enjoy seasonal favorites freshly harvested from the farm. Quite small, this local favorite packs in winemakers and in-the-know travelers. Call 707-523-4814. Website: www.zazurestaurant.com.

OTHER CONTACTS

Forestville Chamber of Commerce & Visitors Center, 6652 Front Street, Forestville. Call 707-869-2958. Website: www.forestvillechamber.org.

Geyserville Chamber & Visitors Center, Call 707-857-3745. Website: www.geyservillecc.com.

Healdsburg Chamber of Commerce & Visitors Bureau, 217 Healdsburg Avenue,Healdsburg. Call 707-433-6935. Website: www.healdsburg.com.

Santa Rosa Convention & Visitors Bureau, 9 Fourth Street, Santa Rosa. Call 707-577-8674. Website: www.visit santarosa.com.

Sebastopol Chamber of Commerce and Visitor Center, 265 South Main Street, Sebastopol. Call 707-823-3032. Website: www.sebastopol.org.

Sonoma County Tourism Bureau, 453 First Street East, Sonoma. Call 707-996-1090. Website: www.sonomavalley.com.

The rugged Northern California coast

7 Highway 1 for Families

Estimated length: 143 miles
Estimated time: 3 hours straight through, or 4 days

Getting there: From San Francisco, travel south on CA 1 to US 101.

Highlights: Photographing the wild Pacific Ocean; walking on the Santa Cruz Beach Boardwalk; visiting the Monterey Bay Aquarium; hiking the rugged cliffs of Big Sur.

Although the idea of taking a road trip with kids often leaves parents in need of a strong cocktail, traveling along CA 1 (Highway 1) between San Francisco to Big Sur offers much to entertain even the squirmiest kiddo, not to mention adults with short attention spans. This ribbon of highway has long attracted wanderers, who find the pounding surf below the ice plant–blanketed cliffs enchanting, not to mention the many outdoor activities, which are sure to inspire.

As you merge onto CA 1 south, San Francisco disappears, and you receive your first glimpse of the Pacific Ocean. If you are lucky, the sun will be glistening off the sea, making the entire carload of folks gape at the beauty beyond; unfortunately, most days the bedroom community of Pacifica is socked in with fog, making it easy to pass through on your way to your first adventure. Just before you reach Half Moon Bay, turn right onto California Avenue in the community of Moss Beach, drive until the street ends, and park in the lot. You'll need to arrive at low tide to best enjoy the Fitzgerald Marine Reserve, the Bay Area's most accessible tide pools (check the website for tide charts). Wear waterproof shoes and trek down the hill to explore these vast pools, inhabited by starfish, anemones, crabs, and the occasional eel. On the rocks just a few feet out, those white blobs you see are actually seals. Kids love this real science lesson—as do their parents.

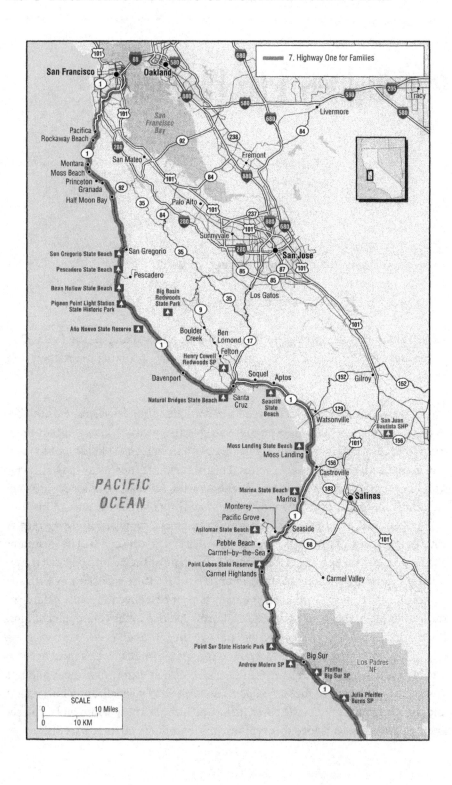

Touch a starfish at the Fitzgerald Marine Reserve.

Back on CA 1, approach the village of Princeton-by-the-Sea; head west on Capistrano and weave through the industrial part of town until you reach the edge of Pillar Point. Park the car and wander along the bird sanctuary path until you arrive at the beach at the end of the trail. This is the sight of the world-famous surf break Mavericks, where kamikaze surfers ride waves taller than buildings (over 100 feet!). This is not a place to learn to surf; in fact, many professional surfers have lost their lives here. But seeing breathtaking waves and the occasional sea mammal is quite the treat. If you are in town when the famed Mavericks Surf Competition occurs, join the crowds on the cliffs to watch daredevils battle mountains of seawater.

Awaiting the perfect wave

If your belly is growling as you approach Half Moon Bay, you are in luck. On the ocean side of CA 1 is the fantastic seafood eatery Sam's Chowder

A Half Moon Bay pumpkin patch

House. Opened by a seasoned foodie a few years ago, the chowder, lobster rolls, and epic oyster selection, not to mention wines and beer, have made locals and tourists line up by day and night. Plus, these guys have crafted the most intelligent kids' menu in the Bay Area. Snag a seat at one of the outdoor fire pits if the weather permits and watch the birds dive into the sea. Or, if you want something a bit lighter, head east toward Main Street and grab a hunk of freshly made pumpkin bread at the Half Moon Bay Bakery. I warn you, my family can destroy a loaf within the hour. Another choice option is the divine—and speedy—Chez Shea. Walk up to the counter and order tacos, salads, or sandwiches, all crafted lovingly with organic ingredients, then weave through the colorfully painted eatery to find the small patio out back. Finally for families who prefer thick sandwiches on fresh-baked bread oozing with mustard and mayo and meats of all varieties, the hole-in-the-wall shop inside the historic San Benito House will not let you down. Grab a sandy and plop down at one of the mosaic-tiled outdoor tables as local musicians strum guitars and kids race up and down the stairs.

Half Moon Bay, once known as Spanishtown, has a rich history in San Mateo County for its agriculture as well as its location as a prime fishing hub. Right in downtown you will meander through historic buildings—none more photo worthy than the tiny jail noticeable from Main Street. Though most tourists crowd the town during pumpkin season, as this is California's pumpkin capital, visiting this seaside village during low season always makes me feel as if I have stumbled upon a secret idyllic village. As you explore the small shops on Main Street, pop into the Half to Have It antique shop to score previously loved toys and the wonderful Coastside Books, which has a fun kids' section, to whittle away a foggy day.

PUMPKIN SEASON

Half Moon Bay considers itself the pumpkin capital of the planet: a hearty title for such a small town. However, come October this community provides plenty of opportunity to pluck your own pumpkins, view the largest orange veggie in the country (weighing over 1,400 pounds), as well as indulging in pumpkin-themed spa treatments, dinners, beer, and more. Below is a collection of my favorite pumpkin-themed events and destinations.

Pumpkin patches run the gamut out here in this aggie-town. From modest roadside venues packed with orange globes (like my fave **Pastorino Farms**) to massive farms complete with corn mazes, train rides, and face painting (the famed **Lemos Farm**).

Usually occurring on the second weekend in October, the **Half Moon Bay Pumpkin Festival** draws thousands from near and far to celebrate the life of this Halloween symbol. The soiree begins with a weigh off to crown the largest veggie in the country and ends with a street party that stretches across downtown.

For food-focused visitors, menus begin showcasing the local superstar in late September. Nearly every restaurant showcases the fall bounty; however, if you have time, tread over to the **Half Moon Bay Brewing Company** for a hoppy dinner of pumpkin-flavored seafood, soups, and pastas paired with pumpkin brews.

Finally, for the wellness crowd, book a pumpkin wrap at the luxurious **Ritz Carlton Half Moon Bay Spa.** Treatments cost a pretty penny, but you deserve to be treated like royalty.

Giant pumpkins in Half Moon Bay

The tent cabins at Costanoa

If you'd like to extend your visit, there are a number of fine family-friendly accommodations in the area. For families wanting to glimpse the ocean out a hotel room window, the nautical-themed Beach House Inn offers spacious quarters, a decent breakfast, and private patios facing the water. Another choice option is the Spanish-style digs at the Half Moon Bay Inn. About 40 minutes south of town off CA 1, Costanoa allows you to pitch your own tent, snuggle up in one of their plush tent cabins (that boast heated beds and in-room art), or rent a cabin; Bay Area families congregate here to roast s'mores in the BBQ pits, watch baseball in the lively restaurant, or enjoy the quiet of this remote but easily accessible location.

Continue south on CA 1, passing fields of yellow flowers spilling into the sea. Just before you reach the miniscule town of Pescadero, look for the famed Pigeon Point Lighthouse. Constructed in 1872, this is one of the tallest lighthouses in the country. Not only can you tour the lighthouse on weekends with a docent, but you can also rent a room, or a bed, at this mellow hostel perched on the tip of land. At night, enjoy the barks of sea lions and the wind ripping through the surrounding trees.

Just east of CA 1 is the pleasant, though unassuming town of Pescadero. Most travelers use the one-street village as a place to pick up house-baked artichoke bread at the Archangel Deli and a bowl of artichoke/green chili soup at the local family-favored Duarte's Tavern. However, the kiddos (and goat-cheese lovers) will become smitten with the gentle goats populating Harley Farms. Tour the property, learn about goat milk production, sample chevre, hold kids, or just chill out in the pastoral ambience. Make a reservation for a two-hour tour, or explore the property on your own.

Depending on the season, a stop at Ano Nuevo State Reserve promises a slice of the Discovery Channel up close, but hopefully not personal. While the highlights of visiting this protected area require about a 3-mile hike, when I brought my three-year-old, he was so stoked about the elephant seals that he walked the entire trail. Yep, this is the main destination in the Bay Area to view those blubbery elephant seals mating, molting, birthing, weaning, and, yes boys, even fighting. The best time to come (though you need a reservation months in advance) is in February, when the males are frisky enough to both mate and fight. It is a bloody mess, so if your child is a little squeamish, this might not be the best option. Also note that you cannot take strollers onto the dunes. If the gore of animal mating doesn't inspire, pretty much any time of year, you'll be able to spot the elephant seals sunning on the sand. Be cautious and respectful; these big guys are bigger—and faster—than you'd imagine.

CA 1 sinews south through the village of Davenport and finally arrives in Santa Cruz, affectionately known as Surf City USA. Her vibrant nature attracts plenty of hippies and environmentalists, as well as the intellects studying marine biology in the redwood-shaded University of California at Santa Cruz. Quite possibly Northern California's most enchanting beach community, Santa Cruz not only offers heaps of outdoor activities but also farm-fresh cuisine and plenty of culture.

Kids at Harley Farms

You enter town on Mission Street, a thoroughfare with some of the best food offerings for families and food lovers. For breakfast and brunch, college students line up for hours for the banana pancakes, acai bowls, and *moquecas* at the lively Café Brazil. Kids and their parents adore the array of burgers served at the aptly named Burger. Burgers are named after 1980s icons like Marky Mark, and after

Dream Inn, Santa Cruz

Elephant seals at Ano Nuevo

you order your meat or veggie slab, fries, and a milkshake at the counter, you are handed a celebrity mug shot (so the servers know where to deliver your basket of goodies) and told to take a seat in the artsy bar. With probably a hundred beers to choose from, sports on the TVs, and a nice collection of families and hipsters, this is an easy spot for picky palates. Finally, for dinner there is no better place to enjoy seasonal pasta dishes than Ristorante Avante. With a friendly staff and a down-to-earth vibe, you feel like you are dining in a casual café in Italy but with only the finest ingredients. Everything I have ever had here has been spectacular, but the gnocchi and ice-cream sandwich win my heart every time.

Check into the beachfront retro digs at the Dream Inn. Kids and their parents adore this newly renovated hotel, especially because of the gifts the front desk offers children on arrival. The inn has a pool and in-house restaurant (Aquarius) and access to the beach and the Santa Cruz Beach Boardwalk. If you'd like accommodations in a quieter location, I have two great options. For those OK with forking over the big bucks, check into the luxurious Chaminade Resort and

Spa, perched atop a hill overlooking the sea. The pool and hot tub are packed with kids, and the big grassy fields are ideal for pickup soccer games. Alternatively, a couple miles south of Santa Cruz in the village of Aptos, the Rio Sands Motel offers sizable (yet affordable) rooms, some with kitchenettes, just steps to a quiet family-friendly beach.

Start your morning with the best coffee in town. Take CA 1 to 41st Avenue and drive west until you see Verve Coffee Roasters. Known for its careful blends and artful presentations of lattes (plus the fabulous collection of Kelly's pastries), this is the locals' choice for reading the newspaper or surfing the Web before spending the day outdoors.

Whether you are a novice or seasoned surfer, you'll want to don your wet suit and test your skills. Beginners should head to Cowell's Beach, close to the boardwalk, while more advanced wave riders should head to the swells between 30th and 36th Avenues off East Cliff. It is helpful to know that local surfers are quite territorial, so use your best surfer etiquette and throw on your toughest skin to handle the possible insults hurled your way when you try to ride a good one. For folks wanting to learn how to ride the waves, see "In the Area."

You'll definitely need a hearty breakfast after burning all those calories, and the harbor-front Aldos serves lumberjack-sized portions of griddle fare and omelets with sass on the dock as you sip strong Bloody Marys. Another local favorite, though with an opposite ambience, is the Silver Spur Restaurant, located in a residential part of Santa Cruz. Popular with hipsters and those nursing hangovers, this ranch-style down-home breakfast (with a fine kiddo menu)

SANTA CRUZ NIGHTLIFE

For night owls looking for some evening fun, Santa Cruz prides itself on having a slew of places to imbibe, hear music, and gather with friends. Most are not kid friendly, but if you happen to have a babysitter (or you are a big kid yourself), you'll want to check out the happenings in the free *Santa Cruz Weekly*. Popular watering holes to hear music include the Catalyst (which hosts alternative and rock events), Kuumbwa Jazz Center, and on Wednesday and Thursday evenings boogie down to live DJs at Clouds Downtown.

In summer, also check listings in the *Weekly* about the boardwalk's Friday night summer music series. They have hosted bands like Sha Na Na, The Fixx, and Flock of Seagulls in the past couple of years.

Santa Cruz Beach Boardwalk

promises to fill the belly with bacon, eggs, pancakes, and a strong cuppa joe.

By this point, the young-uns are probably itching to get to the Santa Cruz Beach Boardwalk. For over one hundred years, this beachfront amusement park has appealed to kids of all ages. Whether you fancy riding the Giant Dipper Roller Coaster; getting dizzy on the century-old carousel; letting the munchkins drive cars, boats, and planes; playing miniature golf; dancing at Dance Dance Revolution; or just sunbathing on the sand, this collection of fun promises to enchant the entire clan.

After spending hours on the prowl for fun, wander out on the pier for a big plate of oysters and a beer at Riva Grill. Quite popular with locals, who populate the bar and then leave with heaping scoops of fresh gelato, you may have to wait for a table by the window, but you won't regret it. Just be sure to stick with the more traditional dishes; occasionally the chef gets a touch too creative with the menu, and I always find these dishes inconsistent, unlike the grill's fish-and-chips.

Jump back in the car for one last beach outing and follow the signs to Natural Bridges State Park. This beloved beach and nature trail shelters the annual butterfly migration that descends upon the central coast in the late fall and winter. Plus, the picturesque stretch of sand, noted for its natural rock bridge

Natural Bridges State Park

(hence the name), attracts birds, passing dolphins, and families camping out for the day. I often come here to watch the sunset over the sea—you can get great photos from the roundabout just above the parking lot.

Eat dinner like the locals and chow down on burritos downtown. For a cost-effective option, line up at Taqueria Vallarta, which also broadcasts soccer games. El Palomar is a touch fancier (and more expensive), with a lively crowd slurping margaritas and grubbing on snapper tacos. On warm evenings, crowds of people stroll Pacific Avenue, streaming in and out of bars, movie theaters, shops, and restaurants, as street musicians serenade the passersby. Whether you crave surf shirts at the locally owned O'Neill Surf Shop, books at Bookshop Santa Cruz, or just wandering through the hemp, crystal, or apothecary stores, you are sure to locate something fun to bring home.

Rise and shine early, jump onto CA 1 for about 30 miles until you reach the village of Moss Landing. Reserve in advance to board your Sanctuary Cruises whale-watching boat. While these trips are not for people with short attention spans (the tours last four to five hours), Sanctuary guarantees whale viewings. On my last trip with these guys, we got so close to the humpbacks we smelled their stinky breath. If you prefer to paddle on your own, you can rent kayaks at Kayak Connection in the Elkhorn Slough. This waterway is home to various bird species, as well as otters, seals, and sea lions. If you are an experienced kayaker, you may even make it out into the bay and sniff yourself a whale.

On the west side of the harbor, you'll find a favorite among Central Coasters at Phil's Fish Market. Located in a corrugated tin roofed warehouse, the super-fresh *cioppino,* daily catches, and fish-and-chips will help replenish the belly after a trip on the water. If you prefer to avoid fish for lunch, order up saucy enchiladas or *carnitas* at the festive Whole Enchilada just off CA 1.

As you travel south on CA 1, the sand dunes and artichoke plants clue you in that you have arrived in Monterey County. Made famous by John Steinbeck, this area might be known for its Cannery Row and tough agricultural history, but today, Monterey and her surrounding sister cities rely on tourism and thus treat their visitors right. The area promises the finest accommodations, golf, attractions, beaches, wineries, restaurants, and parkland between San Francisco and Los Angeles, and you'll find it hard to tear yourself (or your kids) away.

There are plenty of fine family-friendly accommodations in Monterey/Pacific Grove. In Monterey, the spacious suites at Mariposa Inn might appear a touch too modern for little fingers, but the cozy touches like a Murphy bed in the living area, an electric fireplace, big tubs, fluffy beds upstairs, and a pool all allow this hillside inn to shine. For families wanting to experience being in the heart of Monterey, the newly renovated Portola Hotel and Spa offers a dash of the resort experience, without the resort prices. Simple touches like a fantastic concierge, a small wind-blocked pool, a selection of in-house restaurants, and easy access to the waterfront enchant.

For some, Monterey might feel too overrun with tourists. If this is the case, you may prefer a room in neighboring Pacific Grove—a timid town filled with precious B&Bs, Victorian architecture, and one of my favorite waterfront beach paths. The Asilomar Conference Grounds, architecturally designed by phenom Julia Morgan, appeals to families craving an outdoorsy experience without luxury—think summer camp rather than tents. With trails leading to a great surf beach, deer wandering past your quarters, and a

Spot whales year-round in Moss Landing.

group breakfast buffet, you can imagine why companies plan retreats here and why families whisper about the existence of this relaxed destination.

Take the kids over to Monterey's Dennis the Menace Playground in the afternoon to run off that car energy. Colorful and huge, kids of all ages (and I am talking to you grown-ups) race down the tall slides, hide out in the maze, and explore the train car. The playground is located in the city's massive El Estero Park, right across from the ocean, and closes at dusk.

Opt for dinner at one of Monterey's fine eateries. If you can snag a reservation at the famous local Monterey's Fish House, grab it. This seafood joint doesn't look like much, but it reels in the locals who swear by the oysters, clam chowder, and simple presentations of oceanic creatures. Foodies, however, should drive straight to Montrio Bistro. Located in a 1910 firehouse, this bistro's innards boast

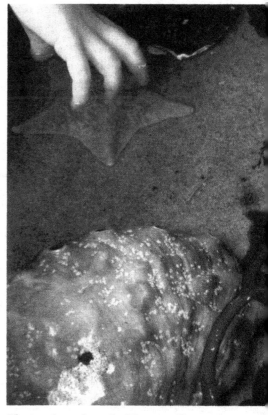

The touch pools at the Monterey Bay Aquarium.

cloud puffs on the ceiling, a convivial bar, and the most knowledgeable servers in the area. Menu items change with the season, but at last visit, my pistachio-crusted halibut and beet salad made me giddy for days. Their kid menu is quite sophisticated, but totally acceptable for picky eaters.

In the morning, a visit to East Village Coffee Lounge will remind you that Monterey is also a college town, packed with laptop toting twenty-somethings slurping lattes in big bowls. They have a decent selection of pastries to indulge in before traveling to Cannery Row for your visit to the world-renowned Monterey Bay Aquarium. Tourists travel from all over the globe to visit this research facility to spot sharks, flamingos, seahorses, jellyfish, and nearly every type of sea life you can imagine. Embedded in the giant kelp forests are hints at how we can take better care of our oceans, eat sustainable seafood (pick up their helpful seafood watch card), and understand the impact of our lifestyles on the oceans. If you get hungry, dine at either their café or restaurant, which have been spruced up by Napa chef Cindy Pawlcyn—though both will take a bite out of your wallet.

After departing Cannery Row, rent bikes at Adventures by the Sea and (depending on the ages and abilities of your kids) take a beachside ride along the 17-Mile Drive (though from the bike rental location at Cannery Row, your trek is an additional 3 miles). While lovely, this stretch of beach is best enjoyed as you pedal alongside the coves searching for sea mammals and whales in the distance, so it is not necessary to travel the entire path.

All that pedaling will get the belly ready for dinner. Right in Pacific Grove, there are some feasible options. Favorites include the modest, though not cheap, Fishwife, which specializes in seafood for families with a Mexican twist. However, my family's favorite is Passionfish—a sustainable seafood restaurant that would be at home in California's finest foodie cities. Though they do not have high chairs or crayons for the little ones, more mature children enjoy the delicate seafood options, like sea scallops with a tomato truffle butter, or land specialties, like the duck confit with honey reduction, which satisfy the palate.

In the evening, this region settles in fairly early, so retreat to your hotel for an evening swim. Then wake up early to line up with the locals at Katy's Place in Carmel. A local favorite for its heaping servings of pancakes and eggs, plus its sweet collection of toys for little guys and the down-home décor, all add up to a casual spot for a morning meal.

If your kids can handle it, explore the lovely shops of Carmel, housed in

The Pacific Grove coastline

Hansel and Gretel cottages. Besides a smattering of candy shops, galleries, and clothing stores, Carmel proffers Thinker Toys, a heaven for children. For parents wanting to tag team a bit of shopping, send the kids to the Harrison Memorial Library, which boasts a brilliant children's room, while a lucky mom or dad explores the snazzy shops.

After Carmel makes you want to spend your kids' college funds, jump back on CA 1 and travel south. You'll wind along a hairy road, across mainstays like the Bixby Bridge, recognizing vistas you've seen in glossy travel magazines, and realize you have arrived in Big Sur, the legendary haunt for writers and artists. Rugged and difficult to explore in a lifetime, let alone a road trip, Big Sur devotes its land to parks rather than houses or resorts, and time spent here requires the ability to stand the summer fog, as well as those windy days that pound these cliffs, resulting in some of the most dramatic beauty in the world.

Pull into Nepenthe Restaurant on the west side of the highway. While not quite cheap, the outdoor tables of this lovely Big Sur institution will make you want to slow down, sip some champagne, and let the kids run along the paths. Favorites include the Ambrosia burger or a big hunk of steak. After eating, stroll down the stairs to the Phoenix Shop, which is cluttered with curiosities for all ages with everything from books to art to toys to clothes.

If you'd like to laze your afternoon away, Pfeiffer Beach, located in the heart of Big Sur, promises a sandy stretch to relax and read while the folks with energy can construct elaborate sand castles or dip their toes in the chilly seas. For something a bit more exerting, continue on CA 1 for 12 miles to Julia Pfeiffer Burns State Park. This amazing park not only offers rugged trails along coastal bluffs, but also the payoff of waterfalls and beaches to explore. A short trail to McWay Falls offers a simple visual feast.

Big Sur provides a number of accommodations, ranging from celebrity worthy to rustic campgrounds. The superfancy resorts do not allow children under 18, so families generally flock to the Big Sur River Inn for overnight stays. If your child is over 6, a real treat is the chance to sleep in a yurt at Treebones Resort.

You'll likely enjoy both dinner and breakfast at the Big Sur Bakery, a low-key house serving up wood-fired pizza in the evenings and yummy pastries and coffee in the morning. Another relaxed option for morning and evening meals is the Big Sur River Inn Restaurant. Nestled under a grove of pines and redwoods, kids can race on the grass while the parents share a bottle of wine. This is the type of joint where you'll eat like you are in the mountains, then feel like a million bucks afterward. Explore the coast on your way back to US 101 along CA 1—the drive doesn't get lovelier than this.

IN THE AREA

ACCOMMODATIONS

Asilomar Conference Grounds, 800 Asilomar Avenue, Pacific Grove. Modest rooms in a Julia Morgan–designed setting. The draw is sleeping in a state park and being steps to the sea for reasonable rates. Call 888-635-5310. Website: www.visitasilomar.com.

Beach House Inn, 4100 North Cabrillo Highway, Half Moon Bay. Nautical-themed rooms situated on the harbor get you up close with the sea. Call 650-712-0220. Website: www.beach-house.com/half-moon-bay-hotels.html.

Big Sur River Inn, CA 1 at Pheneger Creek, Big Sur. Family-friendly rooms in a natural setting. Call 831-667-2700. Website: www.bigsurriverinn.com.

Chaminade Resort and Spa, 1 Chaminade Lane, Santa Cruz. Resort style with a kid-friendly vibe in a former Catholic school. Offers views of the ocean in an oft-fogless setting. Call 800-283-6569. Website: www.chaminade.com.

Costanoa, 2001 Rossi Road at CA 1, Pescadero. Tent cabins with heated beds, rooms, spots to pitch a tent, and plush cabins suit most tastes. Dine at their in-house restaurant and hike to the sea. Call 650-879-1100. Website: www.costanoa.com.

Dream Inn, 175 West Cliff Drive, Santa Cruz. Comfortable and stylish rooms steps from the sand and the Santa Cruz Beach Boardwalk appeal to families. Call 831-426-4330. Website: www.dreaminnsantacruz.com.

Half Moon Bay Inn, 401 Main Street, Half Moon Bay. Smallish rooms decked out in Barcelona style. Front rooms can have some excess noise from the downstairs restaurant, so reserve one in the back. Dogs and kids are welcome. Call 650-726-1177. Website: www.halfmoonbay.com.

Mariposa Inn, 1386 Munras Avenue, Monterey. Suites are the way to go in this mod Monterey hotel. You get tons of space, a continental breakfast, and a pool. Call 831-649-1414 or 800-824-2295. Website: www.mariposamonterey.com.

Portola Hotel and Spa, 2 Portola Plaza, Monterey. Located in the heart of Monterey, this resort promises sophisticated rooms, a small pool, and a restaurant with farm-fresh food. Call 831-649-4511 or 888-222-5851. Website: www.portolahotel.com.

Rio Sands Motel, 116 Aptos Beach Drive, Aptos. Modest, though newly renovated, rooms with kitchenettes across the street from the ocean. Call 831-688-3207. Website: www.riosands.com.

Treebones Resort, 71895 CA 1, Big Sur. Sleep in a yurt on the coastal bluffs. Call 805-927-2390. Website: www.treebonesresort.com.

ATTRACTIONS AND RECREATION

Adventures By the Sea, 299 Cannery Row, Monterey. Rent bikes, kayaks, and more. Call 831-372-1807. Website: www.adventuresbythesea.com.

Ano Nuevo State Reserve, 1 New Years Creek Road, Pescadero. Reserve early to tour the elephant seal mating and nesting grounds. Call 650-879-2025. Website: www.parks.ca.gov/?page_id=523.

Bookshop Santa Cruz, 1520 Pacific Avenue, Santa Cruz. Call 831-423-0900. Website: www.bookshopsantacruz.com.

Catalyst, 1011 Pacific Avenue, Santa Cruz. Call 831-423-1338. Website: www.catalystclub.com.

Clouds Downtown, 110 Church Street, Santa Cruz. Call 831-429-2000. Website: www.cloudsdowntown.com.

Club Ed International Surf School & Camps, 101 Beach Street, Santa Cruz. Call 831-464-0177. Website: www.club-ed.com.

Coastside Books, 432 Main Street, Half Moon Bay. Call 650-726-5889. Website: www.coastsidebooks.com.

Dennis the Menace Playground, 777 Pearl Street, Monterey. Call 831-646-3860. Website: N/A

Fitzgerald Marine Reserve, 200 Nevada Avenue, Moss Beach. Call 650-728-3584. Website: www.fitzgeraldreserve.org.

Half Moon Bay Pumpkin Festival, Main Street, Half Moon Bay. Call 650-726-9652. Website: www.miramarevents.com/pumpkinfest.

Half to Have It, 131 California Avenue, Half Moon Bay. Call 650-712-5995. Website: www.halftohaveit.com.

Harley Farms, 205 North Street, Pescadero. Make reservations to tour the property in spring when the kids are born at this goat dairy. Call 650-879-0480, Website: www.harleyfarms.com.

Julia Pfeiffer Burns State Park, 47225 CA 1, Big Sur. Call 831-667-2315. Website: www.parks.ca.gov/?page_id=578.

Kayak Connection, 413 Lake Avenue #3, Santa Cruz. Call 831-479-1121. Website: www.kayakconnection.com.

Kuumbwa Jazz Center, 320 Cedar Street #2, Santa Cruz. Call 831-427-2227. Website: www.kuumbwajazz.org.

Lemos Farm, 12320 San Mateo Road, Half Moon Bay. Call 650-726-2342. Website: www.lemosfarm.com.

Monterey Bay Aquarium, 886 Cannery Row, Monterey. California's finest aquarium showcases what you'll find in the Monterey Bay, as well as treats like coral reef fish, jellyfish, flamingoes, and sharks. Their educational mission can feel pervasive, but its worth it to view the vast collection of sea life housed here. Call 831-648-4800 Website: www.montereybayaquarium.org.

Natural Bridges State Park, Swanton Boulevard and West Cliff Drive, Santa Cruz. Call 831-423-4609. Website: www.parks.ca.gov/?page_id=541.

Pastorino Farms, 12391 San Mateo Road, Half Moon Bay. Call 650-726-6440. Website: www.pastorinofarms.com.

Phoenix Shop, 48510 CA 1, Big Sur. Call 831-667-2347. Website: www.phoenixshopbigsur.com.

Pigeon Point Lighthouse, 210 Pigeon Point Road, Pescadero. Call 650-879-0633. Website: www.norcalhostels.org/pigeon.

Ritz Carlton Half Moon Bay Spa, 1 Miramontes Point Road, Half Moon Bay. Call 650-712-7000. Website: www.ritz-carlton.com/en/Properties/HalfMoon Bay.

Santa Cruz Beach Boardwalk, 400 Beach Street, Santa Cruz. Call 831-423-5590. Website: www.beachboardwalk.com.

Santa Cruz Surf School, 131 Center Street #1, Santa Cruz. Call 831-426-7072. Website: www.santacruzsurfschool.com.

Sanctuary Cruises, 7881 Sandholdt Road, Moss Landing. Call 831-917-1042. Website: www.sanctuarycruises.com.

Thinker Toys, Seventh and San Carlos Avenues, Carmel. Call 831-624-0441. Website: www.thinkertoys.com.

DINING/DRINKS

Aldos, 616 Atlantic Avenue, Santa Cruz. Harbor-front dining attracts locals wanting stiff drinks with their breakfast fare. Call 831-426-3736. Website: www.aldos-cruz.com.

Archangel Grocery, 287 Stage Road, Pescadero. Known for freshly baked breads, including a rich artichoke variety. Call 650-879-0147. Website: www.normsmarket.com.

Big Sur Bakery, CA 1, Big Sur. A good choice for breakfast and wood-oven-baked pizzas. Call 831-667-0520. Website: www.bigsurbakery.com.

Big Sur River Inn Restaurant, CA 1 at Pheneger Creek, Big Sur. Family-style dinners served under a canopy of trees. Call 831-667-2700. Website: www.bigsurriverinn.com.

Burger, 520 Mission Street, Santa Cruz. Burgers and fries, milkshakes and microbrews, need I say more? Call 831-425-5300. Website: www.burgersantacruz.com.

Café Brazil, 1410 Mission Street, Santa Cruz. Yummy specialties from South America include *gallo pinto*, acai bowls, and *moquecas* served in a colorful setting. Call 831-429-1855. Website: www.cafebrazil.us.

Chez Shea, 408 Main Street, Half Moon Bay. World-fusion cuisine in a casual atmosphere provides healthy food for discerning palates. Call 650-560-9234.

Duarte's Tavern, 202 Stage Road, Pescadero. Old-school bar and diner that seems like it jumped off a film set. Sit with the locals in the bar and order homemade soup and pie. Call 650-879-0464. Website: www.duartestavern.com.

East Village Coffee Lounge, 498 Washington Street, Monterey. Coffee, pastries, and brooding college students, plus open-mike nights and poetry slams. Call 831-373-5601. Website: www.eastvillagecoffeelounge.com.

El Palomar, 1336 Pacific Avenue, Santa Cruz. Filled with margarita drinkers wanting enchiladas to soak up the tequila. Call 831-425-7575. Website: www.elpalomarcilantros.com.

Fishwife, 1996 ½ Sunset Drive, Pacific Grove. Decent-sized seafood dishes served in a casual setting. A bit over-priced, but wildly popular all the same. Call 831-375-7107. Website: www.fishwife.com.

Half Moon Bay Bakery, 514 Main Street, Half Moon Bay. Their pumpkin bread is worth the trip alone. Call 650-726-4841.

Half Moon Bay Brewing Company, 390 Capistrano, Half Moon Bay. Fancy food served on a patio heated by fire pits along the harbor. Pub grub rules the appetizers, while freshly caught seafood populates the dinner menu. Call 650-728-2739. Website: www.hmbbrewingco.com.

Katy's Place, Mission Street between Fifth and Sixth Avenues, Carmel-by-the-Sea. Heaping plates of breakfast fare in a quaint dining room. Parents, send your kids to find the small collection of toys by the entrance. Call 831-624-0199. Website: www.katysplacecarmel.com.

Monterey's Fish House, 2114 Del Monte Avenue, Monterey. Known for its fresh seafood, this place gets so busy on summer nights that you must reserve weeks in advance. Call 831-373-4647.

Montrio Bistro, 414 Calle Principal Monterey. Located in a former fire-house, this hub of haute cuisine is unmatched in Monterey. Menus change with the season as do their cocktails.

Call 831-648-8880. Website: www .montrio.com.

Nepenthe Restaurant, 48510 CA 1, Big Sur. Expensive burgers and sandwiches served high above the Pacific Ocean. You're paying for the views, kids. Call 831-667-2345. Website: www.nepenthe bigsur.com.

Passionfish, 701 Lighthouse Avenue, Pacific Grove. A must for foodies. Passionfish serves sustainable seafood in a classy atmosphere. Call 831-655-3311. Website: www.passionfish.net.

Phil's Fish Market and Eatery, 7600 Sandholdt Road, Moss Landing. A celebratory vibe permeates through the corrugated tin roof, even when musicians aren't strumming guitars. Seafood is as fresh as can be. Call 831-633-2152. Website: www.phils fishmarket.com.

Ristorante Avante, 1711 Mission Street, Santa Cruz. Local wines, produce, and meats round out the Italian offerings in this casual restaurant. Call 831-427-0135. Website: www.ristorante avanti.com.

Riva Fish House, 31 Municipal Wharf #500, Santa Cruz. Fish-and-chips served on the Santa Cruz wharf, paired with a beer and gelato. Call 831-429-1223.

Sam's Chowder House, 4210 Cabrillo Highway North, Half Moon Bay. On warm evenings, the parking lot overflows as diners head to the fire pits overlooking the Pacific to sip vino, listen to music, and dine on fresh seafood. Call 650-712-0245. Website: www.sams chowderhouse.com.

San Benito House Deli, 356 Main Street, Half Moon Bay. Huge sandwiches best enjoyed on the adjoining patio while local musicians strum guitars. Call 650-726-3425. Website: www .sanbenitohouse.com.

Silver Spur, 2650 Soquel Drive, Santa Cruz. Hearty breakfasts served in a cowboy-themed dining room. Call 831-475-2725. Website: www.scsilverspur .com.

Taqueria Vallarta, 1101 A Pacific Avenue, Santa Cruz. Your typical taqueria: Order at the counter, pay a couple bucks, and watch soccer as you eat tacos. Call 831-471-2655. Website: www.taqueriavallartarestaurant.com.

Verve Coffee Roasters, 816 41st Avenue, Santa Cruz. Hands down the best coffee in Santa Cruz. Call 831-475-7776. Website: www.vervecoffeeroasters.com.

Whole Enchilada, 7902 CA 1 Moss Landing. Seafood heavy, this Mexican restaurant looks like someone washed the world with color, making it a festive spot for a meal. Call 831-632-2628. Website: www.wenchilada.com.

OTHER CONTACTS

Half Moon Bay Chamber of Commerce, 235 Main Street, Half Moon Bay. Call 650-726-8380. Website: www.half moonbaychamber.org.

Monterey County Convention & Visitors Bureau, 765 Wave Street, Monterey. Call 831-657-6400. Website: www.seemonterey.com.

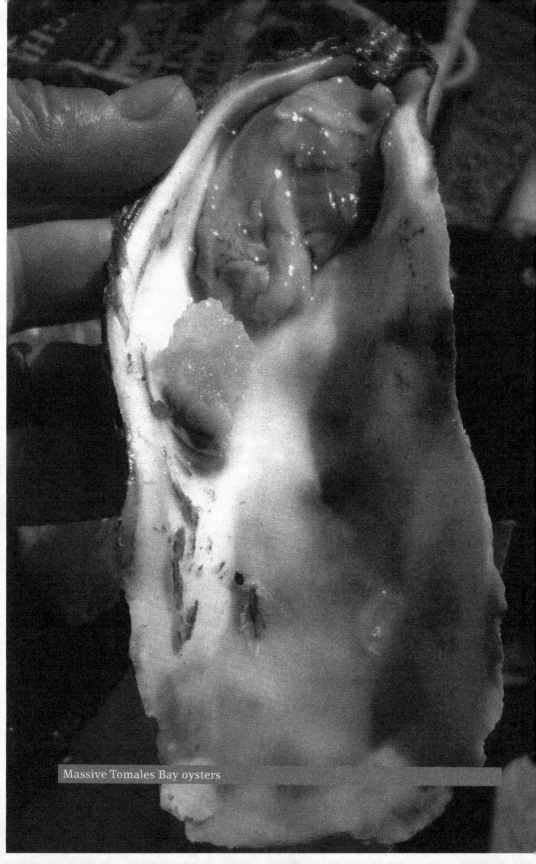

Massive Tomales Bay oysters

8 The Pacific Oyster Trail

Estimated length: 127 miles

Estimated time: 5 hours straight through, or 2 days

Getting there: From San Francisco, cross the Golden Gate Bridge take US 101 north. Exit CA 1 north and follow the signs toward Stinson Beach/Mill Valley. Once in Bodega Bay, take CA 116 east back to US 101.

Highlights: Wind surfing under the Golden Gate Bridge; eating impossibly tasty fresh oysters; watching whales, seals, and rare birds; kayaking in Tomales Bay.

Though often frigid, most coastal Northern Californians have a relationship with the sea. Some surf the massive waves, others dive for abalone, and the less intrepid might merely enjoy the bounty of seafood plucked fresh from the waters of the Pacific Ocean. Whatever your flavor, this stunning route takes you past some of the most lovely oceanfront picnic spots in the world, with plenty of recommendations of places to enjoy the bounty of the Pacific.

For adventurers, begin your journey by windsurfing under the Golden Gate Bridge, a popular pastime for locals who embrace the chilly summer temps. Be sure to don your warmest wet suit as the water temperature averages out at about 52 degrees Fahrenheit. However, if the idea of freezing before breakfast sounds worse than plucking off each of your toenails with your teeth, then instead, at Fisherman's Wharf, catch the ferry to Alcatraz and take the southwest trail down to the sea to explore the thousands of nesting seabirds as well as the most overlooked tide pools in Northern California. Sure you can tour the former prison, but the gardens and wildlife are way more enchanting. Spot anemones, starfish, and crabs from your unobstructed perch just east of the Golden Gate Bridge. Check local tide listings to be sure to arrive at morning low tide.

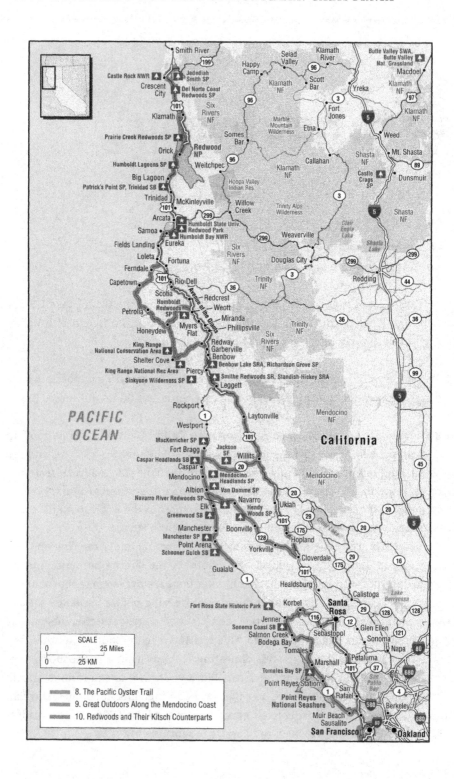

SCALE
0   25 Miles
0   25 KM

8. The Pacific Oyster Trail
9. Great Outdoors Along the Mendocino Coast
10. Redwoods and Their Kitsch Counterparts

DETOUR: A STROLL PAST EGRETS, SNAKES, AND A SHIPWRECK

For a fun and relatively easy hike, favored by local parents and joggers, take a detour to the **Tennessee Valley Trail** (turn left onto Tennessee Valley Road, just 0.5 miles off CA 1 and drive 1.5 miles to the parking lot). Wander through native greenery, passing bobcats, deer, snakes, and egrets, to a lovely beach cluttered with picnicking families. If you are lucky, you might catch a glimpse of the shipwreck to the southern side of the beach; however, I have been here countless times and have yet to see it. The round-trip hike is 3 miles and will likely take you a couple hours.

Tennessee Valley Trail

When your belly begins to sing, travel across the Golden Gate Bridge onto US 101 north. You arrive in Marin County, San Francisco's affluent northern neighbor. Once the hotbed of hippie culture, now Marin houses iPhone-toting lawyers and execs who populate the drool-inducing houses lining the hills. Luckily, some of the best real estate in the county is reserved for parks and public spaces. The community of Sausalito boasts one of the Bay Area's best seafood joints. Exit on Rodeo Avenue and turn right; head left on Nevada Street and then turn left at Bridgeway; make a right on Harbor Drive and take your third right into the parking lot. Fish might not be fancy (you order at the counter and share a picnic table with hungry birds), but the selection of fresh caught seafood is as mouthwatering as you can ask for—especially as the sea lions bob past your waterfront table and you sip beer under the shining sun.

Back on US 101, travel north for less than a mile and exit on CA 1 Stinson Beach/Mill Valley. Follow the signs to CA 1 north traveling away from Mill Valley; a precious suburb nestled in the shadows of redwoods. Wind along the lip of

Whether you windsurf under it or cross it via car, the Golden Gate Bridge is a sight to behold.

CA 1, which offers splendid views of the Pacific raging below, for almost 15 miles to reach Stinson Beach—an oceanfront community that grew after the 1906 earthquake, when refugees started planting roots outside San Francisco. Today, traffic creeps through the smattering of seaside shops and seafood restaurants as travelers look for parking to gain access to the stretch of beach connecting Stinson with her illusive neighbor Bolinas. On warm days, gaggles of beachgoers gather on the sloping sand to frolic in waves and construct sandcastles. Despite the conglomeration of tourists passing through in summer, Stinson Beach's food offerings pale in comparison to those just north in Point Reyes Station, so unless you are in serious need of a burger, fish-and-chips, or a pricey plate of sanddabs, hold off.

Farther north, the town of Bolinas doesn't bother letting you know you've arrived—well, to be frank, the county lets travelers know by hanging a sign, which locals quickly discard. The community of Bolinas is known for its colorful characters and is a great location to spot seals and rare birds. For those in good shape, the trek to Alamere Falls is a worthwhile hike. Turn left on the unsigned Bolinas

Road and veer right for 1.8 miles to Mesa Road (turn right); travel 4.7 miles to the Palomarin Trailhead. For this hike, you'll need plenty of food and water and probably your swimsuit, as the journey to this dynamic waterfall spilling onto the beach is 8.7 miles round-trip, passing wildflowers, a popular lake, and, if you are lucky, plenty of wildlife, including (in winter) views of spouting whales.

Back on CA 1, just 9 miles north brings you to **Point Reyes National Seashore**—a Bay Area treasure. Exploring Point Reyes is best experienced with extended time. Inside the park, you may camp (though you need a permit) or stay at the **Point Reyes Hostel**. Just outside the park, cozy up in a cottage in the town of Point Reyes Station at **One Mesa**. Or for a real treat, check into **Nick's Cove**, a fanciful collection of fishing cabins transformed into chic urbanite retreats on the shores of Tomales Bay.

The village of Point Reyes Station brings to mind a time before cell phones and social networking, when people met at the local feed barn (which also houses the Saturday farmers' market, a coffee shop, and an organic grocery) and chat about everything from the weather to the new Jonathan Franzen novel. Your cell reception likely won't work here, but luckily, the effusive locals will point you to the best morning pastries (**Bovine Bakery**), the choice spot to grab picnic fixings (**Cowgirl Creamery**), and the best dinner within miles (for this you'll get a

An egret in Point Reyes National Seashore

A kayaker on Tomales Bay

split result, either Osteria Stellina's farm-to-table Italian cuisine or impossibly good oysters at Nick's Cove, just up the road on Tomales Bay). Point Reyes Books hawks good reads in addition to hosting world-renowned authors. To purchase some art, head over to Gallery Route One, created by 26 local artists in the 1980s. Many of the multimedia installations reflect the inspiring rural setting of the local creative folks. After morning pastries, grab picnic fixings and head out to explore the National Seashore. At this 71,000-acre parkland, that John F. Kennedy saved by calling it a national treasure, you can drive past bucolic settings populated with dairy farms, visit a working lighthouse, view whales spouting in the distance, hike through abundant wildflowers to wetlands and beaches, and spot elk. Check into the Bear Valley Visitor Center for trail information and a map to get your bearings. Favorite destinations include Limantour, the lighthouse (though it is helpful to know that the trip from the visitors center to the lighthouse is about one hour), Pierce Ranch, and Drake's Beach.

After touring Point Reyes National Seashore, your legs might be tired, so an alternative to hiking is a kayak trip with the venerable Blue Waters Kayaking. Take a guided tour past the shores of Inverness as you paddle along Tomales Bay aiming to spot leopard sharks, harbor seals, bat rays, gray whales, osprey, sea lions, and tule elk.

Just north on CA 1, you'll feel as if you stumbled upon a secret society at the Tomales Bay Oyster Company. On summer afternoons, masses of oyster lovers populate the picnic tables, the muddy beach, and the not-so-grassy hill to shuck their own freshly harvested bag of oysters. This is no fancy affair. You either bring your own oyster knives, or purchase them from the farm. Picnickers are responsible for lugging in their own sauces, charcoal for the barbecues, drinks, and side dishes. Tables fill quickly on weekends (as does the parking lot). But the views, the insanely fresh shellfish, and the fun crowd make this a definite stop.

CA 1 weaves inland about 15 miles, arriving in the blink-and-you'll-miss-it town of Valley Ford. Hidden in this nondescript village are the historic Valley Ford Hotel and the hotel's fun restaurant Rocker Oysterfeller's. If you couldn't stomach shucking your own oysters, then cozy up in the outdoor patio and prepared to be wowed by the creative presentations of that feisty pearl maker. Entrées like flash-fried crab or fried chicken, best enjoyed with a Bloody Mary, might clog those arteries, but they taste so darn yummy. Check in to one of the hotel's six rooms to snuggle in a bed triple-sheeted with fancy linens and watch the sun set over the cattle pastures in the distance.

Just a few miles west, the ocean appears as you enter the coastal community of Bodega Bay; made famous by Alfred Hitchcock, whose masterpiece *The Birds* was filmed here. Though the town lacks creepiness, it is pretty sleepy—ideal for couples wanting to escape it all or families wanting to commune with the 17 beaches strewn along 12 miles. Notable accommodations include the former Holiday Inn turned nautical hotel, the Bodega Bay Lodge, which not only offers lofty quarters with views of the sea but also a hot tub with views of the waterways teeming with avian species as the sun descends into the Pacific.

Grab a bag of oysters at the Tomales Bay Oyster Company.

Breakfast in Bodega Bay won't impress, so check with your accommodations to see if a morning meal is included. If not, take a lovely drive north on CA 1 past the prehistoric-looking beach boulders and turn right onto CA 116/East River Road. The road weaves along the Russian River, taking you to the tiny town of Duncans Mills, home to a trucker-sized breakfast spot—Cape Fear Café. Order up giant portions of omelets, seafood Benedicts, and griddle fare, then return to Bodega Bay to work off that hearty meal by exploring locally favored beaches. For a mellow morning of bird-watching and beach hiking, head to Doran Beach Park (just at the southern edge of town). Throw on your thickest wet suit to surf the big waves at Salmon Creek Beach (a touch north of Bodega Bay); or from December to March, whale watch from your perch at Bodega Head (head west on Westshore Road).

Near Bodega Head on Westshore Road, you might smell the Spud Point Crab Company before noticing the über-popular crab shack. Sonoma County locals swear by the crab sandwiches of this joint, populated with a hungry—and a fairly salty—lunch crowd. Order at the counter (and fork over a bigger sum for lunch than you probably wanted to pay), then plop down on the rickety picnic tables, with the ocean breeze and harbor aroma, and delight in one of the finest seafood tributes west of Boston.

Before heading home, try your luck at snagging your own fish to fry with Bodega Bay Sportfishing Center to catch albacore tuna, salmon, cod, halibut, crab, giant squid, and more. Who knows, you might even spot whales passing your boat.

To return to San Francisco, travel north on CA 1 and turn right onto CA 116/E River Road. The road weaves through redwood parks and along the Russian River, passing Monte Rio and the quirky town of Guerneville—a summer haven for gay and lesbian weekenders (for more information see chapter 6). Along the stretch of commercial venues are a few crystal and tie-dye sellers, but you can also be sure to find cafés with Wi-Fi. Continue east for 5 miles and turn left on Westside Road; travel for 12 miles and follow the signs back to US 101.

Nautical-themed rooms grace the Bodega Bay Lodge.

IN THE AREA

ACCOMMODATIONS

Bodega Bay Lodge, 103 CA 1, Bodega Bay. Spring for the ocean-view option in these nautical-themed rooms. Call 707-875-3525. Website: www.bodega baylodge.com.

Nick's Cove, 23240 CA 1, Marshall. Nautical-themed fishing cabins with heated floors, soaking tubs, and views of the bay. Ooh la la. Call 415-663-1033 or 866-63-NICKS. Website: www.nicks cove.com.

One Mesa, 1 Mesa Road, Point Reyes Station. Country décor, prolific gardens, and a Jacuzzi with a view of Point Reyes—need I say more? Call 415-663-8866. Website: www.onemesa.com.

Point Reyes Hostel, 1390 Limantour Spit Road. Share a room, or reserve the private family room well in advance. Call 415-663-8811. Website: www.norcal hostels.org/reyes.

Point Reyes National Seashore, from CA 1, turn left onto Bear Valley Road and look for the big red barn. The four hike-in (and one boat-in) campgrounds are fitted with a pit toilet, faucet, picnic table, and barbecue grill. You need a permit to camp, which can be obtained at the Bear Valley Visitor Center. Website: www.nps.gov/pore.

Valley Ford Hotel, 14415 CA 1, Valley Ford. Lay your head in an 1864 farmhouse with views of the pastoral landscape. Call 707-876-1983. Website: www .vfordhotel.com.

ATTRACTIONS AND RECREATION

Alcatraz, Alcatraz Landing ticket office at Pier 33, The Embarcadero, San Francisco. Reservations can be made 30 days in advance. Call 415-981-ROCK. Website: www.nps.gov/alcatraz.

Blue Waters Kayaking, 60 Fourth Street, #C, Point Reyes Station. Two-hour half-day guided kayak trips in Tomales Bay to seek out wildlife. Call 415-669-2600. Website: www.bwkayak .com.

Bodega Sport Fishing Center, 1410 B Bay Flat Road, Bodega Bay. Trips depart depending on the weather and season. Call 707-875-3344 for details. Website: www.bodegabaysportfishing.com.

Gallery Route One, 11101 CA 1, Suite 101, Point Reyes Station. Call 415-663-1347. This inspiring collection of local art is open 11–5; closed Tues. Website: www.galleryrouteone.org.

Point Reyes Books, 11315 CA 1, Point Reyes Station. One of Northern California's best locally owned bookstores carries many nature and hiking guides to the park. Open daily 10–6. Call 415-663-1542. Website: www.ptreyesbooks.com.

Point Reyes National Seashore, from CA 1, turn left onto Bear Valley Road and look for the big red barn. This 71,000-acre park contains pastoral landscapes, cheese farms, beaches, waterfall trails, and wildlife viewing. Visiting the park is free. There are no food services. Website: www.nps.gov/pore.

Sonoma Coast State Park, located between Jenner and Bodega Bay on CA 1. A stunning collection of 17 beaches stretched between 12 miles of coastline. Highlights include whale watching at Bodega Head, spotting the endangered snowy plovers at Salmon Creek, hiking around Shell Beach, and camping at Wright's Beach. $8 day-use fee. Website: www.parks.ca.gov.

Tennessee Valley Trail, Golden Gate National Recreation Area, Mill Valley. From US 101, take the CA 1 exit toward Mill Valley; turn left on Tennessee Valley Road. Website: www.nps.gov/goga.

DINING/DRINKS

Bovine Bakery, 11315 CA 1, Point Reyes Station. Whether you crave a freshly baked croissant or a greasy slice of pizza smothered in local produce, you will not regret a stop to this hole-in-the-wall. Open daily at least 7 am–5 pm. Call 415-663-9420. Website: www.savorcalifornia.com.

Cape Fear Café, 25191 CA 116, Duncans Mills. A country kitchen with supersized portions of eggs Benedict with peppered grits, burgers, and griddle fare. If you're staying in Bodega Bay or along the west side of the Russian River, this is the best breakfast you'll stumble upon. Open Mon.–Thurs. 10–3; Fri. 10–8 ; weekends 9–9. Call 707-865-9246.

Cowgirl Creamery, Located in Tomales Bay Foods, 80 Fourth Street, Point Reyes Station. The go-to spot to grab picnic fixings and hunks of creamy cheese. Call 415-663-9335. Website: www.cowgirlcreamery.com.

Fish, 350 Harbor Drive, Sausalito. A local favorite for sustainably caught seafood. Don't miss the catch of the day, served a gazillion ways, or the fish tacos. Nonfish eaters will not go hungry. Open daily at least 11:30–8:30; summer/weekend hours are extended. Website: www.331fish.com.

Nick's Cove, 23240 CA 1, Marshall. Dine atop the sea, and relish in the take-no-prisoners oyster bar or the creative (and occasionally comical) takes on traditional entrées. Open daily for lunch and dinner; breakfast served on weekends. Call 415-663-1033 or 866-63-NICKS. Website: www.nickscove.com.

Osteria Stellina, 11285 CA 1, Point Reyes Station. This Italian eatery practices an "unwavering commitment to organic produce," a haughty motto that never fails to inspire. Settle in and enjoy beef stew, locally foraged mushrooms, cheese drizzled in just-harvested honey, and fine wine. Open daily for lunch and dinner. Call 415-663-9988. Website: www.osteriastellina.com.

Rocker Oysterfeller's, 14415 CA 1, Valley Ford. If Bloody Marys, spicy oyster concoctions, and hearty fried chicken are your game, Rocker Oysterfeller's is a must. The bar gets rowdy in the evenings, while dinner is served in a more subdued atmosphere. Open Wed. through Sun. for dinner; lunch is served on Sat.; brunch on Sun. Call 415-876-1983. Website: www.rocker oysterfellers.com.

Spud Point Crab Company, 1860 Westshore Road, Bodega Bay. Dress warmly and order up the freshest crab sandwich and clam chowder west of Cape Cod. Open 9–5; closed Wed. Call 707-875-9472. Website: www.spudpoint crab.com.

Tomales Bay Oyster Company, 15479 CA 1, Marshall. More of a fish stand than a restaurant. Buy a bag of freshly caught oysters (and a knife if you don't have one), then shuck 'em and slurp 'em. Bring your own drinks, sides, and plates. Open daily at least 9–5. Call 415-663-1242. Website: www.tomalesbay oysters.com.

OTHER CONTACTS

Marin Convention & Visitors Bureau, 1 Mitchell Boulevard, Suite B, San Rafael. Call 415-925-2060. Website: www.visitmarin.org.

San Francisco Visitor Information Center, 900 Market Street, San Francisco. Website: www.onlyinsanfrancisco.com.

Sonoma County Tourism Bureau, 850 CA 1, Bodega Bay. Call 707-875-3866. Website: www.sonomacounty.com.

The rugged Sonoma Coast.

Mendocino Headlands

9 Great Outdoors along the Mendocino Coast

Estimated length: 111 miles
Estimated time: 3 hours straight through, or 3 days

Getting there: From US 101 travel west on CA 128 through Anderson Valley and north on CA 1.

Highlights: Exploring the historic town of Mendocino; playing in the sand at Russian Gulch State Park; spotting vibrant flowers at the Mendocino Coast Botanical Gardens; hunting for treasures at Glass Beach; eating like royalty at the farm-fresh restaurants.

Romantic urbanites whisper about the existence of the Mendocino Coast—a wonderland of Victorian architecture, art galleries, haute cuisine and some of the most dramatic natural environments in Northern California. While locals and repeat visitors know that this region was "found" after Mendocino housed the television drama *Murder She Wrote*, somehow this community has preserved its dignity. Maybe it is because of its moody weather, as fog generally hides the coast from seeing the sun for what seems like half the year. Or maybe because cell service is spotty, halting big wigs from descending on the town. Whatever the case, this region promises to slow you down, inspire your inner artist, and typically lures folks to check real estate listings before departing.

The locals however look a bit different than the dollhouse communities perched atop cliffs. Mendocino happens to be one of the most progressive counties in California—which likely means the entire country—taking on issues like GMO foods and medicinal marijuana. You begin to understand the vibe when you hear local radio stations announce that the DEA is flying over the mountains searching for marijuana growers—a popular occupation in these parts—or, while

A glimpse of the Mendocino Coast

tramping through Boonville, hear the locals speaking their native tongue Boontling, a language that only exists in this redwood-shaded hamlet.

Your journey begins as you wind through the idyllic Anderson Valley, which is an unlikely mix of granola types and winemakers (including the creators of the champagne Cristal). Slow down as you enter the town of Boonville—a tightly knit community known for its take on organic cuisine. Most tourists stop here to sample brews at the Anderson Valley Brewery, or dine at the Boonville Hotel Restaurant (the owner was a disciple of French Laundry and crafts award-winning cuisine). However, if you prefer to spend a night in the woods and get to know the local flavor, check into the Boonville Hotel (I recommend the cottages by the creek, which are not located on the main road). If you plan to spend the day exploring the inland arteries of the county, grab a picnic at the Boonville General Store before heading west for about 8 miles to the community of Philo, where a number of winemakers craft dynamic whites and Pinot noir. Local favorites to sample include Handley Cellars, Husch Vineyards, Navarro Vineyards, and Roederer Estate. From here, explore the redwoods at the Hendy Woods State Park. A hermit (the park's namesake) once lived in the huts you view from the interpretive trail. And this smallish park is relatively mellow compared to the coastal options.

As the trees get taller, and the fog thickens, you approach the coast and the famed CA 1. Travel north, passing the renegade village of Albion (if you can double back here for dinner later, the lovely Ledford House is one of the gems of the region—imagine ocean views, live jazz, and superfresh seafood with an Italian twist, yum!) to arrive in Van Damme State Park. Here you can access a pleasant beach in a sheltered cove. The water's cold, but the beach draws plenty of families when the sun shows its face. Cross the highway and hike to the pygmy forest, a collection of miniature conifers (cypress and pine trees) complete with

Gualala's beach   *Seaweed harvesters in Mendocino*

miniature cones. I can just hear the leprechaun jokes churning; nope, there are no pots of gold up here, sorry. By the way, when visiting California state parks, remember to *save* your parking pass. On the same day, your pass will be valid at other state parks that do not charge higher fees.

As the highway winds along the coastal bluffs, offering sweeping views of the ocean, you approach a collection of remote and well-oiled resorts primed for visitors looking for that something special. Catering to suited executives from LA and Silicon Valley, the plush Stevenswood Spa Resort offers 10 spruced-up quarters boasting the finest technological amenities in the whole county. Throw in an organic spa, a dining room fit for record industry moguls, and the remote

DETOUR: CA 1'S SOUTHERN CHARM

Estimated length: 32 miles
Estimated time: 52 minutes straight through, or 2 days

While the herds trample the northern Mendocino coast, in-the-know travelers often head south. If you have extra time, veer south on CA 1 to the community of Elk (though it is also confusingly called Greenwood). Here are a few chic B&Bs like the **Griffin House Inn** and the **Harbor House Inn,** as well as the locally favored **Queenie's Roadhouse Café,** where Queenie herself slings organic breakfasts and lunches punctuated by strong coffee and a crackling fireplace. After your meal, cross the highway and travel down the path to Greenwood State Beach, where you'll find seaweed harvesters working on a lovely remote stretch of coast.

Farther south, at mile marker 17, head west to explore the **Stornetta Public Lands** (which has a wealth of endangered species, hiking trails, and 2 miles of beaches) and the **Point Area Lighthouse** (a great place to spot whales and spend the night). Continue traveling south on CA 1 and then west on Iverson Avenue and drive until you reach at sea. Here you'll find **Arena Cove,** popular with abalone divers, tide pools, a pier (you don't need a license to cast your line here), and the enchanting **Coast Guard House**—an Arts and Crafts–movement B&B. Travel inland and you'll approach the town of Point Arena, which has seen better days but is still quite cute for a short stroll. Pop into **Franny's Cup and Saucer** for pastries and coffee. If you are sleeping in the location out of Mendocino town, and you understand why folks pay the big bucks for a night here. A fit option for families and folks traveling with Fido is the Stanford Inn by the Sea, perched above a meadow overlooking Mendocino Bay. The timbered inn is known for Big River Nurseries, its California-certified organic gardens where vegetables, herbs, ornamentals, and flowers are grown. The gardens supply Ravens' Restaurant, the inn's award-winning organic vegetarian restaurant.

For travelers craving the authentic Mendo experience, complete with a precious B&B and the ability to walk everywhere, continue north on CA 1 until you reach the historic town of Mendocino—yes, the entire town has been deemed a

area, check the listings at the **Arena Theater,** which is the only theater for miles and shows art house films and hosts live music.

Back on CA 1, travel south to mile marker 11; here you'll find the striking **Bowling Ball Beach.** Hike the 0.5-mile trail to the beach during low tide to spot huge boulders that look like bowling balls—hence the name. Alternatively, if you happen to arrive at high tide, take the trail to **Schooner Gulch State Beach** to do some whale watching (December through March), surf, or just frolic in the sand.

CA 1 continues south, passing Anchor Bay. Just before you arrive in Gualala, you may notice a Russian-inspired castle, complete with minarets and domes; that's **St. Orres,** an institution in the area, not only for its lovely cottages but also for the unlikely creations that come out of the kitchen in the lofty dining room. While the menu changes seasonally, on any day, the chef may add up to 10 specials ranging in style from garlic flan to blueberry waffles with venison. Go big. You won't be disappointed.

As you end your tour of the southern stretch of CA 1 (though you can continue through Sonoma and Marin Counties back to San Francisco—see chapter 8), you will arrive in the town of Gualala, which in any other area might look like a hiccup but here feels like you just arrived in a *city*. Cypress trees and boulder-covered beaches inspire families, who bed down at the revamped **Surf Motel Gualala,** stroll in and out of the few shops lining CA 1, and slurp brews as they grub on wood-pit-smoked BBQ sandwiches at **Bones Roadhouse.** This isn't the classiest town on the coast, but it sure is fun.

The precious Sea Gull Inn

National Historic Preservation District, and for good reason. Take some time to explore the landmark architecture of every building west of CA 1.

Check into the affordable, and quite adorable, rooms at the Sea Gull Inn, where breakfast is served in a garden fit for gnomes. Another choice option is the funky Alegria Inn and Cottages, the only accommodation directly atop the Bay. While each guest room varies—you'll get everything from a lofty artist retreat to a cottage fit with a soaking tub and bamboo floors—the ambience is typical Mendocino: kind, accommodating, and hands off.

A stroll around town guarantees entertainment. Explore the World of Suzi Long, a fun gallery in a skinny water tower; enjoy the stacks in the Gallery Bookshop; or duck into Dick's Place for a pint of lager. Sample mushroom-flavored ice cream at the wildly popular Frankie's Handmade Ice Cream, or just glide in and out of clothing stores and galleries on your way to the Mendocino Headlands State Park, quite possibly the most alluring part of the coast. Gentle trails along a rugged coastline guide you to secluded beaches, hidden sea caves, and grottoes.

Restaurants like the Mendocino Café promise a fitting glimpse at town culture. Here you can have a Thai-inspired burrito, a heaping plate of pasta, or a hunk of cake on a pitch-perfect patio surrounded by butterflies and flowers. Another good option is the small but lively Moosse Café, which provides diners with an upscale palate of fresh seafood and meat without breaking the bank. For coffee and breakfast fare, the Mendocino Bakery and Café serves basic pastries and breads.

Farther along CA 1, you'll come upon the dramatic Russian Gulch State Park, where you can walk to a 60-foot blowhole (best at high tide) or a fern-covered area straight out of the Mesozoic Era. You can camp here. Another site to behold, just a touch up the road, is the Jughandle State Preserve Ecological Staircase. Climb the 2.5-mile staircase to a pygmy forest that displays the ecological succession and landscape evolution. After your geological exploration, take a walk around the lovely sands on Jug Handle Beach.

Just before you reach the town of Fort Bragg, you'll spot the Mendocino Coast Botanical Gardens. And even if you are not a fan of plants, flowers, and

Historic Mendocino

trees, a visit here should not be missed. They are the only coastal botanical gardens on the West Coast, and they sure take advantage of those Pacific Ocean vistas. A jaunt along the coastal bluffs is sure to make you appreciate fog, gardeners, and the outdoors.

Finally, you arrive in Fort Bragg, the largest city in the area. Once a thriving logging town, Fort Bragg is now trying to redefine itself as an ecofriendly tourist destination. Parts of town may feel a bit bleak, but it is worth your time to get to know the community. There is no better place to start than Headlands Coffee House—the central meeting point for events, grub, and coffee. If your poison at the moment requires a pint of microbrew, you are in luck; head over to the North Coast Brewing Company for an Old Rasputin with a Kobe beef burger in a family-friendly atmosphere. If you choose to stick around for the night, check into the comfy Beachcomber Motel. Join dialed in families who gather around BBQs at sunset, enjoying views of MacKerricher State Park—a 9-mile stretch of coastline and the pride of Fort Bragg.

Explore Mendocino's hidden nooks.

Fort Bragg's Glass Beach

In the morning, grab breakfast at Eggheads, a Wizard of Oz–themed restaurant that might just be the best greasy spoon in California. Then head over to Glass Beach, where you can troll the cove for sea glass, while watching dolphins and seals playing in the sea. When you can handle returning to reality, take CA 20, which snakes through a sea of redwoods between Fort Bragg and Willits all the way to US 101.

IN THE AREA

ACCOMMODATIONS

Alegria Inn and Cottages, 44781 Main Street, Mendocino. About 200 feet from the beach, this B&B includes a hot tub, lovely gardens, a delicious breakfast made with local produce, and a history that dates back to 1861. Call 707-937-5150 or 800-780-7905. Website: www.oceanfrontmagic.com.

Beachcomber Motel, 111 North Main Street, Fort Bragg. This motel is great for pet lovers; it even offers a dog day camp. Most rooms offer an ocean view, fireplace, and private deck. Call 707-964-2402 or 800-400-7873. Website: www.thebeachcombermotel.com.

Boonville Hotel, 14050 CA 128, Boonville. Offers 12 rooms accommodating different party sizes, including a family suite and a room just for two. Call 707-895-2210. Website: www.boonvillehotel.com.

Coast Guard House, 695 Arena Cove, Point Arena. A 1901 Cape Cod–style home, featuring rooms with fireplaces in the main house and two private cottages with fireplaces and whirlpool spas for two. Call 800-524-9320 or 707-882-2442. Website: www.coastguardhouse.com.

Griffin House Inn, 5910 South CA 1, Elk. Choose from eight cottages, four of which overlook the ocean. A full breakfast is delivered to your room each morning. Call 707-877-3422. Website: www.griffinn.com.

Harbor House Inn, 5600 South CA 1, Elk. The inn is surrounded by a botanical garden, large redwoods, and the ocean. Accommodations are available in either the historic lodge furnished with antiques or in private luxury cottages that feature fireplaces and private decks. Call 800-720-7474. Website: www.theharborhouseinn.com.

Sea Gull Inn, 44960 Albion Street, Mendocino. An 1878 B&B with nine guest rooms that feature private baths, ocean views, and an organic breakfast. Call 888-937-5205. Website: www.seagullbb.com.

Stanford Inn by the Sea, located at the intersection of Coast Highway and Comptche Ukiah Road, Mendocino. This popular ecoresort offers timbered rooms, an organic vegetarian restaurant, and a pool, plus a kayak, canoe, and bike rental shop. Call 800-331-8884. Website: www.stanfordinn.com.

Stevenswood Spa Resort, 8211 North CA 1, Little River. Rooms in the main lodge feature a modern Italian vibe with wood-burning fireplaces. Spa, restaurant, and plenty of privacy served here. Call 800-421-2810. Website: www.stevenswood.com.

Surf Motel Gualala, 39170 South CA 1, Gualala. Enjoy 1 of the 14 rooms with an ocean view and a full breakfast each morning in the motel's lobby. Creative metal artwork inspired by marine life, wildflowers, and Adirondack deck chairs contribute to the ocean-side atmosphere. Call 888-451-7873. Website: www.surfinngualala.com.

ATTRACTIONS AND RECREATION

Arena Cove, 790 Cove Port Road, Point Arena.

Arena Theater, 214 Main Street, Point Arena. Enjoy popular movies and art house films, as well as live entertainment such as mime troupes and music. Call 707-882-3456. Website: www.arenatheater.org.

Bowling Ball Beach, located 3 miles south of Point Arena at the intersection of Gulch Road and CA 1. Call 707-937-5804.

Gallery Bookshop, at the corner of Main and Kasten Streets, Mendocino. Call 707-937-2665. Website: www.gallerybookshop.com.

Glass Beach, 320 East Oak Street, Fort Bragg. Gather sea glass or check out the interesting array of tide pools that house crabs, mollusks, and a variety of aquatic plants. Call 707-813-1396.

Hendy Woods State Park, located 8 miles northwest of Boonville, 0.5 mile south of CA 128 on Philo-Greenwood Road. The site includes 25 picnic sites near the banks of the Navarro River, which runs the length of the park. Call 707-895-3141. Website: www.parks.ca.gov.

Jughandle State Preserve Ecological Staircase, located adjacent to CA 1, 1 mile north of Caspar. Known for the Ecological Staircase, a 2.5-mile self-guided nature trail that explores wave-cut terraces formed by glacial, sea, and tectonic activity. Call 707-937-5804. Website: www.parks.ca.gov.

MacKerricher State Park, located 3 miles north of Fort Bragg on CA 1, near the town of Cleone. Offers a variety of habitats including beach, bluff, headland, dune, forest, and wetland. More than 90 species of birds make nearby Cleone Lake their home. Call 707-964-9112. Website: www.parks.ca.gov.

Mendocino Coast Botanical Gardens, 18220 North CA 1, Fort Bragg. The botanical gardens is the perfect place to view native flora habitats, including fern-covered canyons, camellias and magnolias, and flower-filled coastal bluffs overlooking the ocean. Call 707-964-4352 . Website: www.gardenbythesea.org.

Mendocino Headlands State Park, from "downtown" Mendocino, follow Main Street up coast past the Mendocino Hotel to Heeser Street. The 5-mile hike is unmarked, but offers beautiful views from the bluffs, seasonal wildflowers, and a beach with a view of Big River and Mendocino Bay.

Point Area Lighthouse, 45500 Lighthouse Road, Point Arena. Guided tours of the light station and self-guided tours of the property are available. If you'd like to stay over, accommodations are available in the historic keeper's home. Open daily 10–3:30. Call 707-882-2777 or 877-725-4448..Website: www.pointarenalighthouse.com.

Russian Gulch State Park, located 2 miles north of Mendocino on CA 1. The park is known for the Devil's Punch Bowl (a large, collapsed sea cave with churning water) and a beach that offers swimming, tide pool exploring, and rock fishing. Inland, there is a 36-foot-high waterfall. Call 707-937-5804. Website: www.parks.ca.gov.

Schooner Gulch State Beach, located 3 miles south of Point Arena, where Schooner Gulch Road intersects CA 1. Hiking, fishing, and surfing are popular activities here. Call 707-937-5804. Website: www.parks.ca.gov.

Stornetta Public Lands, 2550 North State Street, Ukiah. A wildlife habitat featuring extensive wetlands, ponds, cypress groves, meadows, and sand dunes. Call 707-468-4000. Website: www.blm.gov.

Van Damme State Park, located 3 miles south of Mendocino along CA 1. Call 707-937-5804. Website: www.parks.ca.gov.

World of Suzi Long, 45098 Main Street, Mendocino. Look for Long's pastel paintings, giclée (art digital) prints, and cards. Call 707-937-5664. Website: www.suzilong.com.

DINING/DRINKS

Anderson Valley Brewery, 17700 CA 253, Boonville. Visit the taproom, tour the brewery, or play a game of disc golf at the course located right on the brewery grounds. Call 800-207-2337. Website: www.avbc.com.

Bones Roadhouse, 39080 South CA 1, Gualala. Pulled pork is a favorite here, and the ribs are excellent. Call 707-884-1188. Website: www.bonesroadhouse.com.

Boonville General Store, 14077 CA 128, Boonville. Specializes in "California Casual" cuisine with a focus on seasonal and local foods. Enjoy a scone for breakfast or soup, salad, sandwich, or pizza for lunch. Call 707-895-9477.

Boonville Hotel Restaurant, 14050 CA 128, Boonville. This family-style restaurant offers daily specials such as grilled pork chops with black olive tapenade and smashed potatoes, or fresh-shucked oysters on Sundays. Call 707-895-2210. Website: www.boonville hotel.com.

Dick's Place, 45070 Main Street, Mendocino. A full bar with a jukebox and lively atmosphere. Call 707-937-6010.

Eggheads, 326 N. Main Street, Fort Bragg. A great breakfast place honoring Dorothy, Toto, and their pals, serving cinnamon bread French toast and pumpkin waffles. Call 707-964-5005. Website: www.eggheadsrestaurant.com.

Frankie's Handmade Ice Cream, 44951 Ukiah Street, Mendocino. Enjoy delicious traditional flavors like cookies and cream, or opt for more nontraditional flavors like mushroom. Call 707-937-2436. Website: www.frankies mendocino.com.

Franny's Cup and Saucer, 213 Main Street, Point Arena. Offers sweet and savory baked goods for lunch and dinner, as well as handmade chocolates, caramels, and truffles. Try the addictive spicy Mexican mocha. Take-out only. Call 707-882-2500. Website: www .frannyscupandsaucer.com.

Handley Cellars, 3151 CA 128, Philo. The 59-acre property features a refurbished ranch house, barn, and original water tower. Enjoy a picnic in the garden courtyard or enjoy the unique display of world folk art. Wine tastings are available by appointment. Call 707-895-3876. Website: www.handleycellars.com.

Headlands Coffee House, 120 Laurel Street, Fort Bragg. Check out this coffeehouse for nightly live music, monthly art exhibits, and a café menu that features everything from burritos to sandwiches. Call 707-964-1987. Website: www.headlandscoffeehouse.com.

Husch Vineyards, 4400 CA 128, Philo. Open daily 10–6. Call 800-554-8724. Website: www.huschvineyards.com.

Ledford House Restaurant, 3000 North CA 1, Albion. Call 707-937-0282. The Mediterranean-style cuisine is subtly accented with Asian and Latin flavors. Enjoy the fisherman's stew with saffron, tomato, orange, fennel, and rouille. Website: www.ledford house.com.

Mendocino Bakery and Café, 10485 Lansing Street, Mendocino. Look no further for a cuppa fair trade, organic coffee and a tasty chocolate coconut macaroon. Call 707-937-0836. Website: www.themendocinocafe.com.

Mendocino Café, 10451 Lansing Street, Mendocino. Features international cuisine with influences from Thailand, Cambodia, Kenya, France, and Italy. The dinner menu includes a Thai burrito, Brazilian seafood stew, and pasta Florentine. Call 707-937-6141. Website: www.mendocinocafe.com.

Moosse Café, 390 Kasten Street, Mendocino. Serves light fare, such as salads and quiche, as well as heartier items, such as ratatouille, burgers, and short ribs. Open for lunch and dinner. Call 707-937-4323. Website: www.the moosse.com.

Navarro Vineyards, 5601 CA 128, Philo. Offers tours twice daily. Enjoy a selection of local cheeses and meats from the vineyard's deli case with a glass of wine. Call 707-895-3015. Website: www.navarrowine.com.

North Coast Brewing Company, 444 North Main Street, Fort Bragg. The taproom and grill features tacos on Tues. nights and a regular menu of steaks and seafood every night. Call 707-964-3400. Website: www.northcoast brewing.com.

Queenie's Roadhouse Café, 6061 South CA 1, Elk. Enjoy classic breakfast dishes such as eggs Benedict or huevos rancheros or lunch specials including paninis and reubens. Open Thurs. through Mon. 8–3. Call 707-877-3285.

Ravens' Restaurant, Stanford Inn by the Sea, located at the intersection of Coast Highway and Comptche Ukiah Road, Mendocino. Serves vegetarian and vegan cuisine, such as tamari-maple-glazed tofu and portobello sliders. Open for breakfast and dinner. Call 707-937-5615. Website: www.ravens restaurant.com.

Roederer Estate, 4501 CA 128, Philo. The tasting room is open daily 11–5, and tours of the estate are available by appointment. The wine here is known for its characteristic body, finesse, and depth of flavor. Call 707-895-2288. Website: www.roedererestate.com.

St. Orres, 36601 South CA 1, Gualala. Features freshly prepared organic and wild foraged food, including fresh seafood, wild mushrooms, and wild game. Call 707-884-3335. Website: www.saintorres.com.

OTHER CONTACTS

Mendocino Coast Chamber of Commerce, 217 South Main Street, Fort Bragg. Call 707-961-6300. Website: www.mendocinocoast.com.

Visit Mendocino County, 120 South Franklin Street, Fort Bragg. Call 707-462-7417 or 866-466-3636. Website: www.visitmendocino.com

Redwood State and National Park

10 Redwoods and Their Kitsch Counterparts

Estimated length: 241 miles.

Estimated time: 5 hours straight through, or up to 5 leisurely days

Getting there: From Ukiah, travel north on US 101.

Highlights: Being dwarfed by the planet's tallest trees; exploring a pre-Triassic-era canyon walled with ferns; viewing an array of wildlife, including nesting seabirds and North America's largest elk; getting to know the distinct wackiness of the far north.

Often written off as too remote for travelers, the northwestern shoulder of California lays claim to some of the most beautiful landscapes on the planet. Imagine far-reaching redwood trees, shrouded in thick ghostly fog, and a rich carpet of ferns, nestling up to the rugged Pacific Ocean, and you begin to envision a picture of the world the way the Native American Wiyots must have first glimpsed it. However, as with most areas of California, this idyllic landscape was not reserved for the original settlers; in the 1700s and 1800s, explorers from as far away as Spain battled for this mystical land. After a series of colorful wars between the native people and the settlers, Humboldt County (namely the region around Eureka) became a bustling lumber community (you can guess which gang won those wars). And while logging used to be the primary draw for the economy up here, today the locals rely on tourism and marijuana crops for their cash flow. Strangely, you wouldn't know tourism was big business from the lack of cushy resorts in these parts. On the flip side, the redwood coast forces visitors to unplug and settle into modest accommodations so they can spend their days in awe of the magic of nature.

Begin your trip south of Humboldt County in Ukiah, the largest city of

Mendocino County. The county seat resides here, but the real draw for most is the array of wineries, as well as the kooky attractions. You'd never guess, but up in the mountains above town resides a massive international Buddhist community billed the City of Ten Thousand Buddhas; tour the property to learn more about this ancient religion. After giving your karma a nudge, grab lunch at one of the only all-organic brewpubs in California, the Ukiah Brewing Company. Prices are steep, but you can revel in the fact that your burger meat came from a happy cow and your hops haven't been sprayed with anything toxic.

If alcohol is your game, make an appointment to tour one of the finest brandy distilleries in the world, Germain-Robin, hidden in Ukiah's abundant community of grape growers. Crafted from an excellent stock of grapes, the artisan distillers use ancient techniques to craft alambic brandy and grappa.

With your head abuzz, head over to the Vichy Springs Hot Springs Resort to soak in the champagne mineral pools. Either score a day-use pass, which gives you the all clear for hiking, soaking, and swimming, or bed down for the night in the modest accommodations on site.

Alternatively, continue north on US 101 to spend the night in Willits, a small collection of cowboy-boot-wearing, tofu-eating folks who not only grow wine grapes but also like a good old-fashioned rodeo. US 101 cuts right through the center of town, slowing you to a crawl as you pass tie-dye shops, cafés, co-op groceries, and locals lounging on the backs of pickup trucks. Check into the Baechtel Creek Inn and Spa, which doubles as a historic hotel decked out in period antiques on one end of the property and a modest motel fit for families on the other side. Whichever room type you select, their morning poolside breakfast is as country slow as you might expect. The last time I stayed here a family of foxes was eating their breakfast just across the creek from the hotel (not to worry though, they were behind a fairly menacing gate and a steep trench).

In the morning, begin your excursion with a bang by boarding the Skunk Train, a historic scenic railroad that once carted lumber between the coastal town of Fort Bragg and Willits. These days, tourists board the steam train to enjoy a scenic chug through the redwood forest as it sprouts skyward from the Noyo River. Trips take four hours, so picky eaters will want to bring a picnic lunch from the Mariposa Market in town.

About an hour north of Willits off US 101 in Piercy, you arrive at a famed Northern California curiosity—Confusion Hill. While kitsch doesn't even begin to scratch the surface of describing this family tourist attraction, you can at least guarantee some entertainment. Consider the minitrain ride through the redwoods, or the wacky Gravity House where balls seem to roll uphill and kiddos

---

THE LAST TRUE CALIFORNIA RODEO

For seven days over the Fourth of July holiday, the town of Willits comes alive with cowboys and cowgirls of all ages. **Willits Frontier Days** is California's oldest running rodeo that not only sponsors trickster riders, the best ropers around, and showy horsemanship, but also a massive carnival, heaps of BBQ, and the good cheer associated with down-home all-American kitsch, er, fun.

---

appear taller than their dads, plus the redwood shoe house and the world's largest freestanding redwood chain-saw carving, and you begin to understand why you might want a rest stop at this retro destination. If nothing else, their snack shack serves organic grub.

Continue on US 101 for 15 miles until you arrive in the town of Garberville. While this small hippie town sleeps its way through most of the year, when the annual Reggae Rising festival arrives, the town swells with dreadlocks and mellow campers. Since the whole community pretty much falls into the kitsch category—glimpsed by the wood carvings lining pickup trucks and the hole-in-the-wall eateries draped in tie dye—you may wonder why this community makes a worthy stop. For one, the historic Benbow Inn, located on the Eel River, happens to be here. If nothing else, it is worth your time to pop into the hotel and tour the property, play a round of golf, or enjoy a coursed dinner. However, if the lost art of relaxing calls your name, check into the elegant quarters and take pride that you may sleep in the same room as Eleanor Roosevelt or Clark Gable.

Garberville also happens to be the gateway to two majestic drives—the Lost Coast (see sidebar) and the 30-mile stretch of old US 101 aptly named Avenue of the Giants. To access this ridiculously photogenic drive, follow the signs off US 101 and travel north through skyscraping trees over 2,000 years old. Redwood trees primarily exist along the northern California coast (the other species of sequoia trees reside in the Sierra Mountains and have thicker trunks than these tall, slender marvels); having the chance to get up close with these giants is an experience you will not forget.

Looking for a dash of kitsch along the drive? Just outside Garberville right before you reach Phillipsville, check out the One Log House, carefully crafted out of the trunk of a sequoia tree. But the real attraction in these parts (save the trees, of course) is the Riverwood Inn. Packed with bikers day and

DETOUR: GET LOST IN THE LOST COAST

Getting to know the aptly named **Lost Coast** takes time, courage, and endurance. For your effort, you will have the chance to experience the vastly unexplored King Range Mountains, which are tied with the Himalayas as the fastest growing mountain range on the planet. Once you reach the Pacific Ocean, wander along black sand beaches, hunt for treasures in tide pools, snap photos of cows leisurely walking near the sea, and hike through dense wilderness. Take note that services here are extremely limited. If you embark on the journey, fill up your car with gas, bring plenty of snacks and water, and understand that the switchback roads can be both dangerous and exhilarating. Drive slowly (it's so beautiful, why would you want to speed?) and inhale the scent of the last remote stretch of California coast.

There are three ways to access the Lost Coast. From Garberville, follow signs to Shelter Cove/King Range National Conservation Area (allow 45 minutes for the 22-mile trip to Shelter Cove). **Shelter Cove** acts as the jumping-off point for 64 miles of trails traveling both north and south. In town there are a couple of inns, including the beachfront **Tides Inn** and **Shelter Cove Inn.** For a simple lunch, pop into the **Deli at the Campground** for sandwiches and a decent plate of fish-and-chips.

To access the center of King Range for some serious hiking, from US 101 take the Honeydew exit. Going west on Mattole Road, one passes beneath the towering trees in the **Rockefeller Forest,** the largest single stand of old-growth redwoods in the world. Follow the signs to Honeydew (23 miles). Turn left in Honeydew to Honeydew Creek Recreation Site and Smith-Etter Road. Allow one hour for the 24-mile trip. You may continue to Petrolia from here and loop north to Ferndale (see below).

Or, if you have a couple of days and want to check out the best of this stretch of coast (with one of the most interesting drives around), from US 101 exit into Ferndale, a storybook collection of Victorian architecture. Get acquainted with the well-kept town, popping in and out of galleries and restaurants where everyone seems to know each other. Both **Curley's Grill** and **Poppa Joe's** make for an interesting meal. For folks who really enjoy the turrets and gables of the architecture, book a night in the fanciful **Victorian Inn.**

Once you've had your fill of exploring buildings, follow the signs to **Petrolia,** the site of California's first oil strike and the main "town" in these parts. Along the way, you'll pass the **Wall to the Wildcat,** which promises spectacular ocean vistas. For people wanting to spend extra time here, book a night in the lovely **Petrolia Guest House.** For hikers, continue driving for a mile past Petrolia, turn right on Lighthouse Road; it is 5 more miles to the Mattole Recreation Site where you can access trailheads. Allow 1.5 hours for the 42-mile trip.

Along the Avenue of the Giants

Gazing up at the redwoods

especially night, this is the last of the old roadhouses, which means this place reels them in. Not only can motorcyclists park their bikes indoors, but they can also experience the 30-plus collection of tequilas (and hopefully not rev their engines afterward), the live musicians that have included greats like John Lee Hooker Jr. and Guitar Shorty, and the excellent Mexican cuisine. If you imbibe too many margaritas, the Miranda Gardens Resort provides quaint cabins with full kitchens as well as economical quarters beneath towering redwood trees.

Continuing along the Avenue of the Giants, in Myers Flat, you'll come to the Shrine Drive Thru Tree, your chance to drive through a redwood tree. It is wise to know that you will line up for quite some time as people

Dwarfed by redwood trees

take what seems like hundreds of photos from inside the tree. But hey, how many times can you say that you drove through the inside of a redwood? Myers Flat also has the finest dining institution in southern Humboldt County, The Groves. Located in a historic barn, the pros crafting the cuisine here draw from the seasonal bounty, attracting food lovers from Mendocino to Arcata and beyond.

Also, noteworthy is the access to the Humboldt Redwoods State Park in Weott. The Rockefeller Forest at the park boasts the largest collection of old-growth redwoods in the world. If you don't plan on hoofing it all the way past Arcata, here's your chance to hike through a bountiful forest. For a real treat, pitch a tent in the Burlington or Hidden Springs campgrounds.

Farther north in Redcrest, stop and marvel at the Immortal Tree—a 950-year-old redwood that has survived everything from numerous lightning strikes to floods, forest fires, and even a logger's ax (it is still stuck in the tree). More than anything, this curiosity makes a decent stopping point to pick up souvenirs or take a bathroom break.

The scenic drive connects to US 101 in Pepperwood, but does not lose its majestic appeal. Continue north on US 101 for 46 miles, passing the former logging towns of Fortuna and Scotia until you reach **Eureka**, the county seat. The largest community in the far north seems divided between its present environmentalist slant and its former conservative logging roots. Perched on the Humboldt Bay, Eureka at first glance appears sleepy, aged, and unworthy of exploration. And while it is true that its sister city Arcata might have the energy of a toddler in comparison, Eureka should not be overlooked.

Eureka's got plenty of historic Victorian buildings to spend the night, but the most stunning display of opulence is the 1880s mansion Carter House Inn, where the antique interiors of the "really nice rooms" (as the inn dubs them) are accentuated by poster beds, lacy bedding, spa tubs, fireplaces, and modern technological amenities. For a less expensive option, the Ships Inn provides families and romance seekers the chance to bed down in a renovated Victorian crafted with creative touches.

Downtown Eureka has slowly morphed into a foodie hub. For a fine meal that you will long remember, make a reservation to dine in the award-winning Restaurant 301. The muted color scheme of the restaurant shines when combined with the straight-from-the-farm produce and fresh seafood alchemized

THE WACKIEST RACE IN THE STATE

The weekend of Memorial Day brings an added dash of the infamous Northern California kookiness to Humboldt County. The annual **Kinetic Grand Championship** invades the area between Arcata to the Victorian Village of Ferndale, sending man-made, people-powered (and often moveable) sculptures along roads and beaches and even through the Humboldt Bay. Since 1969, when artist Hobart Brown challenged Jack Mays to a foot-powered race down Ferndale's Main Street, this race has entertained the crowds, growing bigger and with more complex creations each year.

That being said, the event planners surely have a sense of humor, offering prizes for the person who finishes the race in the middle (the aptly named Mediocre Award) as well as the Dinosaur Award for the first sculpture to break down after the starting line, the Poor Pitiful Me Award, and the Ace Award for folks who complete the 42-mile course without cheating or pushing their creation. Race planners invite spectators to follow the course on their own bikes.

If you miss the actual event, pop into the **Kinetic Sculpture Race Museum** in Ferndale to see some of the former entries.

To really understand the girth of these giants, these are the roots.

into divine creations. Their wine list might be the best in the county. For the superhungry, head across the bay to the Samoa Cookhouse—the last surviving cookhouse in the West. Tables decked out in red and white checked tablecloths with mismatched chairs overlooking downtown Eureka draw devotees who line up for gigantic plates of seafood or meat paired with more sides than your belly can handle. Don't say I didn't warn you. Back in Eureka, beer lovers gather in the famed Lost Coast Brewery to sample their popular Downtown Brown, paired with a burger or pasta. Locals fill this watering hole for lunch and dinner, making this a fun place to meet new friends. For decent coffee, live entertainment on weekends, and a luxurious collection of chocolates, Old Town Coffee collects its share of a fun crowd morning and night.

After a restful evening, continue north on US 101 to the college town of Arcata. Here you'll see more dreadlocks than cowboy boots, especially in the town square during the weekend farmers' market. That being said, Arcata caters to all types, be it the college professors hanging out in local bookstores, the outdoorsy crowd congregating at Adventure's Edge, a popular sporting goods shop, families catching a Humboldt Crabs baseball game at the Arcata Ballpark, or our future marine biologists hitting the books in the best café north of Mendocino—Café Brio (pop in here for a morning latte and pastry). If the vibe here is more your scene, Hotel Arcata, with its historic (and unfortunately small) rooms, is at the center of town, making it easy to explore this happening community without having to drive.

Like Eureka, there is no shortage of food options around here. Students sing the praises of the unique offerings of Los Bagels, a bakeshop that takes bread to a whole new level. Try the Thai bagel, sushi bagel, or slug bagel (which is not exactly what it sounds like). Another funky restaurant is the wildly popular Renata's Creperie. Originating as a crêpe cart that popped up in local markets, now this sit-down restaurant packs in locals who swear by her crêpe creations. Giant paintings of Ani DiFranco and Michael Franti hang over hippies enjoying their Nutella-filled pancakes.

The food offerings beyond Arcata are slim, so before you jump back in the car, grab picnic food at the North Coast Co-Op. As you travel north along US 101, if there is no fog, it is worth a stop to veer off toward the beach town of Trinidad. While this town won't get you close to curiosities, it delivers spectacular views from Trinidad Memorial Lighthouse as well as access to Patrick's Point State Park, a beachfront redwood park complete with a Native American village (though it's a fake), hiking trails to the sea, Wedding Rock (which has been hosting weddings for over a hundred years), Agate Beach for wading in the frigid water, a native plant garden, and even camping. If you adore this beach town and want to stay the night in a lovely B&B, the Lost Whale Inn provides all the comforts of beach living, including large windows, seascape color schemes, and a good breakfast. There are a handful of restaurants in town, including the Larrupin Café (which specializes in brisket and pork ribs) and the beachfront Seascape Restaurant for fish-and-chips and blackberry pie.

Continue north on US 101 for the real show—entrance to the Redwood State and National Park about 20 miles north of Trinidad. One mile south of Orick, begin your exploration with a visit to the Kuchel Visitor Center to grab a map and get a permit to enter the Tall Trees Grove (the park only offers a limited number each day on a first come, first served basis), which, as the name suggests, has the largest trees on the planet. Alternatively, walk the mile trail through the Lady Bird Johnson Grove.

From Orick, travel north for 15 miles on US 101 to the Newton B Drury Parkway, a 10-mile drive through ancient redwoods. Pop into the visitors center to get a map of this stretch of the park. Depending on your stamina, highlights include a hike along the 30-foot-tall canyon of ferns (whose ancestry dates 325 million years—a fun fact for dinosaur lovers to note) at Fern Canyon; glimpsing North America's largest elk in Elk Meadow; camping at Gold Bluff Beach; or you may opt to experience an ecotour through Redwood Adventures—this outfit provides travelers with mountain bike tours, kayaking trips, and guided hikes. If your vehicle (or your bladder) can handle it, the rough road of the Coastal Drive offers splendid views of the Pacific with glimpses of thousands of nesting seabirds. For travelers who cannot get enough of this area, book a night (or week) at the new Elk Meadow Cabins—a former logging camp, now morphed into luxury cabins with full kitchens.

Farther north, you'll reach the end of Humboldt County and the wacky

The view from Trinidad Memorial Lighthouse

former logging community of Klamath. Here redwood trees seem to blend into the Pacific as whales migrate along the coast. Plus, one of northern California's most curious attractions can be found up here—the legendary Trees of Mystery. Guarded by statues of a 50-foot-tall Paul Bunyan and Babe the Blue Ox, a grove of redwood trees juts up to the sky. Ride the Sky Trail through the tops of the giant redwoods, peruse the gift shop, grab a snack at the Forest Café, or sidle up the road to drive through the Klamath Drive-Thru Tree—hey, it is all about kitsch up in these parts.

At the tip-top of the state, as US 101 reaches Del Norte County, the Del Norte Coast Redwood State Park and the Jedediah Smith State Park guard the most unexplored sequoia groves in the world. Whether you hike the 8 miles of rugged coastline along the Damnation Trail or head inland to the manageable Stout Grove, a collection of old-growth giants lining a river, you won't find scenery more stunning than this. Unfortunately, the community of Crescent City (the largest this far north) has been consistently beaten down by Mother Nature and the demise of the logging industry. If you make it this far north and plan to stay the night, you'll want to bring your own food and camping gear. Travel south along CA 101 to return to Arcata and Eureka.

IN THE AREA

ACCOMMODATIONS

Baechtel Creek Inn and Spa, 101 Gregory Lane, Willits. This hotel is nestled on a quiet creek-side setting. The 45 rooms include access to the hotel's heated pool and hot tub, free breakfast, and wireless Internet access. Call 707-459-9063 or 800-459-9911. Website: www.baechtelcreekinn.com.

Benbow Inn, 445 Lake Benbow Drive, Garberville. Humboldt County's only full-service resort is an attractive option if you aren't keen on sleeping outdoors. Since 1926, this resort has welcomed everyone from Hollywood stars to RV campers, offering a caliber of service not found in many places. Rooms evoke another time, with rich red velvet, deep wood, and doors painted by Eva Benbow. Call 707-923-2124. Website: www.benbowinn.com.

Burlington Campground, located next to the visitors center on the Avenue of the Giants, approximately 2 miles south of Weott. The campground has 57 sites and a short nature trail that leads to a river where you can swim or fish. Call 707-946-1811. Website: www.humboldt redwoods.org.

Carter House Inn, 301 L Street, Eureka. One of the finest inns in the area, this 1880s mansion comprises four restored Victorian buildings. Imagine four-poster beds, wooden antiques, lacy bedding, and modern amenities like flat-screen TVs and DVD players. Call 707-444-8062. Website: www.carter house.com.

Elk Meadow Cabins, located in Redwood National Park. Six cabins, each with three bedrooms and two bathrooms, include kitchenettes, washer and dryer, Jacuzzi, fire pit, and a back porch with grill. Call 866-733-9637. Website: www.redwoodadventures.com.

Hidden Springs Campground, located 5 miles south of the visitors center on the Avenue of the Giants, just south of Myers Flat. Situated on a hillside in a mixed forest, the 154 campsites offer plenty of privacy. Call 707-943-3177. Website: www.humboldtredwoods.org.

Hotel Arcata, 708 Ninth Street, Arcata. Located on the town square of historic Arcata. Thirty-two small rooms offer turn-of-the-century décor, including claw-foot tubs and period antiques. The hotel is well priced, in a good location, and offers continental breakfast. Call 800-344-1221. Website: www.hotel arcata.com.

Lost Whale Inn, 3452 Patrick's Point Drive, Trinidad. This four-room inn combines all the aspects that make Trinidad exceptional under one roof— sea colors, earthy accents like plants and wood floors, big windows, and a full breakfast. Call 707-677-3425 or 800-677-7859. Website: www.lostwhale inn.com.

Miranda Gardens Resort, Avenue of the Giants, Miranda. Sixteen cottages and rooms nestled in a grove of redwoods, with deer wandering through the playground and around the pool, are both homey and rustic. Families will like the ones with full kitchens and barbecue areas. Call 707-943-3011. Website: www.mirandagardens.com.

Petrolia Guest House, 888 Mattole Road, Petrolia. The guest house, also known as the Lost Inn, offers a suite of three rooms including a bedroom, sunroom, and glassed-in kitchenette porch. The inn is located just 1 mile from the Mattole River. Call 707-629-3394.

Shelter Cove Inn, 118 Dolphin Drive, Shelter Cove. The inn offers oceanfront suites with granite countertops, marble tubs, stone fireplaces, Jacuzzi tubs, and private decks. Call 707-986-4030. Website: www.sheltercoveinn.com.

Ships Inn, 821 D Street, Eureka. Lovely renovated rooms in an old Victorian stand out from the crowd with their individual flavor and thoughtful details. The Mission Room, a tribute to Frank Lloyd Wright, relies on soft colors to show off the oversized king bed and wooden antique furnishings. Call 707-443-7583 or 877-443-7583. Website: www.shipsinn.net.

Tides Inn of Shelter Cove, 59 Surf Point, Shelter Cove. Every room in the inn has an ocean view, which is great for whale watching and viewing the family of sea otters that live right by the inn. Call 707-986-7900 or 888-998-4337. Website: www.sheltercovetides inn.com.

Victorian Inn, 400 Ocean Avenue, Ferndale. The inn's rooms allow you to dip into another era of Jane Austin novels and romantic poets. Dream away in comfy beds, surrounded by plush linens and floral wallpaper. Call 707-786-4949 or 888-589-1808. Website: www.a-victorian-inn.com.

ATTRACTIONS AND RECREATION

Adventure's Edge, 650 10th Street, Arcata. A great store for outdoor enthusiasts with hiking, biking, paddling, and rock climbing gear. Call 707-822-4673. Website: www.adventuresedge.com.

Arcata Ballpark, F and Ninth Streets, Arcata. Watch a Humboldt Crabs game at the ballpark, or participate in one of the many community events sponsored by the park. Call 707-826-2333. Website: www.humboldtcrabs.com.

Arcata Farmers' Market, located at Arcata Plaza at Seventh and G Streets. Held seasonally April through Nov., Sat. 9–2. Call 707-441-9999. Website: www.redwoods.info.

Avenue of the Giants, located off US 101 from the south, the drive is north of Garberville, take the Phillipsville exit; or from the north take the Pepperwood exit. This 31-mile scenic road takes you deep into the forest through 51,222 acres of redwoods and along the Eel River. Allow at least two hours for the drive. Website: www.avenueofthe giants.com.

City of Ten Thousand Buddhas, 4951 Bodhi Way, Ukiah. Visit the organic garden, the vegetarian Jyun Kang Restaurant on the property (try some veggie favorites such as curry noodle soup or roasted eggplant with basil), and check out the bookstore/gift shop. Call 707-462-0939. Website: www.cttbusa.org.

Confusion Hill, 75001 North US 101, Piercy. Attractions include the Gravity House, the world's tallest freestanding redwood chain-saw carving, and a miniature mountain train ride. Call 707-925-6456. Website: www.confusion hill.com.

Del Norte Coast Redwood State Park, headquarters for the redwood parks in the area are located in Crescent City at 1111 Second Street. These 8 miles of rugged coastline are hugged by zillions of old-growth mossy redwoods. Call 707-465-2146. Website: www.parks.ca .gov.

Immortal Tree, take US 101/Redwood Highway, exit 667, drive east, then turn north onto the Avenue of the Giants. The tree is a little north of Redcrest. This famous 950-year-old tree still stands today, near a gift shop and picnic tables. Call 707-722-4396.

Jedediah Smith State Park, located 9 miles east of Crescent City on US 199. Drive the rough Howland Hill Road. It'll take you to Stout Grove, the spot with the tallest trees in this northernmost area of the redwood park. Call 707-458-3018. Website: www.parks.ca.gov.

Kinetic Sculpture Museum and Race, 580 Main Street, Ferndale. Call 707-786-9259.

Klamath Drive-Thru Tree, 430 CA 169, Klamath. One of only three drive-through trees on the North Coast. Call 707-482-5971.

Kuchel Visitor Center, US 101, Orick. Provides information, exhibits, a film on Redwood State Park, and a picnic area. During the summer season, patio talks and coastal walks are available. Call 707-465-7765. Website: www.nps.gov.

One Log House, 705 US 101, Garberville. You can get an espresso here and connect to the Internet for free. Call 707-247-3717. Website: www.one loghouse.com.

Patrick's Point State Park, 4150 Patrick's Point Drive, Trinidad. Hiking, camping, biking, exploring a recreation of a Native American village, picnicking, beachcombing, and walking through a native plant garden. Call 707-677-3570. Website: www.reserve america.com.

Redwood Adventures, 7 Valley Green Camp Road, Orick. This tour group offers deals for individuals and groups interested in hiking, biking, fishing, kayaking, or horseback riding in the Redwood National Park. Call 866-733-9637. Website: redwoodadventures.com.

Redwood State and National Park, located on US 101, from Orick to Crescent City. Many of these coastal redwoods have lived here for over 2,000 years; they grow to over 370 feet tall (higher than a 30-story building!); their bark resists fire and disease; and better yet, the tallest recorded tree in the world—the Hyperion—lives in this massive redwood park. Call 707-464-6101. Website: www.parks.ca.gov.

Rockefeller Forest, located in the Humboldt Redwoods State Park. This forest is the largest remaining old-growth redwood forest in the world. Call 707-946-2409. Website: www.parks.ca.gov.

Shrine Drive Thru Tree, follow the signs off US 101 in Myers Flat. Here's your chance to drive through a tree. Expect to wait awhile because people stop and take pictures of their cars inside the tree.

Skunk Train, 299 East Commercial Street, Willits. This 3.5- to 4-hour round-trip on a vintage rail cruiser climbs to the summit of the line at 1,740 feet and descends into the Noyo River Canyon. Call 866-457-5865. Website: www.skunktrain.com.

Trees of Mystery Sky Trail, 15500 US 101, Klamath. Most people come for the seven-minute ride in an enclosed six-person gondola through the redwoods. Others stop at Ted's Ridge for views of redwoods and the beach or to photograph Paul Bunyan and the blue ox. You can hike back down through redwoods and visit the museum at end of trail. Call 707-482-2251 or 800-638-3389. Website: www.treesofmystery.net.

Trinidad Memorial Lighthouse, located at the end of Main Street, Trinidad. Though it doesn't actually function as a lighthouse anymore, this tower marks one of the best views of the sea on a sunny day. Inside is a 2-ton fog bell. Call 707-677-0223.

Vichy Springs Hot Springs Resort, 2605 Vichy Springs Road, Ukiah. This unique, 177-year-old historic hot springs offers naturally warm, carbonated Vichy mineral baths. Cottages are available for overnight stays. Call 707-462-9515. Website: www.vichysprings.com.

Willits Frontier Days. The celebration includes rodeos, a parade, a horseshow, contests, and delicious beef BBQ. Call 707-459-6330. Website: www.willitsfrontierdays.com.

DINING/DRINKS

Café Brio, 791 G Street, Arcata. A great little coffeehouse with excellent cappuccinos and pastries. The café also serves sandwiches for lunch. Call 707-822-5922. Website: www.briobaking.com.

Curley's Grill, 400 Ocean Avenue, Ferndale. On the ground floor of the historic Victorian Inn, this is a popular choice with locals and tourists. The grill is best known for its daily specials, often featuring fresh fish. Reservations recommended. Call 707-725-1595.

Germain-Robin, Ukiah. If you're looking for a traditional brandy, this distillery offers spirits made using 19th-century techniques and equipment. Call 800-782-8145 for appointment. Website: www.germain-robin.com.

The Groves, 12990 Avenue of the Giants, Myers Flat. Located in an old barn attached to a tasting room, here you'll get the finest food and wine between Mendocino and Eureka. Imagine a wood-oven-roasted rack of lamb with rosemary couscous and wood-fired pizzas that will blow your mind. Reservations recommended. Call 707-943-9930. Website: www.riverbendcellars.com.

Larrupin Café, 1658 Patrick Point's Drive, Trinidad. Famous for their beef brisket and pork ribs, both served with the Larrupin barbecue sauce, which is bottled and sold on the premises, folks come from around the Humboldt Bay for finger-licking cooking. Call 707-677-0230. Website: www.larrupincafe.com.

Los Bagels, 1061 I Street, Arcata. This place is packed—all the time. Locals come for bagels with Mexican toppings; visitors tend to stick to traditional lox and cream cheese. Call 707-822-3150. Website: www.losbagels.com.

Lost Coast Brewery, 617 Fourth Street, Eureka. This is a favorite watering hole, lunch spot, and dinner pub. The food is hearty and pretty good, but the highlight is the beer. Their signature Downtown Brown ale has won numerous awards. Call 707-445-4480. Website: www.lostcoast.com.

Mariposa Market, 500 South Main Street, Willits. This market has organic produce, specialty foods, and a good selection of gluten-free products. It also features a juice bar, coffee bar, and deli. Call 707-459-9630.

North Coast Co-op, 811 I Street, Arcata, and 1036 Fifth Street, Eureka. The bakery, deli, espresso bar, vegan and vegetarian food, meat and seafood selection, and bulk items are the best around. Call 707-822-5947 or 707-443-6027. Website: www.northcoastco-op.com.

Old Town Coffee, 211 F Street, Eureka. Located in a historic brick building, this coffee shop is where locals gather to catch up on events, read the paper, drink fine coffee, and hear live music on weekends. They also offer tea, fudge, and chocolates. Call 707-445-8600. Website: www.oldtowncoffeeeureka.com.

Poppa Joe's, 409 Main Street, Ferndale. This is where to find hearty breakfasts. Since 1880, this building has been a gathering spot for locals; today you can still get coffee for a buck and traditional American-style breakfasts of eggs, bacon, and toast. Call 707-786-4180.

Renata's Creperie, 1030 G Street, Arcata. Savory crêpes like spinach and almond or the supersweet Righteous Babe with raspberries, strawberries, and Nutella rule the menu. Call 707-825-8783.

Restaurant 301, 301 L Street, Eureka (at the Carter Inn). A seasonal California-style menu with specials such as cocoa-cumin-crusted rack of lamb and strawberry risotto. Call 707-444-8062 or 800-404-1390. Website: www.carter house.com.

Riverwood Inn, 2828 Avenue of the Giants, Phillipsville. A biker-favored Mexican restaurant, with live music on most Friday and Saturday nights, this rustic stop serves surprisingly good grub. Call 707-943-1766. Website: www.riverwoodinn.info.

Samoa Cookhouse, 908 Vance Avenue, Samoa. The last surviving cookhouse in the West serves an abundance of good food, in the style of a lumber camp: red and white checkerboard tablecloths, mismatched chairs, and a big plate of fish or meat, salad, veggies, potatoes, bread, and dessert. Call 707-442-1659. Website: www.samoacookhouse.net.

Seascape Restaurant, 1 Bay Street, Trinidad. This place gets mixed reviews, but there isn't any other place around where you can have these views (when it isn't too foggy) and eat clam chowder, fish-and-chips, and blackberry pie. I prefer breakfast here. Call 707-677-3762.

Shelter Cove Campground Store and Deli, 492 Machi Road, Whitehorn. A basic convenience store offering standard campground food as well as beer and plastic utensils. The deli serves items such as fish-and-chips and sandwiches. Call 707-986-7474.

Ukiah Brewing Company, 102 South School Street, Ukiah. The brewery serves organic pub fare such as fish-and-chips and burgers and also caters to vegetarians who will enjoy menu items such as the BBQ tofu sandwich and falafel. Enjoy a brew of pilsner, stout, or IPA with your meal. Call 707-468-5898. Website: www.ukiahbrewing co.com.

OTHER CONTACTS

Greater Ukiah Chamber of Commerce, 200 South School Street, Ukiah. Call 707-462-4705. Website: www.ukiah chamber.com.

Humboldt County Convention and Visitor's Bureau, 1034 Second Street, Eureka. Call 800-346-3482. Website: http://redwoods.info.

Mendocino Coast Chamber of Commerce, 217 South Main Street, Fort Bragg. Call 707-961-6300. Website: www.mendocinocoast.com.

Visit Mendocino County, 120 South Franklin Street, Fort Bragg. Call 707-462-7417 or 866-466-3636. Website: www.visitmendocino.com.

The Bigfoot statue in Willow Creek

11 Bigfoot Scenic Byway

Estimated length: 194 miles

Estimated time: 4 hours straight through, or 2 days

Getting there: From US 101 in Arcata, travel east on CA 299 for about 40 miles to CA 96 north—aka the Bigfoot Scenic Byway. Take CA 96 east toward Yreka and connect to I-5.

Highlights: Getting lost in the least traveled part of California; searching for the legendary Bigfoot; swimming in crystal clear swimming holes; meeting friendly local folks.

Depending on who you talk to, Bigfoot, Sasquatch, or, as crypto-zoologists call him, Gigantopithecus not only exists but also thrives in Klamath River country (the stretch of prosperous peaks generously dotted with forest and kept hydrated by gushing rivers populated by steelhead and trout between the Humboldt coast and the Shasta Cascade). From the beginning of their inhabitance of these lush and wild mountains, the native Hoopa and Karuk tribes have long believed that a species of man-apes has thrived in the upper reaches of the Marble Mountain Wilderness and Trinity Alps. In fact, only the most skilled and sacred medicine men ever dared to enter the areas where the legendary Madukarahat (aka Bigfoot) lived.

That being said, the local people have continuously had plenty of lore about the existence of these big guys. Enough so that when the Chinese immigrants (pushed out of Eureka by the then racist logging community) and gold miners looking for alternate business began populating the region, their sightings became a normal part of conversation. It seemed everyone who spent enough time up in these scarcely populated mountains had had an encounter with Sasquatch.

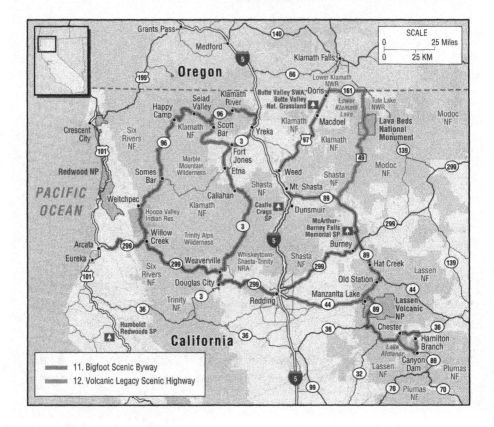

Soon, news of Bigfoot traveled down these mountains toward Redding and Eureka, garnering interest from scientists. In the late 1950s, a team of Bigfoot researchers set out on the two-year Pacific Northwest Expedition to find the illusive creature. These guys were the first to cast footprints (of which there are now many), but otherwise returned with not even a strand of hair to show for their efforts. Then in 1967, Roger Patterson and Robert Gimlin set off on horseback up to the Bluff Creek region in the Six Rivers National Forest (just above the Hoopa reservation) and allegedly filmed a female walking. Though this film has been highly debated for its authenticity, this sparked a huge resurgence in Bigfoot interest.

There have been plenty of hoaxes though. People have admitted to creating false footprints, and more recently, a local man teamed up with an entrepreneur and claimed to have "found" Bigfoot, which turned out to be a man in a costume, causing locals to grimace in anger about losing face in the international community.

In light of these setbacks, Bigfoot researchers still spend their time hiking through the forest searching for any sign of the big guy. And travelers will find that some time spent up in these mountains—if you chat up enough people—will leave you, if not exactly believing in the existence of Bigfoot, accepting that there very well could be a species of man-ape that humans have not been able to prove the existence of . . . yet. And if nothing else, the exploration of this virtually un-chartered territory in Northern California promises interactions with abundant wildlife, clear swimming holes, and quirky locals.

CA 299 sinews east, away from the giant redwood trees of Arcata, and snakes up the dense wooded area of the Six Rivers National Forest and past the gushing Trinity River, popular with kamikaze rafters and fishermen. Travel 40 miles (about an hour of driving) along this stunning route until you arrive in the small town of Willow Creek, ground zero for Bigfoot sightings and lore. Originally named China Flat, this town was a distribution center for pack trains carrying gold mining supplies between Eureka and Siskiyou County. Soon logging companies founded no less than 16 lumber mills, which have since disappeared, creating an economic wasteland.

Today Willow Creek houses its share of mountain people living off-the-grid

Taking a break among the greenery

and retirees eager to cash in and own that large property in nature. Though to outsiders the actual town might appear lacking for services, one conversation with a local and you begin to see why people are drawn to this community.

Begin your Willow Creek adventure at the free China Flat Museum to spot local antiques, and in the back, you'll find the Bigfoot room. Now, don't go expecting skeletons or even hair follicles. Instead, you'll view your share of foot casts (one made by the museum's curator Al Hodgson) as well as amicable tributes to Bigfoot by way of sketches and models and toys. On my visit, I got to tour the site with levelheaded Hodgson, who explained what to look for if you go on a Bigfoot trek: a woven nest of sticks and leaves, an amazingly horrid stench, piled up rocks, twisted-up tree limbs, and, of course, massive tracks. Some people claim to have had spiritual encounters that leave them in tears; others say Bigfoot is quite shy and bolts at the sign of humans, but rarely has anyone claimed the beast to be cruel. At the museum, you'll find plenty of Bigfoot paraphernalia, including shirts and books. Plus, you can snap a photo of the Bigfoot sculpture outside and at least brag to your friends that you saw the big man, just not the breathing one—yet.

If you are really in the market to get schooled, pop into Bigfoot Books. Owner Steven Streufert is an avid Bigfoot scholar. His shop is piled high with new and used titles, with a healthy collection of Bigfoot memorabilia. Streufert knows everything about both the mythology and reality of a species of man-ape living in the uninhabited forests above his house and, if you are game, will sell you a map of Bigfoot sightings.

When you are hungry, know that there are few options up here. Grab sandwich fixings at River Song Natural Foods (which has a limited schedule, so call for hours) or Ray's Marketplace. The local pub Raging Creek serves burgers and fries at a reasonable price. Or you can get traditional Mexican food at Gonzalez Mexican Restaurant. Whatever you

Peruse the stacks at Bigfoot Books.

Coho Cottages

choose, it is good to stock up on food because Willow Creek has no breakfast restaurants and the pickings are virtually nonexistent as you make your way north into the wilderness.

Surprisingly, however, there is a luxurious lodging option in town. Coho Cottages provides guests with self-contained cottages packed with urban amenities. Flat-screen TVs, plush bedding, rain showers, deep soaking tubs, BBQs, and refrigerators populate the riverfront cottages. To really get up close with nature, pitch a tent at the Boise Creek Campground, which is open from May through October ($10).

If the weather permits, travel up CA 96 0.25 mile to Big Rock, a great place to swim and relax by the Trinity River. You can also access the river for rafting, kayaking, and fishing, since trying to bag steelhead is a popular endeavor in these parts. Hopefully, you'll snag a fish to barbecue for dinner.

After sleeping to the tune of silence up here in this natural haven, travel north on CA 96—the Bigfoot Scenic Byway. This very remote road meanders along the Trinity River and then the Klamath River, inching past peaks blanketed with verdant trees and yellow fields dotted with lupines. For nearly 80 miles, this byway takes you as far from civilization as you can get in California without hiking into the backcountry of these mountains—which you can, just check with the

Lower Trinity Ranger Station in Willow Creek for information about back-country hiking and camping.

The first stretch of civilization you come to is the Hoopa Indian Reservation, the largest reservation in California. If you remember, these are the people who wouldn't dare put themselves in the way of Bigfoot, who, they believe, lives high in the hills over their community. However, other people have, among them Forest Service workers, who came to the area to construct Go Road (now called Eye-see Road), located just above the reservation. After the crews had begun work on the road, they returned to the project site in the morning to find their bulldozers

BIGFOOT SIGHTINGS

A collection of stories as told to Steven Streufert, the owner of Bigfoot Books and a local Bigfoot scholar. Streufert has chosen to keep his sources anonymous for the most part.

A sane and sober father of two is out fishing at a local lake when he looks up to see an upright apelike creature stalking the opposite shore. A family is driving home up CA 96 when a large, hairy biped stands up along the side of the road and paces down into the forest. Another fellow sees one outside the Hoopa-area dump. While out camping in the Trinity Alps area, a fellow's tent is pelted periodically for hours with small rocks hailing down from the forested hillside, and strange wood knocks ring out in the night. Unknown chatter and howls are heard off in the dark mountain distance.

A local business owner's father had the following experience. Early in the morning, arriving to open his shop, the lifelong Willow Creeker heard something he had never heard in all his years out in the woods and hills: a loud howling, beastly yell, clearly not human but from no known animal, echoing off the canyon walls up from the river across CA 299. This was strange, but he had a business to run. A short time later, a government worker, either Forest Service or Fish and Game, came into his shop with an air of panic and wild-eyed excitement. Camping down on that same area of the river, he had been awakened by the same ominous howl. Looking out his tent flap, he saw a big hairy creature, walking along the bank. Walking? Yes, upright, walking, bigger than a man, and taller, at about 7 feet. This was no bear!

turned over, 500-pound tires thrown down the mountain, and giant footprints littering the scene. The Hoopa shrugged in the I-told-you-so manner of the knowing, and soon after, Bigfoot hunters began arriving like crazy.

These days, depending on the weather, you can brave the road to Bigfoot's stomping ground by traveling to Orleans and turning onto Eyesee Road; drive the rough 16-mile trek up the mountain and then turn onto 12N13. Stop at the mouth of Bluff Creek and look around for the big hairy dude. If you don't see him, you can at least take a dip in the creek before heading back down the mountain.

Continue north along this stretch of untouched natural beauty only found in

---

One man described seeing a family of Bigfoot (two large males, a female, and a juvenile) when he was a child back in the 1950s, at a Willow Creek area rural country dance. The several other kids at the dance, playing on the perimeter of the property, saw them, too. The creatures watched from the edge of the forest for a while, with obvious interest in what the playing human kids were doing. Nothing else happened. They just retreated slowly back into the woods. This fellow, a former logger, seemed an utterly sensible and down-to-earth chap. It took much coaxing to get him to tell his story.

Quite often someone tells of having seen a Bigfoot in his or her yard, perhaps eating from the blackberry bushes, or seen one crossing the road or a creek or digging in a trash can. A woman working one of the forest fire lookout stations in the area is said to have seen a big hairy biped moving through some underbrush near Friday Ridge Road. This was after some footprints and a peculiar semiwoven nest made of bay tree leaves was found in the area. Sean Fries, an investigator out of Weaverville, was with his girlfriend up on Aikens Creek when they heard a noise in the brush. Not seeing anything, she took a photo. Later, when they put the image on their laptop, they noticed a strange brown form behind some trees. When enhanced digitally, this form showed features that looked surprisingly like the head and upper torso of a humanoid creature. They returned to the spot and found that, when viewed from the same location and angle, the brown form was no longer there.

For more helpful (and intriguing) Bigfoot information, visit http://big footbooksblog.blogspot.com. Or find updates via Facebook: www.face book.com/bigfootbooksblog.

the middle of nowhere—though Bigfoot may argue otherwise. On my last jaunt up here, we passed a baby black bear, a bobcat, herds of deer, and a dense collection of birds along the road, but alas, no Bigfoot.

Twenty-three miles north of Orleans is the Dillon Creek Campground, known for majestic summer camping as well as access to one of the area's best swimming holes—Dillon Creek. After picnicking by the water, hop back in the car and continue north until you reach the town of Happy Camp, a former logging town rich with Bigfoot lore (or kitsch, depending on your perspective). Turn right off CA 96 toward Elk Creek Bridge, where there have been plenty of Bigfoot sightings. Whether you see the big guy or not, you'll be treated to picture-post-card views of the river gushing through the forest, surrounded by varieties of green unseen in even the most thriving botanical gardens. It becomes clear why Bigfoot apparently selected these particular mountains to live. Not only does the landscape make it easy for him to hide, but it is also exceptionally wild and beau-tiful, putting Yosemite to shame. Elk Creek promises an easy place for kiddos to cool off as well.

Though battered by the economy, Happy Camp lives up to its name, promis-ing effusive locals eager to share their interactions with Sasquatch. But that's not all they share. Give a shout, and locals will guide you to Clear Creek, the local swimming hole that rivals swimming holes in Tahiti, then lead you down the river

Elk Creek Bridge   *Public art in Happy Camp*

on a raft to spot bald eagles (or Sasquatch, if you're lucky).

Check into the Bigfoot RV and Cabins, owned by film producer Rita King, de facto mayor of Happy Camp; though the guest quarters are far from plush (you'll have to continue on for fancy digs), the effusive hostess and general kindness offered by the Happy Campers gets you into the heart of this small community. The full kitchens and wood-burning stoves don't hurt either. For dinner, either grab some grub to prepare in your cabin at Parry's Market or join the locals for beers and burgers at the Frontier Café (though I prefer their diner-style breakfasts).

In the morning, schedule a rafting trip with Klamath River Rafting to explore the swollen rivers teeming with trout, bald eagles, bears, and maybe even old Yeti himself. These seasoned rafters can guide you onto the granny run or the more challenging Class III rapids. Some packages include lunch.

BIGFOOT DAYS:

A Celebration of All Things Sasquatch

If you can get to Willow Creek over Labor Day weekend, the annual **Bigfoot Days Celebration** honors the big hairy dude in all his glory. Though the living breathing man-ape has yet to grace the parade, BBQ, and general party scene of this celebration with his presence, you'll see plenty of floats, characters, and people dressed in their hairiest duds. Rumor has it that the next few parades will showcase a Bigfoot kiddo, since in 2010 the big dude had himself a sweetheart.

History buffs may want to visit the Karuk tribe's People's Center Museum, which contains a vast array of Native American artifacts, including hand-carved canoes and instruments. There are plenty of photos of local history, and ask around as the local tribesmen have plenty of Bigfoot lore to share. Another worthy stop is the Klamath Siskiyou Art Center, which at press time was under construction but promises to be a gathering place for local artists. Plans include a restaurant (serving healthy food!) and rotating art exhibits as well as a theater to host traveling performers.

Just before you pull out of town, get your camera ready, because there he stands in all his glory—Bigfoot. Well, a massive junk metal sculpture crafted by locals eager to at least deliver a fine photo op for travelers. You will finally see the big guy, though probably not the living breathing one. This fine specimen of art lives on the corner of CA 96 just across from the lone gas station in town. (Tip: Fill

DETOUR: THE MARBLE MOUNTAIN WILDERNESS
TO REDDING

Estimated length: 159 miles
Estimated time: 4 hours straight through, or at least 3–5 days to fully enjoy this experience

For those of you game for exploring even more remote landscape, traverse into the **Marble Mountain Wilderness**. Just past Hamburg on CA 96, take Scott River Road toward Etna, a one-lane paved road through 7,000-foot peaks, glacier-carved lakes, and diverse wildlife. You'll travel along the Scott River, continuing to where the Scott River Road meets CA 3; continue on CA 3 and you will see the Kingdom Hall, and then you will turn right and see a miniature version of an old west town, ideal for toddlers to explore. Then continue on to Etna to refresh at the famed **Etna Brewing Company**, where you'll likely make friends with some people who've spotted the hairy hominid. If you are not a fan of microbrews, their root beer puts most varieties to shame. And the food ain't too shabby either.

CA 3 winds south from Etna past Trinity Lake and the Trinity Alps, famous for fishing and spectacular country. Be warned: You will have difficulty driving as there is so much to see. If you are here in summer, I highly recommend booking a week at the **Trinity Mountain Meadow Resort,** a family camp nestled in the most remarkable stretch of wilderness. Or if you prefer to camp, drop into the ranger station in Coffee Creek to get a free permit. Note that there is only backcountry camping, meaning you need a strong back to lug your gear into the forest.

Drive south on CA 3 until you reach Weaverville, a funky historic mountain town that boasts the oldest continuously used Chinese temple in California— the **Weaverville Joss House State Historic Park**. The building was constructed in 1874 as a Taoist center of worship and now showcases a decent collection of Chinese artifacts from the gold rush era.

Back on CA 3, the road ends at CA 299 as you reconnect with the Trinity Scenic Byway, this time traveling east until you reach **Whiskeytown National Recreation Area.** Here day-trippers trek to waterfalls, swim or kayak in the lake (rangers offer free guided kayak trips on weekends, so call for reservations), picnic, or try to snag some trout for dinner.

Seven miles east of Whiskeytown, you'll come across the largest city in the far north—**Redding**. For more information, see chapter 12.

Bigfoot has been spotted by this stretch of Elk Creek.

up here. and if you don't have a credit card, go bang on the owner's door and offer up some cash.)

Continue on CA 96 north toward the Seiad Valley, stopping at the Seiad Café to take the pancake challenge: Consume 5 pounds of pancakes in one hour and your breakfast is free (though you may not be able to walk afterward). Here CA 96 begins to head east, carving its way along the Klamath River Canyon, an area favored by fly-fishermen, mushroom-hunting enthusiasts, and hikers. The byway officially changes its name to the State of Jefferson, a tribute to the residents' determination to secede from California and become the 51st state. For your purposes, it serves to know that folks here are as friendly as they come, yet they carry the battle scars of living in virtual isolation up in these mountains—there is a feeling of lawlessness, coupled with a subtle lip curling at city folk. Even more notable is the fact that nature rules the roost up here. The bear population is double the human count, and you'll likely catch sight of bald eagles, bobcats, snakes, and other mountain-dwelling creatures. So be sure to slow down and soak up the unmatchable beauty as your car sinews through these mountains—as the old bootleggers once did—crossing 1901 Ash Bridge along the Klamath River on CA 263 toward Yreka, where you can connect with I-5 and return to civilization.

IN THE AREA

ACCOMMODATIONS

Bigfoot RV and Cabins, 63709 Crumpton Street, Happy Camp. Affordable and modest cabins with kitchens and private baths in a casual and friendly atmosphere. Don't expect luxury, but owner Rita does everything in her power to make you feel at home. Call 530-493-2884. Website: www.thehappy camp.com.

Boise Creek Campground, located 1.5 miles from the town of Willow Creek along CA 299. Facilities include drinking water, but showers and electric/water/sewer hookups are not available. Reservations must be made at least three days in advance. Call 530-629-2118. Website: www.reserve america.com.

Coho Cottages, located off CA 299, behind Ray's Market in Willow Creek. Surprisingly sophisticated cottages along the river provide guests with high-tech amenities like radiant-heated floors, deep soaking tubs, flat-screen TVs, and convenience kitchens. Call 530-629-4000 or 800-672-1511. Website: www.cohocottages.com.

Dillon Creek Campground, from the south, take CA 96 north and proceed for 60.2 miles. Book well in advance as these 21 campsites fill quickly. This area also houses one of the best swimming holes along the byway. Call 530-627-3219. Website: www.reserveamerica .com.

Trinity Mountain Meadow Resort, Star Route 2 Box 5700, Trinity Center. These 10 guest cabins feature shower, toilet, and sink as well as use of the lodge, which boasts a large stone fireplace. Rates are all inclusive with meals, child care, and plenty of activities. Call 530-462-4677. Website: www.mountainmeadowresort.com.

ATTRACTIONS AND RECREATION

Bigfoot Books, 40600 CA 299, Willow Creek. General purpose used bookshop specializing in books about Bigfoot. Call 530-629-3076. Website: www.bigfoot books.webs.com.

Bigfoot Days Celebration, in Willow Creek. Enjoy a parade, BBQ, and kid-friendly activities. Website: www.red woods.info/showrecord.asp?id=3689.

Big Rock, located near the Lower Trinity Ranger District at Six Rivers National Forest in Willow Creek. Features a boat access site and recreational swimming area. Call 530-629-2118.

Klamath River Rafting. Happy Camp. Offers private party whitewater rafting, day and overnight trips, as well as horse-assisted backcountry trips into the Marble and Siskiyou wilderness areas. Call 530-493-2207. Website: www.klamathrafting.com.

Klamath Siskiyou Art Center, 63633 California 96, Happy Camp. Features regular art shows on the last Friday of each month. Call 530-493-5668. Website: www.ksartcenter.org.

People's Center Museum, 64236 Second Avenue, Happy Camp. Check out the exhibition gallery and basket-weaving classroom. Call 530-493-1600, ext. 2202. Website: www.karuk.us /peoples center/peoplescenter.php.

Weaverville Joss House State Historic Park, 630 Main Street, Weaverville. Stop by in Feb. during Chinese New Year or during Fourth of July weekend for a Lion Dance celebration. Call 530-623-5284. Website: www.weavervillejosshouse.com.

Whiskeytown National Recreation Area, 14412 Kennedy Memorial Drive, Whiskeytown. An excellent spot for swimming, water skiing, kayaking, rowing, and fishing. Call 530-246-1225. Website: www.nps.gov/whis/index.htm.

Willow Creek China Flat Museum, 38949 CA 299, Willow Creek. Operates May through Oct., but is open by appointment during the rest of the year. Call 530-629-2653. Website: www.bigfootcountry.net.

DINING/DRINKS

Pickings are slim in these parts. Your best bet is to pop into one of the markets in Willow Creek or Happy Camp to stock up on supplies.

Etna Brewing Company, 131 Callahan Street, Etna. Pub-style food including burgers, sandwiches, and wraps. Call 530-467-5277. Website: www.etnabrew.net.

Frontier Café, 64118 Second Avenue, Happy Camp. Cluttered with curiosities

Happy Camp's Bigfoot statue

from a long-forgotten era, hungry travelers and locals flock here for a home-style breakfast, hearty lunch, or dinner. After dark, the saloon in the back makes for a fun night. Call 530-493-2242.

Gonzalez Mexican Restaurant, 38971 CA 299, Willow Creek. Traditional Mexican cuisine in a casual setting. They are known around town for their ceviche. Call 530-629-3151.

Parry's Market, 143 Davis Road, Happy Camp. Call 530-493-2359.

Raging Creek Pub & Eatery, 38939 CA 299, Willow Creek. For a decent burger and fries, sandwiches, or a pint of beer, this locally favored spot works. Open for lunch and dinner. Call 530-629-1147.

Ray's Marketplace, 38195 CA 299, Willow Creek. Call 530-629-2457.

River Song Natural Foods, 39057 CA 299, Willow Creek. Specializing in local and organic foods. Call 530-629-3148.

Seiad Café, 44719 CA 96 Seiad Valley. Pop in for pancakes and typical diner grub. Call 530-496-3360.

OTHER CONTACTS

Happy Camp Chamber of Commerce, 35 Davis Road, Happy Camp. Call 530-493-2900. Website: www.happycampchamber.org.

Redding Convention and Visitors Bureau, 777 Auditorium Drive, Redding. Call 530-225-4130 or 800-874-7562. Website: www.visitredding.org.

Welcome to Redding, 777 Cypress Avenue, Redding. Call 530-225-4060. Website: www.ci.redding.ca.us.

Willow Creek Chamber of Commerce. Call 530-629-2693 or 800-628-5156. Website: www.willowcreekchamber.com/visitor-info.html.

The road to Lassen Volcanic National Park in spring

12 Volcanic Legacy Scenic Highway

Estimated length: 399 miles
Estimated time: 8 hours–5 days

Getting there: From Redding, drive east on CA 44 for 47 miles; travel south on CA 59 south to Lassen Volcanic National Park (59 miles). Travel north on CA 89 to Mount Shasta (166 miles). Travel north on I-5 to CA 97 north. Drive east on CA 161, then south on CA 39. Head west on CA 89. Return to Redding via I-5 south.

Highlights: Exploring one of three U.S. deemed All-American Roads (the highest federal standing for scenic byways) of California; touring Lassen Volcanic National Park; seeing gushing waterfalls; being wowed by the least populated swath of California; marveling at Mount Shasta, Lava Beds National Monument, Medicine Lake, and Santiago Calatrava's Sundial Bridge.

The Volcanic Legacy Scenic Byway yawns languidly for 500 miles from the bottom of the Cascade Range and up through lower Oregon. The landscape is both harsh and ridiculously beautiful, crafted by the alchemy of volcanic eruptions and the splendor of arboreal wilderness. Lakes, gushing rivers teeming with fish to snag, abundant waterfalls, swimming holes, and hot springs hide beneath the shadows of stratovolcanoes and amid seas of Douglas fir, black oak, and cedar.

This least populated part of California defies most stereotypes of the Golden State—here people hunt, fish, slow down to chat, and tend to vote conservatively. That being said, the Shasta Cascade has its share of crystal-wearing, tarot-card-reading hippies, especially circling the majestic Mount Shasta—a mountain believed to carry healing properties in its waters. Native American settlers swore that this great volcano was so sacred that they had to be purified before ascend-

The Volcanic Legacy Scenic Byway

ing beyond the tree line. Today, folks of all persuasions gather to revere the mountain's power, climb it, and soak in its healing hot springs.

You'll begin your exploration of this scenic byway just east of Redding by following CA 44 (a country road) for 49 miles, then turn right on CA 59 and you are on the byway. Soon you'll arrive at Lassen Volcanic National Park. With 106,000 acres to explore, you can easily stay here for an entire week and still feel you've not really experienced this remote landscape. Grab sandwiches at the Manzanita Lake Campground Store and enjoy a picnic lunch on the western shores of Manzanita Lake with a view of Lassen Peak. Pop into the Loomis Museum to learn about how this area was once a meeting spot for four major Native American tribes. Lassen Peak was the last volcano to erupt along this byway in 1914–1915, and the photos taken by B. F. Loomis are on display in this small museum. Local rangers will also assist with trip planning, if you'd like some additional guidance.

If learning about this rarely explored national park makes you want to stay the night (or three), you can camp in the Manzanita Lake Campground, or if you prefer a bed, the Manzanita Lake Camping Cabins provide a rustic roof over your head (order the camper's package if you are not traveling with a stove or bedding). Cabins include heaters for cold nights and bear boxes.

Lassen Volcanic National Park's Bumpass Hell Trail

Depending on the length of your stay, I recommend two hikes that really show the unique geography of this park. The first (for people planning on passing through Lassen to greener pastures that day) is a short hike through the Devastated Area. Ideal for families or people with limited mobility, this easy interpretive walk shows the volcanic effects upon the land and often feels like walking on the moon. If you plan to stay the night (or take the detour—see the sidebar—around Lake Almanor), do not miss the chance to check out Bumpass Hell, the largest collection of hydrothermal features in the entire park. Take CA 89 south to the Lake Helen parking lot and follow the signs for Bumpass Hell Trail, an easy 1.5-mile hike. Named after an early settler whose leg was severely burned in one of these bubbling mud pools, these richly beautiful pools of water, stained hues of orange, white, and South Pacific ocean, remind you that all that glitters may not be worth getting too close to.

Follow CA 89 north for 29 miles until you reach the Subway Caves. Grab a warm sweatshirt and flashlight to travel underground in a lava tube to see the spectacular route carved in the earth by lava. You walk for 0.3 mile into the cave, so folks afraid of the dark (or critters) might sit out this adventure.

By this point, you'll likely be in the mood for some sustenance. About 20 miles north of the caves, you'll find the tiny town of Burney. This one-street town (turn

The majestic Mount Shasta

Lassen Volcanic National Park in spring

left on CA 299 from CA 89) houses a number of small-town eateries slinging lumberjack portions of fine food. Angelina's Restaurant at the Rex Club has been in business since the 1920s, serving popular dinners of filet mignon, halibut, and pasta in a classic dining room. For something a bit more down to earth, Chatty Cathy's draws locals, who attempt to devourer the massive sandwiches (I have to admit that I prefer breakfast here). Another healthy breakfast option is Blackberry Patch (though they also serve lunch).

The town itself doesn't offer much by way of shopping or entertainment; however, a visit to McArthur-Burney

DETOUR: LAKE ALMANOR

To really get yourself off the beaten path, travel south through Lassen Volcanic National Park on CA 89 (this merges with CA 36 east) through the Lassen National Forest for 57 miles. Quite lovely, this stretch of the scenic byway hosts nature at its finest. Bald eagles nest atop pine, fir, and incense cedar; fall brings a Technicolor display of seasonal change; and in summer, lakes and rivers beg you to jump in.

Veer off onto CA 36 and arrive in the small town of **Chester,** located at the northern tip of Lake Almanor, which houses a startling number of galleries for its size; take a stroll down the main drag and find locally crafted goodies. In town, there are a few restaurants to curb your appetite, though don't expect too much. Local favorite **Knotbumper Restaurant** specializes in meat-heavy dishes and chili served in a logging-themed cabin. For something a bit more ambitious, sample the organic goods at the **Red Onion Grill.**

For hikers, travel south on CA 89 to Humbug Road, pull off, and take the 11-mile easy paved loop around the lovely **Lake Almanor.** The trek takes three hours each way, passing through pine forests and offering plenty of places to take a dip to cool off.

Rest your head on the eastern shores of Lake Almanor at the **Dorado Inn.** To get here, travel south around the lake until you reach CA 147, then veer north. These modest condos and cabins include full kitchens, woodstoves, and even boat slips, if you travel with your own watercraft. Or to return to the byway and retrace your route through Lassen Volcanic National Park.

Falls is a must! If you've arrived too late in the day to fully explore these massive falls that Teddy Roosevelt called "the eighth wonder of the world," then check into one of the campy, yet clean motels along CA 299. The Green Gables Motel attends to most needs, including providing a small continental breakfast in the morning, a heated pool, and free Wi-Fi. If you reserve in advance, snag a campsite in McArthur-Burney Falls Memorial State Park, just a few miles north of Burney on CA 89.

After breakfast, plan to spend the morning at the park, which was crafted by volcanic activity. You can swim, kayak, or boat in Lake Britton. However, the real draw is the chance to hike the short trail down to the 129-foot waterfall. Mist shrouds this pounding flow of water, but you can get up close and feel the power of all that liquid rushing down the mountain.

Lassen Volcanic National Park's Bumpass Hell

Back along the byway, the road weaves north toward McCloud, a proud mill and lumber town, huddled in the shadows of Mount Shasta. Quite picturesque, with a working tourist railroad and historic buildings and the mountain in the background, McCloud invites travelers to slow down and stay awhile. My favorite stop for a meal is the White Mountain Fountain, serving traditional American grub in a friendly diner setting—be sure to check out the original soda fountain dating back to the 1930s. Afterward, stroll through the classic McCloud Mercantile Hotel (a lovely old hotel renovated with plenty of TLC and well worth the cash to stay over for a night), then explore the stacks of the McCloud River Mercantile Co., a store carrying vintage oils, blankets, soaps, candy, toys, wines— you name it.

Want to see another waterfall? Travel east on CA 89 for 5.5 miles. Find the turnoff for Fowler's Camp; turn right and locate the picnic area 1.2 miles down the road. The 3-mile trek along the trio of waterfalls that make up McCloud Falls are not only scenic, but also provide you with a place to jump in the water and cool off.

Return to CA 89 headed northwest until you reach I-5; travel north and exit

The town of McCloud

on the Central Mount Shasta off ramp (12 miles). After exploring the innards of the Cascade region, this small town feels like a metropolis. Curiously adorable houses, cluttered with wine bars, breweries, eateries, and, of course, those famed crystal shops, populate the stretch of downtown Mount Shasta City. Since the dawn of humanity, people have traveled to this rich natural tableau to soak up the fresh air and healing properties of the sacred mountain.

Follow Lake Street east to Mount Shasta Boulevard. Turn right, park, and stretch your legs as you explore this funky community. Get your aura read at Crystal Wings, a metaphysical shop carrying an abundant collection of Vogel crystals. Then tour the many art galleries lining the boulevard. The Gallery showcases natural art, highlighting the mountain of course, as well as serving glasses of wine. Grab a cup of coffee or tea at the Seven Suns Coffee House.

Check into the Mount Shasta Resort, a popular spot for golfers, honeymooners, and families wanting to sleep in chalets by Lake Siskiyou. Woodsy accommodations offer plenty of privacy, with decks facing the lake or forest, indoor fireplaces, and full kitchens. Dine at their lakefront dining room, on traditional mountain cuisine (à la chicken, steak, and hearty veggies). Or head back to town

A Mount Shasta Resort chalet   *McCloud's candy store*

to sample the organic Japanese cuisine at Vivify—a relatively new addition to the area. When the owner found out she had cancer, she and her husband moved from San Francisco to this healing town and opened a version of her successful Bay Area restaurant in a house just off the main drag. Dine outside or beneath the giant paintings in the dining room, and enjoy delicately crafted cuisine that will make you eat until you cannot bear another bite.

Breakfast at the local favorite Lily's, which specializes in Mexican-tinged egg dishes, griddle fare, salads, and other yummy treats served in a garden full of friendly, happy diners. Then pop into the Mount Shasta Super Market and stock up on picnic fixings and plenty of snacks—you are headed into no man's land for the day. Also, be sure to grab warm clothes and hard-soled shoes, and then fill your gas tank before heading north on I-5 to exit in the town of Weed. Travel farther north on CA 97 through the Butte Valley Region, an arid desert hugged by volcanoes and adored by a loving population of bald eagles, especially in the Butte Valley National Grasslands. This marshland provides plenty of safe habitats for nesting birds, so keep an eye out.

You'll pass through small towns like MacDoel and Dorris (whose claim to fame is having the tallest flagpole west of the Mississippi) as you approach the Oregon border. Travel east on CA 161, passing through the Klamath National Wildlife Refuge and the Tule Lake Wildlife Refuge areas—California's best spots to peep birds (75 percent of the Pacific Flyway species touch down here).

Birders, stop in the visitors center to get a feel for which avian species you'll likely spot and where they hide.

The real reason you trekked all the way up here requires a bit more driving. Travel south on CA 39 until you arrive at Lava Beds National Monument, a treat for both geologists and history buffs. To start there are more lava tubes here (435!) than anywhere else in North America. Check into the visitors center to see which tubes and caves are open for exploration, and if you happen to visit in winter, the frigid tour of the Crystal Ice Cave will blow your mind. For those interested in history, this region hosted a 30-year war between the Modoc Indians and the U.S. Army; ask the rangers to point you in the direction of the war sites.

To complete the circle, you can travel south on CA 39, on a rough road past Medicine Lake. Though there are no known outlets in the lake, the water manages to stay pure, inciting Native Americans to believe that this lake embodies healing properties. Continue south for 25 more miles until you reach McCloud. From here, retrace your drive to I-5, this time traveling south to Dunsmuir, an artsy village perched on the Upper Sacramento River. I always breathe a sigh of love when pulling into the mural-lined downtown, once a railroad hub, to find fine food (Café Maddalena serves gourmet Italian cuisine for dinner, or Cornerstone Bakery and Café slings fancy versions of baked goods, spinach omelets, and heaping sandwiches with fresh ingredients) and galleries (favorites include the Brown Trout and Ruddle Cottage) hidden in an unassuming stretch of Northern California. Plus, ask around; this town hosts the region's best swimming holes, but ssshhh, don't tell anyone.

The curious town of Dunsmuir

For an unusual overnight experience, check into the Railroad Park Resort: Sleep in one of 26 cabooses turned into hotel rooms. Backed by Castle Crags State Park, the property promises to indulge your reveries of campfire evenings, morning swims in their pool, on-site dinners, and easy access to dramatic hiking and rock climbing bested in Nor Cal only by Yosemite National Park.

Travel south on I-5 toward Redding, the largest city in this neck of the woods. Redding seems to be in the process of a reinvention that was inspired just after famed architect, Santiago Calatrava, constructed his Sundial Bridge. A modern spectacle to behold crossing the Sacramento River, this bridge actually works as a sundial and day or night poses beautifully for photos. If you are traveling with children or nature buffs, you may consider a pit stop in the Turtle Bay Exploration Park to learn about local fish and plants in an educational museum and arboretum. Or if the weather is not too hot (which it is in the summer), you may walk or bike the Sacramento River Path, a paved ribbon connecting the Sundial Bridge to the Shasta Dam.

There are many restaurants scattered throughout downtown Redding, though many charge way more than they should. Local favorites include Buz's Crab, a hopping restaurant near the river, specializing in all things seafood; the seasonal cuisine at Moonstone Bistro; or the very popular Market Street Steak House — try the hunks of meat topped with blue cheese.

If you don't have a plane to catch, stay the night at one of Redding's lovely B&Bs. Located in a historic building, the Bridgehouse Bed and Breakfast defies the expectations of traditional B&Bs by offering rooms on the more modern edge of the spectrum — think flat-screen TVs and no doilies. On the other side of the scale, the Tiffany House B&B accentuates its Victorian roots with plenty of antiques, floral touches, a full breakfast spread, and an English-themed garden complete with a gazebo.

Redding's Sundial Bridge

IN THE AREA

ACCOMMODATIONS

Bridgehouse Bed and Breakfast, 1455 Riverside Drive, Redding. Simple muted colors decorate this B&B and its interior. Rooms provide comfort and charm, blending a Pottery Barn aesthetic with comfy touches like in-room candles and river views. Call 530-247-7177. Website: www.reddingbridgehouse.com.

Dorado Inn, 4379 CA 147, Westwood. Located on the east shore of Lake Almanor, cabins include full kitchens, fireplaces, and boat slips. Call 530-284-7790. Website: www.doradoinn.com.

Green Gables Motel, 37371 CA 299 East, Burney. A roadside motel that defies the Psycho jokes by decorating the exteriors with potted flowers and providing a friendly ambience. Rooms are small. Call 530-335-2264. Website: www.greengablesmotel.com.

Manzanita Lake Campground and Cabins, Lassen Volcanic National Park. Camping cabins opened in 2011, which added an option for families uninterested in pitching their own tents. Note that it is still a rustic option. Call 877-444-6777. Website: www.recreation.gov.

McCloud Mercantile Hotel, 241 Main Street, McCloud. Historic rooms in a lovely old hotel offer claw-foot tubs, sloped ceilings, and classic antiques. Downstairs are a few shops and a restaurant, making this building the center of McCloud. Call 530-964-2330. Website: www.mccloudmercantile.com.

Mount Shasta Resort, 1000 Siskiyou Lake Boulevard, Mount Shasta. Luxurious chalets line Lake Siskiyou just outside Mount Shasta City. One-bedroom chalets come with private balconies, full kitchens, and spectacular views. Call 530-926-3030. Website: www.mountshastaresort.com.

Railroad Park Resort, 100 Railroad Park Road, Dunsmuir. Sleep in a former train caboose near a pool and in the shadow of Castle Crags State Park. Rooms are small, but chances are you'll spend most of your time exploring nature. Call 530-235-4440. Website: www.rrpark.com.

Tiffany House B&B, 1510 Barbara Road, Redding. Classic bed & breakfast vibe overlooking Mount Lassen range, with a fine breakfast spread and antique decorated rooms. Spring for the private cottage if romance is in the cards. Call 530-244-3225. Website: www.tiffanyhousebb.com.

ATTRACTIONS AND RECREATION

Butte Valley National Grasslands, 1312 Fairlane Road, Yreka. Call 530-842-6131.

Castle Crags State Park, 20022 Castle Creek Road, Castella. Camp or hike in among the granite cliffs. Call 530-235-2684. Website: www.parks.ca.gov/?page_id=454.

Crystal Wings, 226 North Mount Shasta Boulevard, Mount Shasta. Call 530-926-3041. Website: www.crystalwings.com.

Klamath National Wildlife Refuge, 4009 Hill Road, Tulelake. Call 530-667-2231. Website: www.fws.gov/klamathbasinrefuges/.

Lake Almanor, 529 Main Street, Chester. Call 530-258-2426. Website: www.lakealmanorarea.com.

Lassen Volcanic National Park, Lassen Volcanic National Park, Mineral. Call 530-595-4480. Website: www.nps.gov/lavo.

Lava Beds National Monument, 1 Indian Well Headquarters, Tulelake. Call

530-667-8100. Website: www.nps.gov /labe/index.htm.

Loomis Museum, 38050 CA 36 East, Mineral. Call 530-595-3399.

Medicine Lake, 800 West 12th Street, Alturas. Call 530-233-5811. Website: www.fs.fed.us/r5/modoc/recreation /camping/medicine.shtml.

McArthur-Burney Falls State Park, 24898 CA 89, Burney. Call 530-335-2777. Website: www.parks.ca.gov/?page _id=455.

Ruddle Cottage, 5815 Sacramento Avenue, Dunsmuir. Call 530-235-2022. Website: www.ruddlecottage.net.

Sundial Bridge, 844 Sundial Bridge Drive, Redding. Call 800-887-8532. Website: www.turtlebay.org/sundial bridge.

Tule Lake Wildlife Refuge, 4009 Hill Road, Tulelake. Call 530-667-2231. Website: www.fws.gov/klamathbasin refuges/tulelake/tulelake.html.

Turtle Bay Exploration Park, 840 Auditorium Drive, Redding. Explore the children's museum, the botanical gardens, grab a coffee in the café, or merely marvel at the Sundial Bridge. This is Redding's big-ticket destination. Call 530-243-8850. Website: www.turtle bay.org.

DINING/DRINKS

Angelina's Restaurant at the Rex Club, 37143 CA 299 East, Burney. Down-home cooking shines at Burney's finest eatery. Eat steak or pasta in a timbered dining room, served by effusive servers. Call 530-335-4184. Website: www.angelinasrexclub.com.

Blackberry Patch, 37453 CA 299 East, Burney. Nothing to write home about, but a decent place to stop for eggs, bacon, or sandwiches. Call 530-335-2888.

Buz's Crab, 2159 East Street, Redding. If you need some seafood in your day, go to Buz's Crab, which has been slinging crab legs since 1968. Chowders, fried or charbroiled fish, and sandwiches draw plenty of locals. Call 530-243-2120. Website: www.buzscrab.com.

Café Maddalena, 5801 Sacramento Avenue, Dunsmuir. In a small woodsy spot overlooking the train tracks, Dunsmuir's best-kept secret serves delicious gourmet pizza, Moroccan chicken, and rib-eye steaks smothered in blue cheese. Call 530-235-2725. Website: www.cafemaddalena.com.

Chatty Cathy's, 37453 CA 299 East, Burney. Typical diner straight out of Twin Peaks, but if you need some grub, they serve burgers, sandwiches, and pancakes. Call 530-335-5152.

Cornerstone Bakery and Café, 5759 Dunsmuir Avenue, Dunsmuir. A fine bakery, where locals dine beneath high ceilings on salads, sandwiches, and breakfast treats. Much of the produce is both organic and sourced locally. Call 530-235-4677.

Knotbumper Restaurant, 274 Main Street, Chester. Honoring the logging roots of the region, the walls are covered with saws and blades, while Mexican and American favorites go by logging terms. Call 530-258-2301.

Lily's, 1013 South Mount Shasta Boulevard, Mount Shasta. Located in a small cottage, this café serves heaping portions of Mexican-style breakfast treats, pancakes, and salads during the day, jazzing up its offerings to include meaty dishes and pastas by night. Call 530-926-3372. Website: www.lilysrestaurant.com.

Market Street Steak House, 1777 Market Street, Redding. An institution in Redding for prime cuts of steak for lunch and dinner. Try the Kobe filet drenched in balsamic vinegar and Guinness. Call 530-241-1777. Website: www.marketstreetsteakhouse.com.

Moonstone Bistro, 3425 Placer Street, Redding. A good option for people who cannot decide what they want as they serve a slew of styles, including organic chicken mole and smoked pork with dumplings. Call 530-241-3663. Website: www.moonstonebistro.com.

McArthur Burney Falls State Memorial Park

Mount Shasta Super Market, 112 East Alma Street, Mount Shasta. Call 530-926-2212.

Red Onion Grill, 384 Main Street, Chester. Burgers and fish-and-chips in a casual atmosphere populate the menu. Call 530-258-1800. Website: www.redoniongrill.com.

Seven Suns Coffee House, 1011 South Mount Shasta Boulevard, Mount Shasta. Good coffee, plenty of art, and a collection of breakfast treats draw mountain climbers, aura readers, and tourists. Call 530-926-9701. Website: www.mtshastacoffee.com.

Vivify, 531 Chestnut Street, Mount Shasta. Organic Japanese sushi, salads, and raw desserts served in a light-filled cottage. A decent wine list and a lovely patio with views of Mount Shasta promise a mellow ambience. Call 530-926-1345. Website: www.vivifyshasta .com.

White Mountain Fountain, 241 Main Street, McCloud. An old-school diner, ideal for sitting at the counter, slurping a soda, and ordering pancakes or a burger. Call 530-964-2005. Website: www.mccloudmercantile.com/fountain .htm.

OTHER CONTACTS

Redding Convention and Visitors Bureau, 777 Auditorium Drive, Redding. Call 530-225-4130 or 800-874-7562. Website: www.visitredding.org.

Shasta Cascade Wonderland Association, 1699 CA 273, Anderson. Call 530-365-7500. Website: www.visitsiskiyou .org.

Welcome to Redding, 777 Cypress Avenue, Redding. Call 530-225-4060. Website: www.ci.redding.ca.us.

Gold Country from above

13 Digging for Gold and Great Reds

Estimated length: Approximately 269 miles

Estimated time: 6 hours straight through, or 3–4 days

Getting there: From the Bay Area, take I-580 east to I-205 east. Merge onto I-5 south and drive for less than a mile to exit on CA 120 east. Follow the signs to stay on CA 120 east for about 50 miles (here you'll be driving on two-lane highways and through small towns). Follow the signs to CA 49 north, toward Jamestown and Sonora, and continue north on CA 49 all the way through Gold Country.

Highlights: Getting to know the Sierra Foothills; exploring Gold Country's rich culinary and wine scene; hunting for gold in picturesque rivers and streams.

Since 1848 California's Gold Country has represented a dusty, gritty world of rough riders aiming to kill, steal, and screw their way to affluence. America's greatest migration was the result of a lucky man named James Marshall, who struck gold in the town of Coloma. Even without Twitter feeds, news spread across the country, and thousands trekked westward to what became known as the mother lode, swelling the population to beyond its capacity. Towns sprang up along CA 49 to house this onslaught of gold diggers.

Today, these towns still exist along the rolling Sierra foothills, but since the amount of gold has dwindled (though there is still some to be found!), local people have had to try their hands at other means of making a living. And lucky us! In addition to some of Northern California's most lovely (and unexplored) green spaces, travelers have access to some of the most innovative red winemakers in the world. And where there's wine, there's always good food, art, and culture. Throw in a historic tour of the area, and your trip along CA 49 can cover all your travel desires.

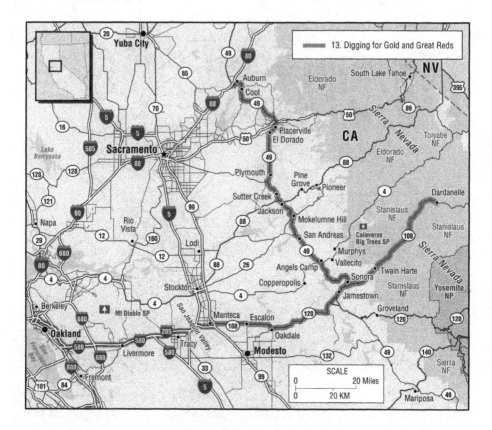

You'll begin your exploration of Gold Country in the town of Jamestown, located just off CA 49. Strung along Main Street, you'll find a handful of restaurants and antique shops and the 1859 Historic National Hotel, home of Flo, a
resident ghost who occasionally plays silly pranks. While Jamestown has not been
lucky enough to experience a modern-day boom like its neighbor city Sonora,
her past booms have been tied to gold, quartz, and the insight to create a railroad
here. In fact, the town's most tourist-worthy destination, Railtown 1897 State
Historic Park, showcases the railroad history of the area, including self-guided
tours of the facilities, a guided roundhouse tour, or a 6-mile-long steam train ride,
ideal for Thomas-loving kiddos. If you are feeling that this stop is slightly Holly-
woodesque, you are correct; in fact, it was Hollywood that saved this train from
demolition—of course, only to use it in the movies.

Hankering to pan for gold? Gold Prospecting Adventures rents materials or
leads people on a variety of expeditions. If you go at it alone, it helps to know
these simple tricks. Start in a river; hopefully, the guys at Gold Prospecting Adventures will offer advice on the best spot (if not, you can try Woods Creek, where

CA 108 crosses over the creek, just north of town, as this was *the* spot for prospectors in 1848). You need a strong 12- to 18-inch gold pan, a small shovel, a bucket, a spoon, a pocketknife, and a little vial for your riches. (Other spots to score this equipment in Gold Country include the Hangtown Gold Bug Mine and Park in Placerville, and Bekearts Gun Shop in Coloma.) Dig where heavy gold might settle—around tree roots, upstream in gravel bars, or around old mines. Tilt, then swirl the water, sand, and gravel in your pan, slowly letting materials fall from the pan until you reach black sand and hopefully gold. Be patient. And don't settle for that fool's gold, which breaks at the touch. If you find some, take a picture and send it to me!

To sample some of the fine wine coming out of the area, pop into Gianelli Vineyards & Tasting Room for a free sample of their Gold ribbon 2008 Dolcello. Then continue along CA 49 to the county seat, Sonora, a bold mix of hippie culture, old-school miners, and renegades uninterested in city living. Sonora's Historic Downtown (located along Washington Street) is home to plenty of antique shops, candy stores, the Old Fashion Soda Fountain Shoppe, wine bars, the Tuolumne Courthouse (1898), and St. Patrick's Church (1975). For lunch, you

Try your hand at panning for gold.

TUOLUMNE COUNTY DETOURS AND DESTINATIONS

For those of you with an extra couple of days, drive up CA 108, the Sonora Pass, to see some of my favorite under-the-radar destinations—albeit without much wine or gold offerings. Start your experience in the hamlet of Twain Harte, named strangely for Mark Twain and Bret Harte, though neither ever stepped foot in this town. Book a night in the **McCaffrey House B&B** and enjoy clean quarters in a homey atmosphere, surrounded by a sea of trees, as well as one of the best breakfasts in eastern California. Twain Harte itself may not be a hub of culture and culinary prestige, but it has a calming alpine vibe, and the **Rock Pub and Restaurant** and the fine Italian-themed **Villa D'Oro** make for decent eats. The real highlight of the area is nature, so throw on that bathing suit and those hiking boots and trek east on CA 108 all the way up to Dardanelle, a popular day-use area in the Sierra Mountains, or picnic (supplies best picked up at **Alicia's Sugar Shack** in Sugar Pine before the road gets too windy) under a canopy of juniper at Donnell Vista. When you tire of hiking, travel west on CA 108 to **Pinecrest Lake,** a lovely alpine lake surrounded by conifers and frolicking birds, ideal for swimming, kayaking, and relaxing in the sand.

can't beat the offerings at the Diamondback Grill. For 20 years, the owners have been serving locally grown produce, grass-fed beef, and surprisingly good wines in a gold rush–era building. Seems every person in town comes for lunch on weekends; their burgers are that yummy.

About 4 miles north of Sonora just off CA 49 (head north on Parrots Ferry Road) is the Columbia State Historic Park, a car-free historic town preserved quite well. In its prime, Columbia was the capital of the area, thriving with "working gals," gunfights, and gold seekers. Stroll into the William Cavalier Museum (Main and State Streets) to learn about this once-rough town. Other notable stops include the Columbia Grammar School and Fallon Hotel. If you are aching for sustenance, there are a couple of restaurants and saloons here, the highlights being the City Hotel and the Fallon Ice Cream Parlor. Alternatively, you may take a ride on the carriage before heading out to a livelier destination.

By this point, you'll likely be in the market for some wining and dining, so continue on Parrots Ferry Road to CA 4 east; drive for 3 miles until you reach the town of Murphys and turn onto Main Street. It wasn't until I stumbled on the precious town of Murphys that I began to believe all the hype about Gold Country being California's hidden gem. Imagine a Main Street littered with gourmet restaurants, wine shops, art galleries, and bakeries that would make an urbanite drool; throw in a town park with a river slicing through it that kids can play in on warm summer days, wineries, and majestic green spaces just a short drive from town; then add sophisticated hotels to lay your head. Yep, Murphys might just live up to her nickname as the Queen of the Sierra Foothills.

Check into the Murphys Historic Hotel, a registered Historic Landmark Hotel (1856) with a modern lodge as well as 29 historic rooms. The historic guest registry can make for a fun read. As long as you aren't put off by some noise from the bar/restaurant and shared bathrooms, you'll appreciate these modest quarters. Otherwise, dive into romance at the Dunbar House 1880, an Italianate home and country inn promising decadent bathtubs and a fanciful breakfast.

From the vegetarian gourmet restaurant Mineral, which convinces carnivores that veggies can be delicious, to the more modest but no less outstanding Firewood, which serves up pizza and pasta in a family-friendly atmosphere, the cuisine in Murphys is quite impressive. Or if you crave modernity, V Restaurant and Bar serves a tasty dollop of mussels in white wine and butter broth or petite lamb chops and desserts like cheesecake or flourless chocolate cake, which draws plenty of appreciative oohs and aahs from the crowd.

In summer and fall, check Ironstone Vineyards' Website; they may be hosting a silent movie night or concert. Favorites like Don Henley, Sammy Hagar, and Willie Nelson have graced the stage. Sit on blankets on the grass and sip Ironstone wines under the stars. Or check to see if Historic Winery Tasting Room, off Sheep Ranch Road, is hosting their Theater Under the Stars at the outdoor Murphy's Creek Theater. This is the oldest winery in Calaveras County, specializing in great red wines.

In the morning, grab flaky pastries and coffee at Aria Bakery, which draws a steady stream of locals throughout the day. Then head up CA 4 to Calaveras Big Trees State Park, just 4 miles past Arnold. This dramatic park was set up in 1931 to preserve the North Grove, home of the giant sequoias. Wander through some of the planet's tallest (and widest trees), soaking up the rich mountain air.

STOMP GRAPES AND SHOP

In October, the town of Murphys hosts the **Calaveras Grape Stomp and the Gold Rush Street Faire**. The annual grape stomp celebrates the wine community, offering everything from competitive grape stomping in Murphys Park to a fun street fair to shop, snack, and people-watch.

Old grape vines

For lunch, grab sandwiches at Alchemy Market then head out to the local wineries for a picnic and wine sampling. The female-owned Chatom Vineyards crafts award-winning red wines. Alternatively, Indian Rock Vineyards churns out fantastic Barbera. Parents can sip by the pond while kids toss bread to feed the trout population. Call ahead to see if they are serving their Saturday BBQ.

Travel west on CA 4 until you reach the county seat of Angels Camp and then hop back on CA 49 north. There's not much to see in Angels Camp, though this is a decent place to stock up on groceries should the need arise. Drive for about 30 miles, passing through the village of San Andreas—which is home to the best sandwich shop in the county, Pickle Patch Deli & Garden, as well as the historic Calaveras County Courthouse (1867)—and the town of Mokelumne Hill, where you can bed down in a historic treasure, the Hotel Leger. If you are hungry for prime rib, this restaurant is famous for its large portions and classy atmosphere.

Farther north on CA 49, you'll find the city of Jackson—the county seat of Amador County. As with most gold rush–era cities, Jackson housed a tribe of lawless gold diggers, who ultimately burned the city to the ground in the 1860s. After rebuilding itself, Jackson continued its mining tradition by using tools to dig the deepest mines on the globe. Today, Jackson seems to be in an identity crisis. The growth of Amador County's wine tradition doesn't blend as seamlessly with the antique shops lining Main Street—though you can score treasures like hand-carved headboards and much-loved china. Check into the historic Gatehouse Inn, which does manage to serve the B&B crowd as well as people craving a solar-heated pool, private cottages, or Jacuzzi tubs. Casual cuisine lines the streets. Café de Coco provides travelers with fine burritos, *pupusas*, and Mexican coffee, or the ever-popular Mel and Fayes Diner serves up burgers and hearty breakfast fare.

In terms of gold history, Jackson won't let you down. You can begin with a self-guided walking tour (grab a map from the visitors center). Meander past the St. Sava Serbian Orthodox Church, or just stroll past the Civil War–era buildings, imagining this town as it once was.

Eight miles east of Jackson on Pine Grove–Volcano Road, you'll find Indian Grinding Rock State Historic Park. The Miwok Indians took up residence in the valley here, and you can still see their petroglyphs. Today, the Miwok gather under the oaks to celebrate acorns throughout the year, with music, dancing, and food. To really engage your local history buffs, visit the Chaw'se Regional Indian Museum to view Native American artifacts. You can also tour the reconstructed Miwok village and hike or camp in the park.

Back on CA 49, drive north a few miles until you reach the well-preserved gold rush–era town of Sutter Creek. If you ignore the modern cars and style of dress, you can almost picture how this town looked back in the day. Almost. Yet these days, Amador's wine vibe is creeping in. Stop for lunch at the Mediterranean-inspired Susan's Place Wine Bar and Eatery. Favorites here include the BBQ pork sandwich, the served-any-way pastas, and the lovely salads, all enjoyed on an outdoor patio. Another option is the Twisted Fork Restaurant, which serves gourmet salads and sandwiches.

Poke around the antique shops, tasting rooms, and galleries in town. Also of note is Monteverde General Store, which is now a museum showcasing items like gold rush–era diapers. When your legs tire, head out to the Sutter Gold Mine. Travel underground and explore this hard rock mine, which helped make Leland Stanford (of Stanford University) rich. Tours culminate with a chance to try your luck at finding gemstones. You might also want to explore the Western Hard Rock Mining Museum on the property, which houses a comprehensive collection of mining artifacts. If you'd like to stick around Sutter Creek for a night, the lovely Foxes Inn of Sutter Creek dates back to 1857 and provides travelers with a touch of luxury, including breakfast served to your room so you don't have to chitchat before coffee. Another option is the four-room Eureka Street Inn, just off Main Street—a craftsman cottage that doesn't look like someone vomited flowers.

Traditional Gold Country architecture

TIME OUT FOR FUN!

Adventure seekers come from around the globe to experience the Class III rapids at the south fork of the American River in Coloma— the only rapids of this caliber to flow year-round. On warm summer days, traffic crowds the river as rafters brave the waters squealing their way along the sinuous foothills. Take some time out of your wine tasting and gold hunting to join **Gold Rush Whitewater Adventures** or **American Whitewater Expeditions** on their exhilarating trips, often padded with camping and cuisine on either end of your trip.

Two miles north of Sutter Creek is the village of Amador City. With a population of 200, you'll likely breeze through the town on the way to brighter pastures, but if you are keen to hang out for a bit, the historic Imperial Hotel and Restaurant (1879) is housed in a lovely brick façade and offers antiques, white-tablecloth dining, a bar serving local wines, and cozy quarters; spring for the cottages as they are quieter. For a small town, Amador City has an ambitious collection of galleries and antique shops.

By now, you are probably itching to sample some vino, and luckily, the Shenandoah wine region is a mere 6 miles north on CA 49. In the town of Plymouth, grab picnic fixings at the Amador Vintage Market on Main Street. Then travel east on Shenandoah Road, where over 30 wineries grace the bucolic setting. Most tasting rooms offer free samples (do you hear the gasp from our Napa friends?) of robust red wines like petite Syrah and Zinfandel. Favorites include Story Winery, TKC Vineyards, and Charles Spinetta Winery (which also showcases a wildlife art gallery). When you begin to feel the buzz of too much wine, head back to Plymouth to experience the seasonal cuisine like oven-roasted guinea hen in the lively dining room at Taste Restaurant.

Or for a real treat, connect to CA 16 east and drive for about 10 miles up a windy road until you real the community of Fair Play. Though it may not look like much at first glance, these pastoral lands provide the ideal growing conditions for a variety of species—from grapes to alpacas. Sample more wine paired with pizza in their wood-fired oven on the lovely deck of the Fitzpatrick Winery (they also rent B&B rooms for people wanting to spend the evening on a vineyard), or have an Italian meal that seems to have traveled across the Atlantic to your plate at the wonderful Bocconato (hint: anything the waiter recommends, order it—their cuisine is superfresh and perfectly prepared).

Experience the rapids along the American River.

Other than eating, sipping, and hiking, Fair Play doesn't offer much, so I rec-ommend traveling back toward Plymouth and then continuing north on CA 49 for 20 miles until you reach Old Hangtown, otherwise known as Placerville. Other than its ideal location between Sacramento and Lake Tahoe, with access to the Fairplay wine region, Coloma, and a dizzying wealth of outdoor activities, Placerville is well worth a visit for its own merit. Historically, like the other towns along CA 49, gold brought folks to the town, but it was a combination of toughness, determination, and innovation that kept Placerville on the map. Sure, its nick-name alludes to a less aesthetic era, and yes, Hangtown's famed judges were rather stringent on unsavory types, but that hasn't left Placerville in the dark ages. Rather, today you'll find a surprisingly sophisticated town, bursting with wine culture, art, live music, and the friendliness of nature lovers.

In town you can tour the Hangtown Gold Bug Mine and Park. Or join the crowds for a glass of locally crafted vino and everything from wild mushroom pizza to Thai-flavored soups at Heyday Café. On the more casual side, the Cozmic Café serves organic cuisine, brews, wines, and coffee throughout the day in a former mine—the cavernous interiors make for a fantastic place to escape the heat outside. Check around as they often host live music in the evenings. When you need a place to rest, the Historic Cary House Hotel provides affordable luxury punctuated by period antiques and regal bedding in the heart of Placerville.

In the morning, you're off to experience the highlight of your gold history education—Coloma's Marshall Gold Discovery State Historic Park. From Placerville, take CA 49 north for 8 miles, and you'll spot one of the most important historical sites in California. You won't have an experience as kitschy as you may have in Columbia; in fact, there is not much here to do, save wander around the rebuilt Sutter Mill, sample ice cream, or tour the Gold Discovery Museum. However, people interested in the spot where James Marshall shouted eureka, drawing the largest migration west that this country has ever know, are sure to be engaged.

The town of Coloma may not seem like much at first glance—there is no real heart or Main Street like other Gold Country communities, yet travelers will not be at a loss for grub or nice accommodations. Hands down, my favorite B&B in Gold Country is the Coloma Country Inn. Owner Marjorie Sanborn has crafted a work of art in her cottages, providing guests with comfortable quarters with plenty of style. The fragrant gardens, often populated with deer in the morning, have a wooden swing and a pond. When your stomach begins to grumble, join the locals under the outdoor misters at Marco's Café for pizza and salad by the river. In the evening, the dazzling Café Mahjaic serves organic seasonal cuisine reminiscent of California's coastal cities—their chocolate chipotle prawns are addictive. Outdoor enthusiasts should stop into the American River Trail Conservancy to explore their interactive nature center and get information about trails and swimming holes.

For most, there is nothing better after a long day of hiking or swimming than sipping a cold brew or glass of Zinfandel (which put this wine region on the map). Luckily, the rolling hills around Coloma are teeming with high-caliber wineries. Favorites include Boeger Winery, David Girard Vineyards, and Gold Hill Vineyards (they happen to also have a brewery on-site for folks craving a more hoppy experience). For dinner, travel back to Placerville to dine at Sequoia, which was constructed in 1853 as the home to Judge Bennett, who was the reason Placerville got its nickname of Old Hangtown; later, the creator of the pony express, Colonel Bee, moved in. Though you cannot see it, in the wine cellar there is a tunnel that once allowed "working gals" to get into Placerville without being seen. Dinners are typical of white-tablecloth restaurants, including a fine grilled fish, steak, or cassoulet. Save room for dessert.

In the morning, give yourself time to linger over coffee before departing the "life is good" attitude of the Sierra foothills.

IN THE AREA

ACCOMMODATIONS

Coloma Country Inn, 345 High Street, Coloma. This 2.5-acre property offers more than just a place to sleep. Explore the rose garden, take a rowboat out on the pond, or play a game of bocce ball on the front lawn. Call 530-622-6919. Website: www.colomacountryinn.com.

Dunbar House 1880, 271 Jones Street, Murphys. If you like B&Bs, this Italianate home and 1880s country inn offers refined coziness. Children over 12 are welcome. Call 209-728-2897 or 800-692-6006. Website: www.dunbar house.com.

1859 Historic National Hotel, 18183 Main Street, Jamestown. Since 1859, this hotel has offered nine elegant accommodations in the heart of Jamestown. All guests have access to the soaking room, buffet breakfast, and restaurant. Call 209-984-3446 or 800-894-3446. Website: www.national -hotel.com.

Eureka Street Inn, 55 Eureka Street, Sutter Creek. Features rosewood wainscoting accented by leaded and stained-glass windows, along with a large collection of early 20th-century antiques and collectibles. Call 209-267-5500. Website: www.eurekastreet inn.com.

Fallon Hotel, 11175 Washington Street, Columbia. Stay in an authentically re-stored 19th-century country inn with an on-site restaurant and bar. Call 209-532-1470. Website: www.briggshospital ityllc.com/the-fallon-hotel.

Foxes Inn of Sutter Creek, 77 Main Street, Sutter Creek. This mid-19th-century inn features chef-prepared cooked-to-order breakfasts using herbs from the inn's garden. Call 209-267-5882 or 800-987-3344. Website: www .foxesinn.com.

Gate House Inn, 1330 Jackson Gate Road, Jackson. Check out the traditional Victorian sitting room with Italian marble fireplace or the formal dining room. Call 209-223-3500 or 800-841-1072. Website: www.gatehouseinn.com.

Historic Cary House Hotel, 300 Main Street, Placerville. This historic hotel dating back to 1857 features period furnishings and antiques. Call 530-622-4271 or 866-906-5207. Website: www .caryhouse.com.

Hotel Leger, 8304 Main Street, Mokelumne Hill. The present hotel is actually three separate buildings, one of which served as the Calaveras County Courthouse from 1855 to 1866 and included the county jail. Relax in the billiards parlor with a game of pool and a drink, or play the antique piano. Call 209-286-1401. Website: www.hotel leger.com.

Imperial Hotel and Restaurant, 14202 CA 49, Amador City. This late 19th-century bed & breakfast offers six rooms within the main guest house and three luxury suites located in a nearby cottage. Call 209-267-9172. Website: www.imperialamador.com.

McCaffrey House B&B, 23251 CA 108, Twain Harte. Well-appointed rooms and a fascinating collection of furniture and art in the common areas of this mountain lodge. Call 209-586-0757 or 888-586-0757. Website: www.mccaffrey house.com.

Murphys Historic Hotel, 457 Main Street, Murphys. A registered Historic Landmark Hotel (1856) with a modern lodge and 29 historic rooms. Call 209-728-3444. Website: www.murphys hotel.com.

ATTRACTIONS AND RECREATION

American River Trail Conservancy, 348 CA 49, Coloma. An excellent spot for hiking, mountain biking, boating, and rock climbing, as well as learning about wildlife in the region. Call 530-621-1224. Website: www.arconservancy.org.

American Whitewater Expeditions, 5981 New River Road, Placerville. With over 30 years of experience, this company offers whitewater rafting tours for ages six and up. Call 800-825-3205. Website: www.americanwhitewater.com.

Bekeart's Gun Shop, located on the grounds of Marshall Gold Discovery State Historic Park, 310 Back Street, Coloma. Offers a selection of gold-panning supplies, leather crafts, and Native American artwork. Call 530-621-0173. Website: www.coloma.com/gold/marshall-park.php.

Calaveras Big Trees State Park, take CA 4 east, 4 miles past Arnold. As a first-timer, you'll want to stroll at least part of the interpretive trail, which introduces you to the Discovery Tree, the first redwood discovered in 1852 among many others. Call 209-795-2334. Website: www.parks.ca.gov.

Calaveras Grape Stomp and Gold Rush Street Faire, Murphys Community Park, 1015 Forest Meadows Drive, Murphys. Get your feet sticky at the grape stomp. Call 209-754-0127. Website: www.calaverasgrapestomp.com.

Chaw'se Regional Indian Museum, 14881 Pine Grove–Volcano Road, Pine Grove. Hike the North or South Trails to explore the oak environment. To camp here, reserve early. Call 209-296-7488. Website: www.parks.ca.gov.

Columbia Grammar School, on the north end of Main Street, Columbia. Features a collection of antique desks, books, and slates dating from the 1860s.

Columbia State Historic Park, 11255 Jackson Street, Columbia. Reminiscent of Disneyland, without the crowds, the high prices, and the mouse. Tour a real Gold Country town. Call 209-588-9128. Website: www.columbiacalifornia.com or www.parks.ca.gov.

Gold Prospecting Adventures, 18170 Main Street, Jamestown. Choose between guided or self-guiding gold-panning adventures. Call 209-984-4653. Website: www.goldprospecting.com.

Gold Rush Whitewater Adventures, 7291 CA 49, Lotus. Offers customizable whitewater rafting trips from beginner to the most advanced. Call 530-295-8235. Website: www.goldrushriver.com.

Hangtown Gold Bug Mine and Park, 2635 Goldbug Lane, Placerville. Enjoy the newest attraction at the Stamp Mill—a working blacksmith shop. Open daily 10–4. Call 530-642-5207. Website: www.goldbugpark.org.

Indian Grinding Rock State Historic Park, 14881 Pine Grove–Volcano Road, Pine Grove. View marbleized limestone with 1,185 mortar holes and a number of petroglyphs. Call 209-296-7488. Website: www.parks.ca.gov.

Marshall Gold Discovery State Historic Park, 310 Back Street, Coloma. The spot where gold was first discovered by California transplants lures hundreds daily. Call 530-622-3470. Website: www.parks.ca.gov.

Monteverde General Store, 3 Randolph Street, Sutter Creek. This museum schools visitors about the history of the region. Walk along the aisles of the store and view the vintage hardware, pharmaceuticals, clothing, and miner supplies. Call 209-267-1344. Website: www.suttercreek.org.

Pinecrest Lake, located in Stanislaus National Forest, Pinecrest. Offers motorboat, paddleboat, kayak, and sailboat rentals. Call 209-965-3411. Website: www.pinecrestlakeresort.com.

Railtown 1897 State Historic Park, Fifth Avenue and Reservoir Road, Jamestown. Known as the movie railroad, kids and adults will find more than a museum of past railroad artifacts here. Open daily: 9:30–4:30 Apr. through Oct.; 10–3 the rest of the year. Call 916-445-6645. Website: www.csrmf .org.

St. Sava Serbian Orthodox Church, 724 North Main Street, Jackson. The oldest Serbian Orthodox church in North America. Call 209-223-2700. Website: www.stsavamissionfoundation .org.

Sutter Gold Mine Tours, 13660 CA 49, Sutter Creek. People like this tour because they can see the mother lode from the inside. Guided tours daily from at least 10–5. Call 209-736-2708. Website: www.suttergold.com.

Tuolumne Courthouse, 41 West Yaney Avenue, Sonora. Dating back to the late 19th century, this courthouse still stands as a landmark today. Call 209-533-6984. Website: www.tuolumne .courts.ca.gov/Historic.htm.

Western Hard Rock Mining Museum, 14207 CA 49, Amador City. Houses a comprehensive collection of mining artifacts. Not recommended for kids under four. Call 209-267-0848. Website: www.minerspick.com.

William Cavalier Museum, Main and State Streets, Columbia. Offers an overview of local history with exhibits,

slide shows, films, and a 45-minute walking tour. Call 209-532-4301.

DINING/DRINKS

Alchemy Market, 191 Main Street, Murphys. A decent place to pick up a picnic before heading to a local wine tasting. The attached dining room serves fancied-up American dishes. Call 209-728-0700. Website: www .alchemymarket.com.

Alicia's Sugar Shack, 24191 CA 108, Sugar Pine. Come here for espresso and sweet treats. Call 209-586-5400. Website: www.aliciassugarshack.com.

Amador Vintage Market, 9393 Main Street, Plymouth. Offers fresh sandwiches, home-style salads, charcuterie, artisan cheeses, and desserts. Call 209-245-3663. Website: www.amadorvintage market.com.

Aria, 458 Main Street, Murphys. Serves well-brewed coffee and espresso drinks; sandwiches, salads, soups, and quiches are served for lunch. Open 7–4; closed Tues. Call 209-728-9250. Website: www.ariabakery.com.

Bocconato, 7915 Fair Play Road, Fair Play. Local, seasonal, and fresh ingredients are the spotlights in the dishes of this traditional Italian restaurant. Call 530-620-2492. Website: www.bocconato .com.

Boeger Winery, 1709 Carson Road, Placerville. Call 530-622-8094. Website: www.boegerwinery.com.

Café de Coco, 140 Main Street, Jackson. Serves coffee and Mexican cuisine. Call 209-223-2626.

Café Mahjaic, 1006 Lotus Road, Lotus. Expect New American cuisine made with organic meats, grains, and produce and fresh fish. Reservations recommended. Call 530-622-9587. Website: www.cafemahjaic.com.

Charles Spinetta Winery, 12557 Steiner Road, Plymouth. Tasting room features gallery-style artwork on the walls. Call 209-245-3384. Website: www.charlesspinettawinery.com.

Chatom Vineyards, 1969 CA 4, Douglas Flat. Tasting room boasts 13 varietals in a Mediterranean setting, with picnic area and beautiful gardens. Call 800-435-8852. Website: www.chatom vineyards.com.

City Hotel, 22768 Main Street, Columbia. The What Cheer Saloon at the hotel offers a casual dining menu and local beers on tap. Call 209-5321479. Website: www.briggshospitalityllc.com.

Cozmic Café, 594 Main Street, Placerville. Find a good selection of vegetarian and organic options throughout the day, plus a healthy selection of beer and wine. Call 530-642-8481. Website: www.ourcoz.com.

David Girard Vineyards, 741 Cold Springs Road, Placerville. Specializes in Rhone-style wines and classic Bordeaux varietals. Call 530-295-1833. Website: www.davidgirardvineyards .com.

Diamondback Grill, 93 South Washington Street, Sonora. Enjoy the vaulted ceiling and exposed original rock and plaster walls as you bite into a half-pound burger of locally raised grass-fed beef. Call 209-532-6661. Website: www.thediamondbackgrill.com.

Fallon Ice Cream Parlor, 11175 Washington Street, Columbia. Serves sundaes, sodas, milkshakes, and espresso drinks. Call 209-532-1470.

Firewood, 420 Main Street, Murphys. If you don't mind the line on busy days, this is a good family locale for a casual lunch or dinner. Their wood-fired pizzas from the centerpiece Italian oven delight kids and adults. Open daily 11–9. Call 209-728-3248. Website: www.fire woodeats.com.

Fitzpatrick Winery, 7740 Fair Play Road, Fair Play. Organically grown wines are the highlight of this winery, along with its Irish bed & breakfast. Call 800-245-9166. Website: www.fitz patrickwinery.com.

Gianelli Vineyards & Tasting Room, 18263 Main Street, Jamestown. Open Thurs. through Sun. 12–5. Call 209-984-1500. Website: www.gianellivineyards .com.

Gold Hill Vineyard, 5660 Vineyard Lane, Placerville. With 11 varietals and a brewery on-site. Call 530-626-6522. Website: www.goldhillvineyard.com.

Heyday Café, 325 Main Street, Placerville. Offers a great selection of soups, salads, pizzas, and paninis and an extensive wine list. Call 530-626-9700.

Historic Winery Tasting Room, 2690 San Domingo Road, Murphys. Visit the oldest winery in Calaveras County and taste the new Red Rover. Open daily 11–5. Call 209-728-0638.

Indian Rock Vineyards, 1154 Pennsylvania Gulch Road, Murphys. Located on a site originally settled by the Miwok tribes, the land itself has a historic feel. Sip a Barbera or a Pinot noir and check out the several year-round springs that feed two large ponds and hydrate the 14 different varietals. Open Fri. through Sun., 12–5. Call 209-728-8514. Website: www.indianrockvineyards.com.

Ironstone Vineyards, 1894 Six Mile Road, Murphys. Tour the historic caverns and the museum (with the largest hunk of gold ever found here; pan gold, shop, or enjoy deli fare on the outdoor patio, overlooking the vineyards. Make sure to check out the pipe organ downstairs. Open daily 10–5. Call 209-728-1251. Website: www.ironstonevineyards .com.

Marco's Café, 7221 CA 49, Lotus. Fill up with pizza and salad along the river under perfectly placed misters to cool you off. Call 530-642-2025.

Mel and Faye's Diner, 31 CA 49, Jackson. Serves traditional country breakfasts and burgers. Call 209-2230853. Website: www.melandfayesdiner.com.

Mineral, 419 Main Street, Murphys. Try the chef's 5 Course Discovery, which includes dishes like a chili hemp fondue with herb salad. Don't leave without experiencing the decadent Indian-spiced fried chocolate. Open Wed. through Fri., 3–9; Sat. for dinner. Call 209-728-9743. Website: www .mineralrestaurant.com.

Old Fashion Soda Fountain Shoppe, 131 South Washington Street, Sonora. A historic antique bar that serves icecream sodas, sundaes, and desserts. Call 209-532-8120.

Pickle Patch Deli & Garden, 577 West Saint Charles Street, San Andreas. They have the best sandwiches and salads in the county. Call 209-754-1978. Website: www.picklepatchdeli.com.

Rock Pub and Restaurant, 23068 Fuller Road, Twain Harte. Serves breakfast, lunch, and dinner seven days a week in a mountain lodge atmosphere. Call 209-586-2080. Website: www.rockoftwainharte.com.

Sequoia, 643 Bee Street, Placerville. Head here for a classically decadent meal of grilled fish, steak, or cassoulet. Reservations recommended. Call 530-622-5222. Website: www.sequoia placerville.com.

Story Winery, 10525 Bell Road, Plymouth. Specializes in Zinfandel wines; some of the vines date back to the early 1900s. Call 209-245-6208. Website: www .zin.com.

Savor the good life in the Sierra Foothills.

Susan's Place Wine Bar & Eatery, 15 Eureka Street, Sutter Creek. Indoor and outdoor seating available, in a setting that includes soft music, greenery, fountains, and even live doves. Call 209-267-0945. Website: www.susans place.com.

Taste Restaurant, 9402 Main Street, Plymouth. Take advantage of the prix fixe menu, which includes three seasonal courses for under $30. Call 209-245-3463. Website: www.restaurant taste.com.

TKC Vineyards, 11001 Valley Drive, Plymouth. Try one of the reds, this vineyard's specialty. Call 888-627-2356. Website: www.tkcvineyards.com.

Twisted Fork Restaurant, 53 Main Street, Sutter Creek. Offers gourmet lunch and dinner menus, including grilled rack of lamb and Tuscan chicken. Reservations recommended. Call 209-267-5211.

Villa D'Oro, 23036 Joaquin Gully Road, Twain Harte. Features a Mediterranean seasonal menu using fresh seafood and organic produce. Call 209-586-2182. Website: www.villadororestaurant.com.

V Restaurant and Bar, 402 Main Street, Murphys. Hearty, savory dishes in a modernist setting; don't leave without trying at least one dessert. Serving Wed. through Sun. beginning at 5. Call 209-728-0107. Website: www.victoria inn-murphys.com.

OTHER CONTACTS

Amador County Chamber of Commerce & Visitors Bureau, 115 Main Street, Jackson. Call 209-223-0350. Website: www.amadorcounty chamber.com.

Calaveras Visitors Bureau, 1192 South Main Street, Angels Camp. Call 209-736-0049 or 800-225-3764. Website: www.gocalaveras.com.

El Dorado County Visitors Authority, 542 Main Street, Placerville. Call 530-621-5885 or 800-457-6279. Website: www.visit-eldorado.com.

Sonora Chamber of Commerce. Call 209-588-9625. Website: www.sonora chamber.com.

Tuolumne County Visitors Bureau, 542 West Stockton Road, Sonora. Call 209-533-4420 or 800-446-1333. Website: www.tcvb.com.

Ghostly quiet in the High Sierra

14 Hunting for Ghosts in the High Sierra

Estimated length: 179 miles

Estimated time: 5 hours straight through, or 5 days

Getting there: From Truckee travel south on CA 89 along Lake Tahoe's western shore and continue (this road may close in winter) to CA 395 south. To get to Bodie from CA 395 south, travel east on CA 270. Retrace your drive to CA 395 south to Mono Lake area, and connect with CA 120 west.

Highlights: Learning about the Donner Party in Truckee; exploring Lake Tahoe's majestic shores and the Bodie Ghost Town; soaking in the Travertine Hot Springs; viewing the ghostly Mono Lake.

The Sierra is, in fact, the longest, highest, and most diverse mountain range in the continental United States. This remote yet well-traversed Northern California landscape has attracted travelers from all over the world, like naturalist and explorer John Muir, whose scientific writings and observations are the reason why we still enjoy the natural resources in these parts. Many a bold pilgrim has felt the High Sierra's spellbinding pull and gone trekking into that wild landscape of diamond crests and sapphire lakes, granite walls and emerald forests. Some returned with grand stories to tell, while others were not so fortunate.

It was in 1846 when some of the bravest of these travelers set out from Independence, Missouri, on a 2,500-mile journey to California. Just a mere 150 miles from their destination at Sutter's Fort, the party was blanketed by a storm in a mountain pass and snowbound for many months. More than half of the original party starved to death, and some of the remaining survivors ultimately resorted to what has become the most infamous and taboo act of survival—feeding on the dead. This tragic bunch was later known as the Donner Party (also the Donner-Reed

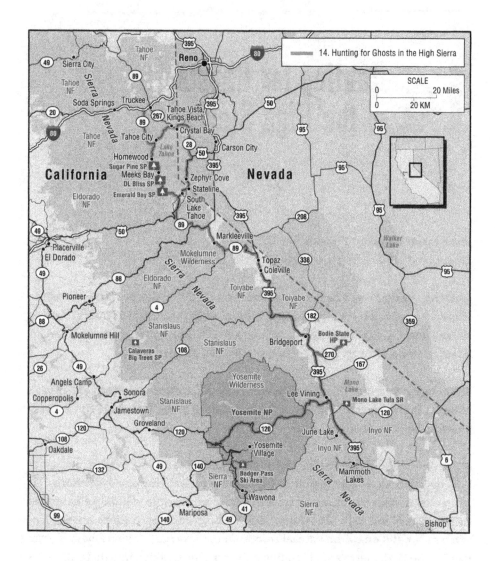

Party), and their story has fed the imagination, if not many a campfire tale.

You will start your ghostly journey at Donner Memorial State Park and Emigrant Trail Museum at Donner Pass Road, off I-80, west of Truckee, where the ill-fated Donner Party had its last supper and where many ghostly sightings have been recorded over the years. Visit the landmark before exploring the museum, which has a slide show about the group, indicating how they never ate family members, only munched on someone else's brother's leg meat.

After touring the park, drive onto Old Highway 40 Scenic Overlook for a fantastic view of Donner Lake, then head back on I-80 into Historic Downtown

Truckee, a true Wild West boomtown where the old refreshingly mingles with the new. Truckee is named for a northern Paiute medicine chief (sometimes referred to as Captain Truckee) and influential prophet who in 1844 guided a grateful emigrant party from Humboldt River to California via the Truckee River, Donner Lake, and Donner Pass. Though under the radar, Truckee is coming into its own with chic hotels and great restaurants coupled with storefront facades, covered wooden walkways, and original buildings. You'll feel like you've stepped back in time without sacrificing modern amenities.

Grab a bite at the Squeeze Inn (it really is 11 by 60 feet!) for an early lunch, or for the claustrophobic, Moody's is a great choice for seasonal farm-fresh cuisine. The Big Ass Pork Platter comes highly recommended. Then mosey onto Jibboom Street, the first road ever built in the Truckee Basin. You'll find the Truckee-Donner Historical Society and Old Jail where two famous residents spent the night here: Ma Spinelli, the first woman in California to die via gas chamber, and famous gangster Baby Face Nelson.

People-watch as you sip on an espresso at the Coffeebar. Or imbibe at the Dragonfly for great happy hour sushi, or at Cottonwood Restaurant & Bar for fantastic views, eats, and the restaurant's signature Frenchy Margarita. At the end of the day, rest your weary bones at The River Street Inn, a former brothel now a quaint B&B. For more decadent travelers, Cedar House Sport Hotel is the hip place to sleep. Mod stylings, hot tubs, and a fab restaurant make for a heavenly stay. For the diehard ghost tracker, The Truckee Hotel is the place to be. Several murders have taken place at this 1870s establishment, where ghostly sightings are frequent. You can request a room on the fourth floor where the spirit of a young girl is said to roam the hallways.

In the morning, grab a hearty breakfast (and some picnic provisions for later) at the Full Belly Deli and travel south on CA 89 to the hauntingly beautiful

---

TRUCKEE'S HISTORICAL HAUNTED WALKING TOUR

With a Wild West reputation like Truckee's, it's not surprising that this historic town would host an annual ghost tour. Part history/part bar crawl, the guided walking tour features ghostly haunts including the Old Jail, Richardson House, and a couple of downtown watering holes like Moody's Bar & Grill. Check www.truckeehistory-tour.com for dates on the next tour at the Truckee-Donner Historical Society, which usually happens in October.

VIKINGSHOLM CASTLE:

A Piece of Scandinavia in the Eastern Sierra

In 1884, a Dr. Kirby bought 500 acres in Emerald Bay and built a resort. A portion of the property was sold to the William Henry Armstrong family, who then sold it to Mrs. Lora Josephine Knight in 1928 for $250,000. Since Emerald Bay reminded her of a Scandinavian fjord, Knight decided to commission her nephew, Lennart Palme, a Swedish architect, to design her a summer home, based in part on 800-year-old wooden houses in Lillehammer, Norway. The house, constructed with massive hand-hewn timbers and a sod roof, would later become Vikingsholm Castle, a 38-room mansion/resort. Motifs and flourishes like intricately carved dragon beams, carvings around the doors, and delicate paintings on ceilings and walls are just some of the striking ornamentation that adorns Vikingsholm.

Emerald Bay State Park. Many claim the park is the residence of some ghosts. One famous spectral resident is Dick Barter who was employed as a caretaker in 1863 for Ben Holladay, a stagecoach magnate who owned lots of land surrounding Emerald Bay. Barter is said to haunt Fannette Island, where he smashed his boat against the rocks and died.

The best hike in the park is the Rubicon Trail (9 miles round-trip); start on The Bliss trailhead for 0.125 mile, then connect to the Rubicon Trail to view dizzyingly dramatic cliffs (600 feet below!). This trail takes you through fields of trees and all the way to Emerald Bay and a great beach with warmish water (in autumn the colors are mind blowing and in spring the area bursts with wildflowers) to Vikingsholm Castle, where you can sign up for a tour. Many have witnessed the ghostly residents that still live there.

Another gorgeous hike to consider is the Balancing Rock Nature Trail, a 0.5-mile trek that shows off granite rocks balancing on small stone bases. You can camp here in summer; reservations are required (www.reserveamerica.com). Just around the bend, you'll find natural formations, like local favorites Sleeping Lady, Gladiator, Frog Rock, and Old King Cole. Or locate the remains of an osprey nest or a tiny wooden lighthouse. From here you can spot Cave Rock. This sacred site of the Washoe Indians is said to be haunted by spirits of the deceased, who can be manifested if the proper ceremony is performed on the summit. It is also presumed to sit above the home of the legendary monster Tahoe Tessie, a

Emerald Bay

60-foot-long serpentine creature sited by locals and scientists alike. Even aquaman Jacques Cousteau took never-seen footage of Tessie that "the world wasn't ready for."

After a day of hiking, motor to Lake Tahoe, the largest alpine lake in North America, which attracts summer adventurers looking to cool off in the waters and winter snow bunnies braving the world-class slopes. Over a mile up in the mountains and split between the states of California and Nevada, this lake has many a ghost story to tell. The resorts, casinos, live music, and tons of people that clutter the lakeshore often eclipse the mellow ambience the surrounding mountains evoke. Since it is 72 miles around the entire lake, you'll find a variety of towns to explore, including Tahoe City, one of the more developed spots on the north shore, and South Lake Tahoe, the biggest town located a few miles south on CA 89 with a stretch of strip malls, resorts, restaurants, and ski lodges.

Grab an afternoon snack at Sprouts Natural Foods Café to take to Kings Beach Plaza for picnicking and relaxation. Then travel onto Tahoe Tessie's Lake Tahoe Monster Museum to learn more about this elusive creature, or visit Gatekeeper's Log Cabin Museum. The original 1910 cabin housed the gatekeepers who regulated Lake Tahoe's water level. The cabin was rebuilt in 1981, after the

Lake Tahoe in winter

MORE GHOSTLY DETOURS ON THE LAKE

About 3 miles north of South Lake Tahoe is **Sugar Pine Point State Park's** Ehrman Mansion where the park rangers believe they have come in contact with a ghostly visitor: Sydney Ehrman himself! Someone found an indentation in the bed of the room he once occupied. Continue the trip around the lake until you reach **Crystal Bay,** the northern border between California and Nevada where a certain sharp-dressed casino dealer has been spotted though, eerily, *not* an employee of the **Crystal Bay Club Casino.** Or meet Molly, a showgirl who committed suicide at the **Biltmore Lodge and Casino** in the '60s. Her ghost still entertains at the casino with late-night appearances in the old ballroom, dressed in full showgirl regalia.

original burned, and exhibits various Lake Tahoe memorabilia, including local rocks and fossils, logging equipment, and vintage newspapers.

For a more laid-back afternoon and coffee boost, refuel at Alpina before heading to Heavenly Village for some shopping on the South Shore, including galleries, clothing boutiques (check out Rainurbana), and jewelry stores. For lakefront dining, feast on Dungeness crab at the Blue Water Bistro. If you want to avoid those long lakeside dinner waits and stomach grumblings, The Cantina is *muy bueno* for tasty margaritas and hearty Mexican fare before bedding down at the cozy Black Bear Inn B&B.

For a heavenly breakfast, start your morning at the Blue Angel Café before setting out to the town of Markleeville. In winter, the only way to explore the ghosts of this historic town is via CA 88, but all other times, take CA 89 over Monitor Pass to reach the mining town of Markleeville, first settled by Jacob Marklee in 1861. On August 2, 1885, fire broke out in the town destroying several buildings, including Harvey and Rask's Butcher Shop and Smokehouse. The building was rebuilt and reopened as Rask's Butcher Shop. You can visit the building today with original structures plus additions built in the 1890s and 1950s. Visit the ghosts of the gold rush past at the Alpine Hotel Alpine County Museum/Historical Complex, which houses a cluster of buildings including the Old Webster School and Old Log Jail (the original cells were in Silver Mountain City and moved here) and re-creations of an old country store and a blacksmith shop. For old-world atmosphere, lunch at Wolf Creek Restaurant and Bar, or for more modern eats, the Stone Fly is your best bet in this one-horse town.

Just 4 miles west of Markleeville is Grover Hot Springs. (It is located at the end of Hot Springs Road at the edge of the Great Basin Province.) The state park features hot springs, swimming pool, picnic area, campground, and gorgeous hiking trails, not to mention the ghost of a Civil War soldier. Dressed in Union regalia, this specter was first spotted by stagecoach passengers in the 1870s and is seen around the backroads.

Next connect to CA 395 south to visit what's popularly considered the jewels of the Eastern Sierra and gateway to Yosemite National Park, Bridgeport and the Bridgeport Valley. In summer, the area is a hotbed of outdoor activities from fishing to boating to hiking to just swimming and lazing in the sun. Bridgeport, located on CA 395, was originally called Big Meadows; this fertile valley offers a spectacular setting of open range and grasslands. High above this lush valley is the Sawtooth Ridge of the High Sierra Crest named for its knifelike spikes of granite piercing the sky. This ridge is also known for its daredevil rock climbs and ski mountaineering routes. Be sure to visit the Mono Basin National Forest Scenic Area Visitor Center if the plethora of outdoor activities overwhelms.

In the town of Bridgeport, you'll want to grab some grub and do some more sightseeing. Mono County Museum features the ghosts of Bridgeport past, with artful displays featuring the area's native, mining, and ranching populations. Grab a drink and a slice at Rhino's Bar and Grille, a popular locals' joint, and then get some R&R at the Virginia Creek Settlement, an authentic roadhouse 5 miles south of Bridgeport. Or try some shut-eye with ghosts of the literary past at the Bridgeport Inn. Rooms look much the same as when Mark Twain visited (and perhaps he still does!) but with modern conveniences. For you city slickers who want a taste of the cowboy way, get along yer little doggies to the 4,400-acre Hunewill Guest Ranch in Bridgeport Valley for a true cattle ranch experience you can brag about to your friends.

Farther along CA 395, start your morning with a relaxing dip in Travertine Hot Springs (I see naked people!), or if that's not your thing, just across the street is Buckeye Hot Springs where clothing is not optional. Be sure to stock up on food and drink supplies at Albert's Meat Market & Deli because your next stop is Bodie, the mother lode of ghost towns, which has nothing but the skeletal remains of a once-booming mining town.

Off CA 395, drive on CA 270 east for 13 miles to reach Bodie State Historic Park (note: the last 3 miles are unpaved). In 1859, one William (aka Waterman) S. Bodey discovered gold at what is now called Bodie Bluff. In 1861, a mill was established and a town was born. By 1881, the town of Bodie was so lawless it was called a "sea of sin" by a reverend, boasting almost 10,000 people and more

GHOST TOWNS:

More Ghostly Haunts off the Beaten Path

Bennetville Ghost Town is located just a quick 1-mile hike from outside Yosemite National Park. This silver-mining ghost town, which dates back to the 1880s, is in a gorgeous area, its mining shacks lovingly restored and preserved by the Forest Service. According to the area's history, a road from Lundy to Bennetville was never completed, and with a little patience and a pioneering spirit, you may find the abandoned equipment left there by the road workers.

Manzanar is located on the west side of CA 395, 9 miles north of Lone Pine and 6 miles south of Independence. In 1942, the U.S. government ordered more than 110,000 Japanese American citizens and resident Japanese men, women, and children to leave their homes and be detained in military-style camps.

Manzanar War Relocation Center was one of 10 remote camps during World War II. The visitors center, where you'll find free self-guided driving tour maps, also houses a museum documenting the area's history.

May Lundy Mine is situated at over 9,000 feet overlooking picturesque Crystal Lake and just northwest of Mono Lake, 6 miles west of CA 395 just north of Lee Vining. Just shy of 4 miles on an old road, this hike is worth the trek. This mine was named after the daughter of W. J. Lundy, and the sawmill incidentally supplied Bodie with lumber. In 1879, with gold findings, Lundy became a boomtown with hotels, saloons, boardinghouses, and even a Chinatown. However, avalanches, which were a common threat in these parts (the cause of many deaths), coupled with the high cost of mining operations were most likely the cause of Lundy's demise.

Prescott Mining District, at almost 10,000 feet, is located on the old Mono Pass Trail at Mono Pass overlooking Mono Lake. In 1852, an army lieutenant pursuing the local indigenous population discovered gold in what was called Bloody Canyon. The area was rediscovered in 1879, and the Prescott Mining District was born. The Old Mono Pass Trail was used by the early miners and starts in Mono Basin, goes over Mono Pass, and ends in Dana Meadows. The hike from Dana Meadows to Mono Pass is 4 miles with an elevation gain of 1,000 feet (a pretty rigorous hike).

MARKLEEVILLE'S DEATH RIDE

Markleeville is best known in the cycling community for hosting the annual Tour of the California Alps Death Ride. The route goes over five passes for a total distance of 129 miles and over 15,000 feet of elevation gain. The Death Ride sounds more grueling than it is. Mountain bikers of all ages and abilities enjoy the single-track trails and downhill runs surrounding Markleeville. In fact in 2010, 3,500 riders entered the race and 2,417 completed all five mountain passes. Hotels do fill up quickly, so be sure to check race dates before scheduling your trip.

---

than 60 dance halls and saloons. With so much drinking, money, and gunslinging, daily fatalities were the norm. In Bodie, "Have a man for breakfast?" was code for "Did anyone get killed last night?" However by 1881, the mines became depleted, and after a major fire in 1892 and another in 1932 that destroyed most of the town, it became a ghost town. This park not surprisingly attracts about 200,000 visitors a year as it's incredibly preserved. Highlights here include Grand Central Hotel, the Schoolhouse, and the Sam Leon Bar and Barber Shop. And, of course, the resident ghosts of Bodie.

After Bodie, travel south on CA 395 to Mono Lake area to eat gourmet cuisine at the Tioga Gas Mart's Whoa Nellie Deli—yep, you read right, good food in a gas station, go figure! Check into the tree-lined Lake View Lodge or the Tioga Lodge in Lee Vining, which offers country cottages and an organic restaurant. Both have views of Mono Lake. Wake to the sunrise over the lake and throw on those hiking boots. If California had its own Dead Sea (without the religious significance but surely containing the restorative powers of salt, endurance, and rejuvenation), it would be Mono Lake. Tufa towers made from calcium carbonate from underwater springs march along the shoreline of this ancient lake, creating a surreal atmosphere. You'll feel as though you are at a portal to the underworld or have taken a trip to the moon. At 700,000 years, Mono is one of the oldest continuously existing lakes on the continent. Its area of 66 square miles is but a fraction of its previous magnitude, for it once was fed by glaciers during the last ice age and reached a size over 60 times greater than today. Head to the Mono Lake Tufa State Reserve for the best up-close views of these limestone pieces of art. Also you might want to spend some time exploring the Panum Crater, Mono Craters, and Navy Beach. Connect with CA 120 west to return to civilization.

IN THE AREA

ACCOMMODATIONS

Black Bear Inn B&B, 1202 Ski Run Boulevard, South Lake Tahoe. The luxury lodge features farm antiques and the best gourmet breakfast around for guests in the five rooms and three cabins. No children allowed. Call 530-544-4451. Website: www.tahoeblackbear .com.

Bridgeport Inn, 205 Main Street, Bridgeport. Mar. through Nov., you can experience 1877 in this restored inn in the heart of Bridgeport with a variety of styled and priced rooms including the cottage (complete with a full kitchen) and a restaurant. Call 760-932-7380. Website: www.thebridgeportinn.com.

Cedar House Sport Hotel, 10918 Brockway Road, Truckee. This 42-room hotel is calling out to travelers who want the ultimate in luxury like German down comforters and heated granite floors plus hot tub and bar to add to the allure. Call 866-582-5655. Website: cedarsporthotel.com.

Hunewill Guest Ranch, 1110 Hunewill Ranch Road, Bridgeport. Founded in 1861 by Napoleon Bonaparte Hunewill. Stay in an authentic cabin, go on a cattle drive, ride horses, sing songs around a campfire, dance, and eat three hearty meals. Call 760-932-7710. Website: www .hunewillranch.com.

Lake View Lodge, 30 Main Street, Lee Vining. Centrally located, this accommodation offers choices of motel rooms or cottages (with Direct TV and private bath). The Garden House Coffee Shop is on the premises. Call 760-647-6543. Website: www.bwlakeviewlodge.com.

River Street Inn, 10009 East River Street, Truckee. This old brothel doesn't disappoint, with 11 rooms offering velvety linens, claw-foot tubs, sloped ceilings, and breakfast. Call 530-550-9290. Website: www.riverstreetinntruckee .com.

Tioga Lodge, 54411 US 395, Lee Vining. The new owners of this one-time tollbooth are attempting to lure ecofriendly travelers into the country cottages with an organic restaurant and country charm. Call 760-647-6423. Website: www.tiogalodgeatmonolake .com.

The Truckee Hotel, 10007 Bridge Street, Truckee. One of the best deals in the area. You'll feel the history as you walk into this 1868 lumber worker hotel, decorated in dark wood and period antiques. Moody's Bistro and Lounge is on the property. Call 530-587-4444 or 800-659-6921. Website: www.truckeehotel.com.

Virginia Creek Settlement, 70847 US 395, Bridgeport. Some of the best deals in the region. John Wayne stayed in this establishment with its seven basic but sweet rooms, restaurant, campground, camp town wagons, and housekeeping cabins. Call 760-932-7780. Website: www.virginiacrksettlement.com.

ATTRACTIONS AND RECREATION

Alpine County Museum/Historical Complex, School Street, Markleeville. Tour the town's historical sites like the Old Webster School and Old Log Jail for free. Call 530-694-2317. Website: www.alpinecountyca.gov/departments /museum.

Biltmore Lodge and Casino, 5 CA 28, Crystal Bay. A tad rundown. Come here for the ghost hunting and kitsch, but not to stay. Call 775-831-0660.

Bodie State Historic Park, CA 270, 7 miles south of Bridgeport off US 395. Truly the best ghost town in America, specter hunters will not be disappointed. Call 760-647-6445. Website: www.bodie.com.

Buckeye Hot Springs, Buckeye Road, Bridgeport. If you're not afraid of a little skin, this free and remote hot springs is a perfect place to soak after a long day. Call 760-932-7070.

Crystal Bay Club Casino, 14 CA 28, Crystal Bay. Funky little remodeled casino that offers a lot more than just ghostly visitors, like live entertainment and a great little coffee shop. Call 775-833-6333. Website: www.crystalbay casino.com.

D.L. Bliss State Park, 3 miles north of Emerald Bay State Park on CA 89, Lake Tahoe. This park is one of the most beautiful stretches of parkland in the Lake Tahoe area where, with reservations, you can camp in summer. Call 530-525-7277. Website: www.parks.ca .gov.

Donner Memorial State Park and Emigrant Trail Museum, Donner Pass Road, off CA 89, west of Truckee. A museum and park commemorating the Donner Party, where you can hike, snowshoe, and cross-country ski while ghost hunting. Call 530-582-7892. Website: www.parks.ca.gov.

Emerald Bay State Park, 4 miles west of Pope Baldwin Recreation Area on CA 89. The most photographed spot in California and possibly the United States, this turquoise blue 3-mile bay surrounds Fannette, Tahoe's only island. Call 530-525-7255. Website: www .parks.ca.gov.

Gatekeeper's Log Cabin Museum, 120 West Lake Boulevard, Tahoe City. The original cabin housed the gatekeepers who regulated Lake Tahoe's water level after the Truckee River was dammed. Call 530-583-1762. Website: www.northtahoemuseums.org.

Grover Hot Springs State Park, 3415 Hot Springs Road, Markleeville. Open year-round, whether sleet or intense heat, these two hot spring pools (and now a visitors center and store) in an alpine meadow and pine forest attracts folks wanting to go on intense hikes 10,000 feet up and then relax the muscles. Call 530-694-2248 or 530-694-2249. Website: www.parks.ca.gov.

Heavenly Village, 1001 Heavenly Village Way, South Lake Tahoe. There is some serious boutique shopping on the South Shore here; plus you'll find movie theaters, miniature golf, an ice rink, and galleries. Call 775-265-2087. Website: www.theshopsatheavenly.com.

Kings Beach Recreation Area, along CA 28, downtown Kings Beach. Tons of stuff to do here like BBQ, swimming, water sports, or visiting summer arts-and-crafts fairs. Call 530-546-7248. Website: www.parks.ca.gov.

Mono Basin National Forest Scenic Area, US 395, Mono Lake. A landscape straight out of Dante's imagination and much like the hoodoos of Utah, Mono Lake's tufas create an eerie setting, jutting out like craggy fingers reaching into the blue sky in this gorgeous park. Call 760-873-2498. Website: www.fs.fed .us.

Mono County Museum, Emigrant Street, Bridgeport. Located in the former Bridgeport Elementary Schoolhouse built in 1880. You'll find Paiute baskets, area artifacts, and mining and farming equipment. Call 760-932-7004. Website: www.monocomuseum.org.

Sugar Pine Point State Park, 7360 Westlake Boulevard, Tahoma. There are 10 miles of trails at this state park, including Ehrman Mansion, which you can tour in summer months. Call 530-725-7982 or 530-525-7982. Website: www.parks.ca.gov.

Tahoe Tessie's Lake Tahoe Monster Museum, 8608 North Lake Boulevard, Kings Beach. Come and hear tales about the legendary Tessie who allegedly trolls the waters of Lake Tahoe or peruse the unique gift shop featuring Tessie T-shirts, souvenirs, and books, and it's free. Call 550-546-8774.

Travertine Hot Springs, Jack Sawyer Road, Bridgeport. Soak your weary bones in beautifully natural hot springs. Call 760-872-5000.

Truckee-Donner Historical Society and Old Jail, Jiboom and Spring Streets, Truckee. A visit to this 1875 jail allows you to experience the 32-inch-thick walls and windowless cells, plus see memorabilia from Truckee's past, all for free. Call 530-582-0893. Website: www.truckeehistory.org.

Truckee's Historical Haunted Walking Tour, 1007 Bridge Street, Truckee. More like a bar crawl, check out the dates for this not-to-be missed annual ghost hunters' dream tour geared for adults only. Call 530-305-4231. Website: www.truckeehistorytour.com.

Vikingsholm Mansion and Visitor Center, 3299 Emerald Bay Road, Tahoma. Magical in location and architecture, the hike is a steep 1.7 miles down (and back up) the mountain but is so worth the trek. Call 530-525-3345. Website: www.vikingsholm.org.

DINING/DRINKS

Albert's Meat Market & Deli, 198 Main Street, Bridgeport. Not for vegetarians, this unassuming deli showcases a humongous selection of sandwiches including a tri-tip to die for. Call 790-932-7177.

Alpina, 822 Emerald Bay Road, South Lake Tahoe. Locals line up for coffee and breakfast pastries, plus there is free Internet access and a special section for kiddos. Call 530-541-7449. Website: www.alpinacafe.com.

Blue Angel Café, 1132 Ski Run Boulevard, South Lake Tahoe. Locals love this healthy breakfast spot for a granola, a frittata, or the infamous British Bob's hangover cure. Call 530-544-6544. Website: www.blueangelcafe.com.

Blue Water Bistro, Boardwalk Pier, Timber Cove Marina, South Lake Tahoe. Reservations are recommended for this lakefront spot specializing in organic seasonal cuisine like sweet potato Dungeness crab cakes and lentil nut loaf. Call 530-541-0113. Website: www.bluewaterbistrotahoe.com.

The Cantina, 765 Emerald Bay Drive, South Lake Tahoe. Hearty burritos, quesadillas, and nachos populate the menu, while the happy hour specials enjoyed at the festive bar or on the patio make for a fun postadventure snack. Call 530-544-1233. Website: www.cantinatahoe.com.

Coffeebar, 10120 Jibboom Street, Truckee. A wide selection of coffee and tea, smoothies, and fresh squeezed juices, plus a vegetarian campagna panini that's to die for. Call 530-587-2000. Website: www.coffeebartruckee.com.

Cottonwood Restaurant and Bar, 10142 Rue Hilltop, Truckee. Winner of numerous local favorite awards, this fine dining establishment overlooks downtown Truckee and delivers on great wines and creative fare like butternut squash enchiladas that beg you to eat with your fingers. Call 530-587-5711. Website: www.cottonwood restaurant.com.

Dragonfly, 10118 Donner Pass, Truckee. Great sushi and California fusion cuisine like flatbreads, Asian-inspired seafood, and Kobe steak. Call 530-587-0557. Website: www.dragonflycuisine .com.

Full Belly Deli, 10825 Pioneer Trail, Suite 103, Truckee. Simply delicious, the menu will satisfy any hungry palette, but do try the signature Dirka Dirka; the $5 daily special is always a great choice. Call 530-550-9516. Website: www.fullbellydelitruckee.com.

Jolly Kone, 178 Main Street, Bridgeport. More than just a roadside hamburger stand, Jolly's serves up yummy American eats like the spicy chipotle black bean burger and, of course, chocolate-dipped ice-cream cones. Call 760-932-7555.

Moody's Bistro and Lounge, 1007 Bridge Street, Truckee. This local fave serves up organic, seasonal fare, like morel mushrooms or antelope, that changes depending on the whim of the chef. Call 530-587-8688. Website: www.moodysbistro.com.

Rhino's Bar and Grille, 226 Main Street, Bridgeport. A kid-friendly locals' joint with billiards and video games and signature Rhino's burgers you can order "hot," meaning topped with a big helping of hot sauce. Call 760-932-7345.

Sprouts Natural Foods Café, 3123 Harrison Avenue, South Lake Tahoe. If you want healthy fare like wraps, rice bowls, and smoothies, Sprouts is it; be sure to bring some cash. Call 530-541-6969.

Squeeze In, 10096 Donner Pass Road, Truckee. Call 530-587-4694. The Squeeze In breakfast spot is not joking about the name, but it also claims to have the 62 "Best Omelettes on the Planet." Open daily for breakfast and lunch. Website: www.squeezein.com.

Stone Fly, 14821 CA 89, Markleeville. With brick oven pizzas large enough for two, you can't beat the arugula, fig, and prosciutto combo capped off with a Meyer lemon soufflé for dessert. Call 530-694-9999.

Whoa Nelli Deli, Tioga Gas Mart, 22 Vista Point Road, Lee Vining. A bit of a novelty in these parts, a Mobil gas station that serves up divine fish tacos, lobster taquitos, smoked trout bagel, and gourmet pizza. Call 760-872-1088. Website: www.whoanelliedeli.com.

Wolf Creek Restaurant and Bar, 14830 CA 89, Markleeville. You can't beat the friendly service and historic setting that serves up delightfully simple fare like avocado sprout sandwiches for vegetarians and yummy burgers that satisfy meat lovers. Call 530-694-2150.

OTHER CONTACTS

Lake Tahoe Visitors Authority, 169 Highway 50, Stateline, Nevada. Call 775-588-5900 or 800-AT-TAHOE. Web Site: www.tahoesouth.com.

Mono Basin National Forest Scenic Area Visitor Center, 1 Visitor Center Drive, Lee Vining. The helpful rangers can guide you toward hikes and campgrounds, plus they offer guided hikes of Mono Lake's South Tufa area, a film depicting the geology of the region, and interactive natural history exhibits. Call 760-873-2498. Website: www.fs.fed.us.

North Lake Tahoe Visitors & Convention Bureau. Call 530-581-8703 or 530-581-8701 or 800-462-5196. Web Site: www.gotahoenorth.com.

Truckee Donner Chamber of Commerce, 10065 Donner Pass Road (downtown in the historic train depot), Truckee. Call 530-587-8808. Web Site: www.truckee.com.

Find hidden mountain lakes in the High Sierra.

CPSIA information can be obtained
at www.ICGtesting.com
Printed in the USA
BVHW011830240421
605634BV00020B/581